TO KILL
A MESSENGER

Television News
and
The Real World

STUDIES IN PUBLIC COMMUNICATION

A. WILLIAM BLUEM, GENERAL EDITOR

"By the late '60's television was no longer safe. The public reacted in frustration and anger. Television's top executives grew fond of noting that ancient Persian generals had messengers killed when they brought bad news."

"*Yet the first bringer of unwelcome news*
Hath but a losing office, and his tongue
Sounds ever after as a sullen bell. . . ."

KING HENRY IV, PART II

TO KILL
A MESSENGER

Television News
and
The Real World

by

WILLIAM SMALL

COMMUNICATION ARTS BOOKS

HASTINGS HOUSE, PUBLISHERS · NEW YORK

First Edition

Copyright © 1970, by William Small
All rights reserved. No part of this book
may be reproduced in any form without
written permission of the publisher.

Published simultaneously in Canada by
Saunders, of Toronto, Ltd., Don Mills, Ontario

SBN: 8038-7094-9
Library of Congress Catalog Card Number: 76-110070

DESIGNED BY AL LICHTENBERG
PRINTED IN THE UNITED STATES OF AMERICA

For Gish, of course.

CONTENTS

PREFACE

CHICAGO in 1968 was probably the turning point. The great American audience turned on television. Resentment against news media existed for some time before that—resentment about news that touched on the revolution of the Blacks, the protests against the war in Vietnam, and the turmoil among the young. The television coverage of the streets of Chicago during the 1968 Democratic Convention brought the audience resentment boiling forth. Television has become fair game for the man on the street and the man who became Vice President. Television has changed America to an indoor country; it delivers everything to the living room and much that comes is neither welcome nor invited. The public has turned its anger on the messenger, the bearer of bad tidings.

Television touches our lives in many ways. Sometimes it merely brushes the senses, sometimes it burns deep. The easy way, the common way, the accepted way is to simply look for the warts, to report the shortcomings. Most books on television, other than text books, tend to follow this well-worn path. The tube is an easy target.

There is a waiting audience, swelled by intellectual snobbery and professional envy, that warmly greets each new attack on television. The snobbery reflects television's role as the common man's medium. The envy reflects television's kidnapping of exciting and powerful roles once exclusively the province of the printed press. Television in the world of reality is too important and too powerful to be left to its practitioners or its critics. It is also too complicated to be reduced to simple generalizations, critical or not. That is the only excuse for this volume rambling over television as it relates to war, to violence, to racial dispute, to politics, to government, and to our very selves in the disorganized, discursive, rambling way of our life.

As many others practicing in the art of non-fiction television, I find reason to be proud of its present state and its bright future. Though there is much that is critical in the pages that follow, my bias is clear, my prejudice is not hidden. There are some things that television can not do well and perhaps some that it can't do at all but, overall, it can and does supply invaluable service to our commonalty.

⌈Television is the first development of consequence in modern history to reverse trends taking public matters away from the public. As other factors—population growth, bigness in business and labor, impersonalization of the printed media, growing sophistication of technology and decision making—tend to minimize individual man, television seeks to personalize government, politics, social change. For the average man, this is literally at his fingertips as he turns on the set. He may turn out or turn off but it is there. Individual man can get a better grasp of the forces that mold his social environment.

This reversal of bigness, this reduction of major forces into elements that Everyman can grasp is not the primary goal nor the major focus of television. It is, I believe, its major accomplishment. In bits and snatches, with false starts and frequent lapses, sometimes too simple and sometimes too quick, it does offer all of us chances to view the whole of which we are all part. Newspapers and serious magazines serve similar functions but none reach Everyman as easily or as often. ⌋

If a sin of commission here is to show television in fits and starts then we are guilty. Our only excuse is that this work hopefully reflects television and its role in society. If it does, it is dealing with a matter that is itself rambling, discursive and not a careful, well-organized, easily studied phenomenon. It is hoped that readers will examine these diverse elements and somehow get their own feeling for the whole.

If there is a sin of omission here, and there is, it involves people. When I told veteran CBS News executive Ralph Paskman that this book was being written, he snarled, "If I'm not in it, it can't be any good!"

We laughed but he was right. He should be in it. So should the hundreds of able broadcast newsmen in the network news operations and in local newsrooms. I am appalled that somehow this much could be written and so little about my colleagues in the Radio Television News Directors Association and so many others to whom I owe so much in my own professional development: Glenn Snyder, Harold Salzman, Victor Sholis, Barry Bingham, Mark Ethridge, Norman Isaacs, Blair Clark, Bill Leonard, Gordon Manning, Ernie Leiser, Bud Benjamin, Don Hewitt, many more, and—of course—Ralph Paskman. Of others—Cronkite, Kintner, Sevareid, etc.—there is some in this volume but not enough. To all these professionals, named and unnamed, my apology.

I would also like to express my gratitude to Mrs. Marjorie Geddes of CBS News, Washington for her tolerance, Mr. Richard Salant of CBS News, New York for his critical eye, and Mr. Russell Neale of Hastings House for his encouragement. To them, my thanks.

INTRODUCTION

ON ONE OCCASION or another over the past decade each of us has despaired over those versions of "reality" which have spilled from the small screen into our living rooms and consciousness. We have either experienced in ourselves or sensed in others a longing for respite from the endless recounting of "things as they are." We have hungered for a quiet, more ordered view of the world around us. Television's curse is that it is simply unable to satisfy this longing. A medium of action, TV carries all the psychological overload as well as the aesthetic power of the motion picture medium whose modes and styles of communication it most closely parallels.

The following, I believe, represent the major criticisms which have been directed against TV as a journalistic medium:

(1) The nature of sight-sound, edited presentation in the medium heightens and attenuates the more surface, visceral aspect of conflict and confrontation in our civilization—the reporting of which, regrettably, is the *raison d'être* of journalism.

(2) As the level of irrationality in an event rises, so television's record of it "heats up," and the camera begins to exchange momentum, as it were, with the forces at work within the very situation it is supposed to be recording.

(3) The medium undoubtedly tends to reward both personality and personability in those who are involved in or actually present the news—a fact which makes it quite simple for those who wish to equate credibility with physical attractiveness or "image" to do so.

It is unfortunate, of course, that the greater number of TV viewers seldom take into account these known and obvious conventions and conditions of the communications situation. Those who do not over-react seem somehow to disappear into that "silent majority" where they become useful pawns in the politicians' endless struggles for power. But what is of far greater significance is that the more articulate, media-sophisticated and forward-thinking of the great audience have also begun to wish for surcease—for the relative "distance" which the print media can put between the reader and the event. These media-sophisticates—including not a few in the academic community—know that it is easier, affectively speaking, to read about riots than to be dragged into them through a small screen. And they know also that the anger and action must be brought into some kind of perspective if productive social outcomes are to result.

If this awareness of TV's powers had given rise to nothing more than Marshall McLuhan's tenuous theorizing, there would be little cause for concern. Unfortunately, social fall-out from the TV information explosion has begun to draw some of our leading thinkers into the despairing and reactionary logic of "stop the machine." Not a few of our social theorists regard television as merely another aspect—albeit an important one—of technology run rampant over the physical and psychic health and welfare of mankind. Their persuasive argument is always made, of course, in the spirit of *pro bono publico* and under the assumption that the great majority simply cannot handle the force and power of what is communicated to them. The greatest danger we face, perhaps, is the growing acceptance of their desperate notion that we must turn back time, reverse the engines, and silence the new voices and machines that now speak to all men in this society.

We dare not, in fact, even assume that we have a choice. We have made massive individual and social commitments to science and technology, and we cannot now suppress aspects of them which disturb or inconvenience us while those we approve are left to flourish. There is no stopping of the machine. We cannot be rid of chemistry because men have used it to produce poison gas, or quit physics because they have produced a nuclear bomb. Nor can we tear down our transmitters, roll up the wires and bring the satellites back to earth merely because those in the intelligentsia who feel we have still not determined what "we should say to India" resent and regret the impact of televised communications upon the mass of men. To some these may seem hard thoughts, but there is no other answer to those who would limit the communicative tools and techniques not only of journalists, but of all who seek to inform and to educate their fellow beings.

If there is an alternative, it is an obvious and recurring one. We must train a generation of citizens to "read" the new media—a task which many in the field of motion pictures have long since undertaken. We cannot assume that an entire civilization will acquire sophistication and knowledge in the conventions and techniques of the medium by accident. If we do not attempt to provide such understanding, the pressure to silence the medium will continue.

It may be noted here that an essential precondition to this kind of citizen education is the creation of a vast library of those records the medium actually has produced. The establishment of a major repository for the sight-and-sound output of the electronic media in this century is long overdue. Such a library and history center must focus its collecting, classifying and disseminating activities not only upon that small proportion of media output which is genuinely worthy of the name Art, but also upon the massive documentation of the social and political life of our times which radio and TV have already created and will continue to create. Until such an institution exists, the task of citizen education perforce must be circumscribed—and until the larger task is undertaken throughout our society there will loom the spectre of an enforced limitation upon what the media are and might become.

For if technology has drastically altered the nature of information structure and flow within our civilization it is yet to be proven that it has mysteriously changed men's designs and intentions when they engage in communication with their fellow beings. These designs can be discerned, isolated and evaluated so long as men are willing to study what others say, why they said it, and the context and manner in which they said it. Central to the study of each of these aspects of communications are the opinions, judgments and insights of the responsible media practitioner. For this reason, *Studies In Public Communication* welcomes the contribution of William Small, who—as Director of CBS News operations in Washington, D.C. throughout the tumultuous 60's—has stood in the eye of the hurricane.

A. WILLIAM BLUEM Ph.D.
General Editor: *Studies in Public Communication*
S. I. Newhouse Communications Center, Syracuse University

CHAPTER 1

HOW TIMID TELEVISION?

AMERICANS watch television too much.

In the average home, a television set is burning for almost six hours a day. On any weekday evening in winter (we watch less in summer) approximately half the population of these United States is found silently watching the little screen at any given hour.

Something like ninety-five per cent of our sixty million homes have television sets. Over one-fourth of these homes have two or more sets. It has been estimated that the average American male will spend the equivalent of 3,000 full days, roughly nine full years of his life, watching television.

Americans watch television too much.

A member of the Federal Communications Commission, Nicholas Johnson, has observed that "the average child before entering kindergarten will have received more hours of instruction from television than he will receive instruction in a college classroom getting his B.A. degree. . . . Most children get more stimulation from television while in school than the school teacher and church combined."

Critics of television are appalled by the amount of viewing. It seems obvious to them that anything so popular must be bad. If Karl Marx could speak from his grave, the sober German would be expected to note that television, not religion, is now the opiate of the masses.

Critics of television are appalled by its content. They chew away at the emptiness of the outpouring. It is shallow, they cry, debasing. But popular theatre has often been this. The miracle of Shakespeare is that he could produce masterpieces within a similar shallow, debasing theatre of his day. If *he* were with us today (and chose to care), he might find puzzling this criticism of vulgarity and violence in television. Some of those matters were the grist of his prolific genius and it was the poetry which survived that mattered. Television has had no Shakespeare and its poets have been few but so were the number who survived the theatre of Shakespeare's time.

One wades through the endless list of criticism. It is barely softened as its few defenders, mostly speaking for the management of television, issue manicured brochures of defense. One recalls Samuel Butler's *An Apology for the Devil*. He wrote, "It must be remembered that we have only heard one side of the case. God has written all the books."

This present volume is not meant to be the Devil's book and will 'dwell considerably on God's ledgers, if that is what the critics are anthologizing. As with a youngster discovering sex, this volume hopes to accomplish two things: to spell out the enormity of it all and to examine that important but limited portion which affects real life. The "tube" as a palliative is worthy of someone's exploration but we will not do that here. Instead, we concern ourselves primarily with television and the world of non-fiction, television and the real world. Television devotes but small measure of its effort in this area yet the impact is unrivalled in the history of mass media. It is of great moment to this nation, these times, and to that most important invention of man's mind—the democratic mode.

Television's years as a force in American life are few. Yet, television has already left marked impression on the American psyche.

Recall some of the remarkable things in twenty-five years of television growth. When John Kennedy was killed, television played a role in stemming a tortuous wound and calming a continuing-on that could otherwise have been eruptive and damaging. When Joe McCarthy, a dozen years earlier, emerged in a different kind of troubled time, television through its greatest journalist, Edward R. Murrow, put the brakes to the demogogic Senator from Wisconsin.

When scandal threatened to destroy Richard Nixon in his first national race, it was his use of television that kept him on the Eisenhower ticket and prevented an early end to a career that culminated with the Presidency in 1968. It was also television that defeated Mr. Nixon in 1960. The "Great Debates" propelled John F. Kennedy to victory over Nixon. The television encounters between the two were neither great, as examination of the texts later revealed, nor debates, at least not in traditional debate form, but they did offer a young, Massachusetts Senator the opportunity to take a quantum step to national prominence, to the Presidency.

When his religion threatened to overwhelm this first Catholic candidate, it was television which permitted him to take a brilliant defense of the religious issue before millions of people. Films of his appearance before Protestant clergy in Houston were played at local stations across the country and defused the anti-Catholicism that threatened his candidacy. It was later suggested that he was really the epitome of the White Anglo-Saxon Protestant President. Some Southern Baptist clergy laughingly called him "a good Southern Baptist President" and that, too, reflected the image in that television film.

When television covered its "first war," in Vietnam, it showed a terrible truth of war in a manner new to mass audiences. A case can be made, and certainly should be examined, that this was cardinal to the disillusionment of Americans with this war, the cynicism of many young people toward America, and the destruction of Lyndon Johnson's tenure of office.

When the opposition to Vietnam and the ruling establishment bubbled forth at the 1968 convention of the Democratic party, television played a major role in portraying internal and external disenchantment with the party in power. It was an element in the under-reported revolution of that year—the rebellion of the good, gray middle class which elected Richard Nixon. He called them the "forgotten Americans." Remembering them elected him. It was a campaign which relied heavily on the use of the medium.

When television examined a different kind of revolution, it was singularly effective in helping bring about the Black revolution. The emergence of Negro militancy half a step behind also is related to the impact of television. It is frequently blamed for the unsightly, often insolent, grindingly frustrating, conscience-tweaking, persistently insulting, repeatedly vulgar and sometimes violent outbursts that shook and baffled white America. It created instant black heroes—and villains.

We shall examine all these matters in this volume.

It is worthy of note that these social and political changes, in which television played a major role, reflect differing use of the medium. Sometimes, as during the Chicago convention, as with the Black revolution, it is television as the common carrier of what is "happening now." Sometimes, as with Nixon's 1952 defense, as with Kennedy's Houston reply to bigotry, it is others making use of the medium. Sometimes, as with Murrow vs. McCarthy or the treatment of Vietnam, it is the power of the television journalist.

Though the list of television contributions to change in the real world is impressive, these contributions must be placed in the context of what television really is and what it isn't. What it is most of the time is fiction, contrived to attract the largest audience possible, designed to carry commercial messages. It is a mass medium with a mass audience. It makes money. Journalism is only part of it.

Edward R. Murrow, in his most famous speech dealing with television, spoke before the Radio Television News Directors at their 1958 convention in Chicago and said:

> One of the basic troubles with radio and television news is that both instruments have grown up as an incompatible combination of show business, advertising and news. Each of the three is a rather bizarre and demanding profession. And when you get all three under one roof, the dust never settles. The top management of the networks, with a few notable exceptions, has been trained in advertising, research, or show business. But by the nature of the corporate structure, they also make the final and crucial decisions having to do with news and public affairs. Frequently they have neither the time nor the competence to do this. It is not easy for the same small group of men to decide whether to buy a new station for millions of dollars, build a new building, alter the rate card, buy a new Western, sell a soap opera, decide what defensive line to take in connection with the latest Congressional inquiry, how much money to spend on promoting a new program, what additions or deletions should be made in the existing covey or clutch of vice-presidents and at the same time—frequently on the same long day—to give mature, thoughtful consideration to the manifold problems that confront those who are charged with the responsibility for news and public affairs.

Those of us involved in the arrangement of that RTNDA convention, still remember Ed's agreement to make that speech. He wasn't making many public speeches those days but he had something he wanted to say. He arrived in Chicago, his remarks carefully prepared. That tall, handsome figure always looked tired—the smile with teeth fighting yellow nicotine stain, the stain already marking his fingers, fingers that held the never-ending chain of cigarettes, cigarettes which ultimately brought lung cancer and death too soon.

His remarks began with mild apology, "This just might do nobody any good. At the end of this discourse a few people may accuse this reporter of fouling his own comfortable nest; and your organization may be accused of having given hospitality to heretical and even dangerous thoughts."

His heresy had charm, his dangerous thoughts were prophetic but there was no rancor, no hate, just a little despair. Perhaps there was a touch of what Anatole France described when he noted that "All good writers of confessions, from Augustine onwards, are men who are still a little in love with their sins."

Murrow said that evening that perhaps the American system could survive, "perhaps the money-making machine has some kind of built-in perpetual motion but I do not think so . . . we are currently wealthy, fat, comfortable and complacent. We have currently a built-in allergy to unpleasant or disturbing information. Our mass media reflect this. But unless we get up off our fat surpluses and recognize that television in the main is being used to distract, delude, amuse and insulate us, then television and those who finance it, those who look at it and those who work at it, may see a totally different picture too late."

Murrow's prime frustration was this uneasy relationship between television's money-making function and its social purpose. "I believe," he said, "that potentially we have in this country a free-enterprise system of radio and television which is superior to any other. But to achieve its promise, it must be both free and enterprising. There is no suggestion here that networks or individual stations operate as philanthropies. But I can find nothing in the Bill of Rights or the Communications Act which says that they must increase their net profits each year, lest the Republic collapse."

At the time Murrow spoke, gross broadcast revenues in television had already approached a billion dollars a year. It has, of course, grown greatly since then and now runs over two billion dollars a year in gross revenues. Adding radio, the gross revenue for broadcasting grew from just under one and a half billion to $3,167,672,000 in the 1958–68 decade.

Someone has estimated that the average American is confronted with 650 advertising messages a day. Someone else has done a study showing that he barely notices one in eight of these. It was Will Rogers who observed that if George Washington was told that the American people today spend two billion dollars yearly on bathing material, he would say, "What got 'em so dirty?"

Cost of Broadcast News

Yet, broadcasting—profitable as it can be—has hardly stinted on expenditures for non-fiction coverage. *Broadcasting* magazine estimated that 1968 expenditures for news coverage at the three networks alone (not counting local stations) probably exceeded 150 million dollars, well over budgets for the year. Something like $30,000,000 was spent on election coverage alone.

In 1969, the three networks budgeted $10 million more, about $140 million plus at least $40 million more for the operation of network-owned local stations. Though the daily half-hour evening newscasts can bring in as much as $34 million a year, the networks still lose millions on news annually. There is "unscheduled" news such as heavy coverage of a Presidential trip overseas. In the closing years of the decade of the 60's, NBC says it has averaged $4 million annually to pay for the unexpected. In March of 1969, when Dwight Eisenhower died, between out-of-pocket costs and the losses due to preempting regular programs (NBC and CBS carried seventeen hours of special coverage, ABC twelve and a half hours), the cost to NBC exceeded $2 million, to CBS about $2½ million and to ABC half a million dollars.

Though all newsmen in broadcasting have felt the need for more funding at times, they certainly have had more financial support than most newspapers. The best in the business have spent immense sums for coverage. Murrow himself said, "I have never had a program turned down by my superiors because of the money it cost."

Two things that worried Mr. Murrow were the failure of local stations to carry some of this programming—a fault that remains—and the frequency with which such programs end up in marginal time rather than prime time on the network schedule. Some of that has changed, some has not, since Murrow's day. The problem: a constant striving by many in television to reach the largest possible audience for everything. Reality is less attractive than fiction to the largest possible audiences.

Though fiction outdraws fact as a day-to-day matter, it is interesting to note that the single biggest audience in every year of the decade of the 60's has been for a news event. In 1960, 1964 and 1966 it was election night which drew the year's largest audience. In 1961, the heaviest single day of viewing was during John F. Kennedy's Inaugural address. In 1962, it was John Glenn's suborbital flight, 1963 the four days of Kennedy's assassination and funeral, in 1965 the Gemini-Titan IV space shot, in 1967 it was Lyndon Johnson's State of the Union address and in 1968 the Democratic National Convention.

The greatest number of viewers during the decade (53,500,000 viewing homes according to the A. C. Nielsen Company) came in 1969 when Apollo XI reached the moon. This was 93.9% of the potential audience. The Kennedy assassination period reached fewer viewers (just under fifty million) but a higher percentage (96.1%) of then available "TV homes".

At least once a year, fact outstrips fiction as television fare. All America yearns to watch its astronauts stride across the surface of the moon. On other days, however, America prefers entertainment.

Heywood Broun had said, "No body politic is healthy until it begins to itch." Murrow had added, "I would like television to produce some itching pills rather than this endless outpouring of tranquilizers . . . Let us not shoot the wrong piano player. Do not be deluded into believing that the titular heads of the networks control what appears on their networks. They all have better taste. All are responsible to stockholders, and in my experience all are honorable men. But they must schedule what they can sell in the public market . . . their business is to sell goods, and the competition is pretty tough."

Yet, in fairness, the networks and the stations have produced, in the midst of this tough competition for the advertising dollar, a remarkable record of memorable moments in the world of reality. Television, a medium for the commercial message, has also delivered messages that helped mold and change our world.

Its influence is due in part to the enormity of its being. In the United States, there are over 4,000 AM radio stations, over 700 television stations, 1,500 plus FM stations, almost one radio set per person in our population of over 200 million Americans, something like seventy million television sets in use, etc.

Over 2,000 different communities have at least one local radio station and over 250 areas have a local television station. The average American family can pick among at least three different television stations and more than half a dozen radio stations.

In cities of size, the average goes way up—New Yorkers have nine television stations, seventeen AM and nineteen FM stations (and only three major, daily newspapers); Chicagoans have an equally large number of broadcast stations (with four major, daily newspapers); and in Los Angeles, you can pick and choose between thirteen television stations, fourteen AM and twenty FM radio stations (but only two major, daily newspapers).

Numbers do not guarantee diversity but the opportunity for diverse presentation of views and reporting certainly seems more ready in broadcasting today than in newspapers. The number of daily newspapers across the country has remained static in the last quarter century, dropping slightly from 1,800 to about 1,750 papers. In contrast, two decades of television has seen a growth from about fifty television stations to some thirteen or fourteen times that number, radio stations (AM) have doubled in number and there has been a fifty per cent increase in FM stations.

Little Study of Impact.

Oddly enough, not enough broadcasters and fewer viewers pay much attention to the social implications of this toy grown immense. Serious research is rare. Popular commentary is common, a reflection of how much a part of our lives television commands, but it hardly contributes to understanding the nature of the animal. Some of it is just plain silly.

The kind of myth that amuses the general public was published in 1966 in the *New York Times* entitled "Births Up 9 Months After the Blackout." It cites a marked increase in new babies nine months after the power blackout that darkened our biggest city on November 9, 1965. It quotes Dr. Robert W. Hodge, a sociologist, as saying, "Our data show that most people wound up at home. They didn't have access to a major source of amusement—television. Under the circumstances, it's not un-reasonable to assume that a lot of sex life went on."

Of all the achievements television might claim, this is probably the most bizarre.

More common, in the daily press, are more ominous evaluations of television's impact. Distinguished semanticist Dr. S. I. Hayakawa com-pared television to a powerful sorcerer who snatches the child from his parents for three or four hours a day and alienates them. The child, he suggests, has a negative reaction to television's material messages and the result is the rioting, drug-taking, alienation and radical politics of young people. Or at least that is the UPI account of his address to the 76th an-nual convention of the American Psychological Association.

"A child sitting in front of a TV set gets no experience in influencing behavior and being influenced in return," said Hayakawa. "Is there any connection between this fact and the sudden appearance in the past few years of an enormous number of young people from the educated and middle class families who find it difficult or impossible to relate to any-body—and therefore drop out?"

On the other hand, psychologist Chaytor Mason of the University of Southern California is quoted in *Time* as fearing that non-watchers of television suffer the same problems as overly obsessive watchers—they tend to become withdrawn, confused and unimaginative. To keep chil-dren from television, suggests Dr. Richard I. Evans of the University of Houston in the same article, is self-delusion in "an electronically saturated world."

Newspapers enjoy criticism of television. FCC members who find fault with broadcasting always get big play. When FCC Chairman New-ton Minow made his maiden speech as Chairman and termed television a "vast wasteland," the phrase was so widely quoted it quickly became a cliche. It is with us still.

The occasion was the 1961 convention of the National Association of Broadcasters in Washington. Minow earned a smile as he began, "I seem to have detected a certain nervous apprehension about what I might say or do when I emerged from that locked office for this, my maiden station break."

The "break" was to last throughout his tenure for Minow told the broadcasters:

> . . . when television is bad, nothing is worse. I invite you to sit down in front of your television set when your station goes on the air and stay there without a book, magazine, newspaper, profit-and-loss sheet or rating book to distract you—and keep your eyes glued to

that set until the station signs off. I can assure you that you will observe a vast wasteland.

You will see a procession of game shows, violence, audience participation shows, formula comedies about totally unbelievable families, blood and thunder, mayhem, violence, sadism, murder, Western badmen, Western good men, private eyes, gangsters, more violence and cartoons. And, endlessly, commercials—many screaming, cajoling, and offending. And most of all, boredom. True, you will see a few things you will enjoy. But they will be very, very few. And if you think I exaggerate, try it.

Ed Murrow had said much the same three years earlier when he noted,

> Our history will be what we make it. And if there are any historians about fifty or a hundred years from now, and there should be preserved the kinescopes for one week of all three networks, they will there find recorded in black-and-white, or color, evidence of decadence, escapism, and insulation from the realities of the world in which we live.

Yet, ten or twelve years after those remarks, television is criticized by contemporaries *not* for protection from the realities but because it exposes us to them. Not the game shows, the blood and thunder, that Minow cites but the game of current life, with all its blood and thunder. Amidst the general entertainment, the show business, the fantasy world that fills most of the TV schedule are the reports of the real world, often as dramatic, even more startling, and terribly important—the medium and its most telling message.

TV Guide once called television "The Timid Giant." It is that no more. The change is due in part to television as a simple mirror to life, showing the country what it really doesn't want to see, but also due to maturation of the television journalist. He is not likely to avoid the controversial. He is more likely to complain he is running out of good subject matter. Timidity has not disappeared but it is hardly the color of the coat television wears.

To be timid was to be safe. By the late '60's television was no longer safe. The public reacted in frustration and anger. Television's top executives grew fond of noting that ancient Persian generals had messengers killed when they brought bad news.

The general manager of the Associated Press, Wes Gallagher, put it this way in a speech in early 1969:

The task of the journalist is to hold a magnifying mirror before our society to show warts and all. The world today is mostly warts: Vietnam, racial rioting, student demonstrations, decaying cities, urban crisis . . . the list is endless.

As the problems have multiplied so have the means of communicating news. Newspapers, television, radio and magazines jam these problems into an already irritated public conscience and the bearer of uncomfortable news is never loved.

The more emotional the time, the greater the rise in the attacks upon the press, or the news media in general. Another maxim governing public reaction is that attacks upon the news media will rise in direct proportion to the intensity of public frustration in meeting the problems of the day.

Reuven Frank, President of NBC News has said, "I gather Americans are tired of television forcing them to look at the world they live in. I refuse to consider that we can do anything else." It is interesting to note that Frank was addressing a convention of the Radio-Television News Directors Association in 1968, exactly ten years after Murrow told the same group in convention that "I would like television to produce some itching pills rather than this endless outpouring of tranquilizers."

Is it true that a single decade has completely changed the nature of television? No. Across the nation, there are still stations run as money machines with only the slightest bow towards public service, a carefully measured "enough" to take care of licence renewal. Networks still have some executives who are more comfortable in the shadow of caution, the dark side of safety. At both the local and the network level, the prime object remains—as it does in all forms of entertainment and/or journalism —to remain solvent, to turn a profit, to show stockholders happy fiscal statements. At the same time, the leaders of the television industry are men of pride. They do savor the honors that television earns in special programming and in news coverage. If the heart of what they control must be common fare, entertainment for the largest mass, it is because— as former FCC Commissioner Lee Loevinger put it—"Television is a golden goose that lays scrambled eggs; and it is futile and probably fatal to beat it for not laying caviar. Anyway, more people like scrambled eggs than caviar." Yet they do not limit themselves to goose eggs. There is a desire to make part of the schedule meaningful and other parts socially significant.

Do top executives enjoy the controversy that has come to television with its young maturity? Very little. It is top management that ends up before the Congressional committee explaining network attitudes toward violence and race relations and political coverage and any other unpleasant items that may have irked a Congressman or his constituent. It would be much easier for networks to stick to the safe and not be sorry, to be the Timid Giant.

Newspapers have traditionally been the bold, not the timid, voice of the community. At least that is the myth fostered by aging editorial writers, journalism textbooks, and every formal meeting of American publishers. The fact is that there are but few great newspapers in this country. The thrust of social purpose in most newspapers takes a halting, stuttering, erratic course. Some matters seem to call for crusades. Others seem to call for silence.

Broadcast News Brings Diversity.

The best thing that has ever happened to the American newspaper, as far as its *readers* are concerned, has been the emergence of broadcast journalism.

In a growing number of communities, it is the local station that is keeping the newspaper honest. In some, it is the local station that supplies information which otherwise would be ignored, sometimes by design, more often by ineptitude. It is the network newscast—in most communities—which fleshes out the newspaper's skimpy coverage of national and foreign news. It is the network newscast—in some communities—which brings first word of social forces at work in this country.

Freedom of the press has been a sacred thing in America. Freedom *from* the press has been rare. Diversity brings that and the trend in newspapers is for fewer, not more.

Fortunately the trend in broadcast journalism is more, not fewer. The "more" is not truly reflected in the figures showing growing numbers of stations as opposed to dwindling numbers of daily newspapers. Many, if not most local stations, tend to give limited service in news. The trend, not easily measurable and not without lapses, is for more of the existing stations to get interested in, enchanted with, and enthusiastic for news and special coverage. The healthy thing about competition and diversity is that local stations want to compete with each other for the news audience even though it is smaller and more costly to capture. Though in city after city, one can cite anecdotes about old movies or new cartoons getting higher ratings than newscasts and documentaries, in city after city station management is cited for its pride in the latter. The competition between stations results in more and better coverage.

Lack of competition among newspapers does not always mean poorer service. Some monopoly newspapers are among the best in the nation. Broadcasters serve to keep these, too, honorable and alert. The health of newspapers is vital, of course. A nation without newspapers is a sick nation. Broadcasting has serious limitations and never in the wildest fantasy could broadcasting replace the printed word. There are many things newspapers do best. The presence of broadcast competition is one goad to do them.

In the last decade, broadcast journalism has tended to be more and more the major source of news for most people. This trend seems likely to increase. Similarly broadcasting seems to be trusted more than newspapers.

While that argument is poor in cities of size with good newspapers such as New York, Los Angeles, Louisville, Denver, St. Louis and Washington, there is a second element. Good television journalism presents news in the most attractive and lucid form yet devised by man. It does so in a manner that appeals to all classes and backgrounds, to men well-read and men poorly educated, to viewers rich and poor, to those interested and those only mildly curious about their world. The package captures the fancy of all. It is easy for all to take.

For the industry-sponsored Television Information Office, Roper Research Associates have been polling this phenomenon since 1959. When they began, six per cent more people (57% vs. 51% with multiple answers accepted therefore a total exceeding 100%) identified newspapers over television as the source for "most of your news about what's going on in the world today." Four years later, in 1963, it was 55% to 53% in favor of television and by 1967, a remarkable 64% against 55% favoring newspapers. In 1969, TV dropped to 59% and newspapers to 49%.

Most sobering for newspapers perhaps is the result of the question, "Suppose that you could continue to have only *one* of the following— radio, television, newspapers or magazines—which one of the four would you *most* want to *keep*?" Television was the choice of 42% in 1959; newspapers the choice of 32% that year. Television, said 50% in 1969; newspapers, said only 24%. Half of America wanted to keep television if they could keep only one medium. One-fourth of America would keep newspapers beyond all others.

The question that was key to the matter of reliability and of trust came as Roper asked, "If you got conflicting or different reports of the same news story from radio, television, the magazines and the newspapers, which of the four versions would you be most inclined to believe?" In 1959, television was a fraction behind newspapers in this believability test. By 1969, 44% of the public trusted television first; only 21% relied on their newspaper first.

Perhaps it has been the trend toward television as the prime source for news, perhaps the believability factor, perhaps the excitement that television alone can generate, that created the young traditions of broadcast courage which emerged with the years. As the decade of the 1960's drew to a close, broadcast management and broadcast journalists were fiercely clinging to this eminence in the world of reporting fact.

Critics are nervous. Too powerful, they say. They once called it the Timid Giant; they now worried more about Frankenstein impulses. FCC member Nick Johnson in a documentary on television journalism produced by the Public Broadcast Laboratory: "I think quite frankly that at the present time there is very little danger of intimidation of the mass media. My own feeling is quite the contrary, that the mass media, the networks in particular, broadcasting in particular, are probably now beyond the check of any institution in our society. The President, the Congress of the United States, the FCC, foundations and universities are reluctant even to get involved. I think they may be now so powerful that they're beyond the check of anyone."

His concern was echoed by Vice President Spiro Agnew in his famous attack on network television in November of 1969. Said Mr. Agnew, "No medium has a more powerful influence over public opinion. Nowhere in our system are there fewer checks on vast power."

A dramatic thought that, but hardly accurate. Broadcasting, as we shall see, is full of internal as well as external checks and balances. Television is powerful because of its nature as a conveyer of images and ideas but we are still learning just how powerful.

Richard Salant, President of CBS News, once noted that the full text of a typical half-hour of news as reported by Walter Cronkite would occupy barely three-fourths of the eight columns that make up the front page of the *New York Times*. The power of television is hardly measured by the number of words or pictures it offers. The power is in *"how"* it does this and *how* it is received. Television, says Marshall McLuhan, is a "cool" medium; it is compressed and condensed. "A cool medium, whether the spoken word or the manuscript or TV, leaves much more for the listener or user to do than a hot medium. If the medium is of high definition, participation is low. If the medium is of low intensity, the participation is high. Perhaps this is why lovers mumble so."

It is dangerous, however, in the present state of the art, to accept McLuhan in simple form. It is certainly premature to believe there is some easy way to use the medium, to prove it is truly the message, to discover a magic mannerism that permits candidates to get elected and soap to be sold and ideas to be accepted simply in how you use television and not what you really say.

At the BBC news office in Washington, a hand-lettered sign reads, "The medium gets in the way of the message."

CHAPTER 2

BEYOND A MINUTE
AND A HALF

THE STRICTURES of time bind tightly. Non-fiction television often seems at the edge of strangulation because there just isn't time enough to tell the story. Even as evening newscasts went from fifteen minutes to half an hour on the networks and to an additional full hour on some local stations, individual items still are often embarrassingly brief.

The dilemma was best described in an anecdote that a Mayor of Milwaukee once told broadcast newsmen gathering in his city. If Moses came down from Mt. Sinai with the Ten Commandments in an era of television, he would certainly be greeted by camera crews.

"What do you have?" they would ask.

"I have the Ten Commandments," replies Moses.

"Tell us about them but keep it to a minute and a half," they would say.

Moses complies and that night on the news, in still more abbreviated form, the story is told. The newscaster begins, "Today at Mount Sinai, Moses came down with Ten Commandments, the most important three of which are . . .!"

Exaggeration? Brevity does indeed haunt the electronic journalist.

The half-hour network newscast is not really thirty minutes long. After commercials and introductions and the like, it is really more like twenty-one or twenty-two minutes of news. On occasion, networks have tried to break free. On August 22, 1968 the CBS-TV "Evening News with Walter Cronkite" expanded to a full hour to handle the heavy news load which included satellite feeds from three continents to handle reports from inside Czechoslovakia which had been invaded by troops from Russia and other Communist bloc countries, from Bogota, Columbia showing the arrival of Pope Paul VI there and by Pacific communications satellite, the rocket attack on the South Vietnam National Assembly building in Saigon. Admirable to expand and meet the measure of the increased news budget? Yes, but some CBS-TV stations were upset. It was an extra half-hour of *their* time, of station time, that was taken over. It meant a cut-back on local programming, mostly news. It meant a loss of revenue for the local station.

NBC-TV News did much the same thing in December of that year to accommodate two major stories, reports from the Apollo VIII space mission around the moon and, from Korea, release of the crew of the captured spy ship *Pueblo*. They, too, found some of the affiliates less than thrilled by the innovation. Early in 1969, NBC went an hour for five straight nights to accommodate coverage of President Nixon's trip to Europe.

In March of that year, as public controversy grew over the decision involving deployment of ABM, anti-ballistic missiles, the Cronkite newscasts on several occasions were again expanded to a full hour. The second half of the hour was devoted to explanations of the ABM controversy and high-lights of Senate hearings dealing with it. This time, CBS-TV presented the second half as "co-op," a system permitting the stations to sell their own commercials and insert them in this 30-minute period.

A newspaper, in theory, can simply add pages to accommodate extra news. Newspapers rarely do so, a reluctance they do not have when they need to add *news* to accommodate a heavier *advertising* budget before Christmas or on similar occasions. Television cannot stretch an hour to exceed 60 minutes. Something has to go if the time is taken beyond normal scheduling.

When television interrupts the schedule, except for brief bulletins, it can get very expensive. Still, interruptions are plentiful. All Presidential news conferences open to live television coverage are carried by all networks. The President's State of the Union message and other major joint gatherings of the Congress are televised. Many special events are similarly carried.

Among the more expensive excursions into live television are Congressional hearings. This is a tradition that goes back to the earliest days of television when Americans were intrigued watching the so-called Kefauver hearings after Tennessee's Senator Estes Kefauver admitted cameras into a Senate inquiry into organized crime. Those hearings were highlighted by a memorable moment when underworld leader Frank Costello objected to being televised and cameras dwelled on a close-up of his hands as the dialogue of the hearing continued. In time, there were to be many more examples of live hearings: a check of the Mafia with Joe Valachi as main witness, many hearings dealing with Vietnam, some portions of the investigation of ex-Senate aide Bobby Baker, and so on. The most famous, perhaps, were the Army-McCarthy hearings in 1954.

When the hearings began in April of that year, CBS settled for filmed highlights in the very late evening and NBC dropped out after the opening excitement. Robert Kintner, a brilliant news buff who was then President of ABC and was later instrumental in propelling NBC News into top prominence, saw it as an opportunity to win attention and prestige for his network. ABC was doing badly during daytime anyway, a poor third in audience and sponsorship. He saw to it that ABC carried it all, as did the small Dumont network.

Live coverage of such a sustained event is a difficult problem for networks. It is costly and it is cumbersome for no one knows where it will lead, how it will end. It can be exciting television for those same reasons. Networks have never solved the problem of how you deal with hearings. They can have long, dull stretches. On the other hand, anticipation of the unexpected helps carry the audience along.

Audiences don't always respond enthusiastically. In the Eisenhower years, when television cut away from regular programming to present the United Nations debating during a world crisis, viewers have called in by the thousands to complain. To television's credit, in times of truly great crisis—as during the Cuban missile crisis, the Six Day War between Israel and its Arab neighbors, and so on—the networks have unfailingly gone to the story. Costs are ignored, ruffled feelings among viewers are accepted with teeth gritted.

In matters less vital to the national good, television has had trouble finding the right road to follow. Taped summaries in prime, evening time have been a suggested answer but these generally attract small audiences, larger than the audience that watched live coverage earlier but small for prime time.

Live coverage has had highly dramatic moments as when attorney Joseph Welch turned on Senator Joseph McCarthy for attacking a young lawyer on his staff. In August of 1968, CBS-TV was carrying an evening session of the Democratic Platform Committee hearings live when Secretary of State Rusk was concluding his testimony and was handed a news report of the invasion of Czechoslovakia which he read aloud. The news was the first word for millions of people including the Czech Ambassador to the United States!

Was there ever a moment in any media of communication to match NBC's live coverage of the shooting of Lee Harvey Oswald in the basement of that Dallas jail?

Television's ability to bring events live, from pictures of the moon to Martin Luther King delivering his "I Have A Dream" speech, is television at its most exciting. Perhaps the key to the excitement remains the lack of predictability. Russell Lynes, distinguished editor of *Harper's,* wrote of television, "It reports ably after the fact, but it is when it is a substitute for one's own eyes, watching action as it happens, that it is more miraculous. Who will ever forget the sun reflected in the eyes of Robert Frost so he could not read his poem at President Kennedy's inauguration? Who will forget the McCarthy hearings, the moment when Ruby shot Oswald, the smoke billowing from burning Detroit last summer? Television is the most remarkable transmitter of news ever devised because it is the first to be instantaneous."

Live television, instantaneous television remains a permanent fixture for political conventions, inaugurations, major Presidential appearances, and many major events. How to find the proper way to handle important Senate hearings and other events that aren't "must" coverage remains a dilemma for television. One internal criticism is that once the judgment to carry is made, the only journalistic decision left is when to stop.

Newspapers, which often seem to be urging more live coverage, don't have that problem. They rarely carry a text in full (with the exception of the *New York Times*) and even then, make that decision after the fact with full knowledge of what the text says, of what they think it is worth.

TV's In-Depth-Reporting.

The journalistic talents of television, its excursions into the real world, take flight in the "specials" and documentaries. TV reports in depth and in detail when it breaks the more confining bounds of the daily newscast. It is in specials that the socially significant can be treated for thirty minutes, an hour, a series of one hour broadcasts and even an entire evening on a network.

Well-known and long remembered is Newton Minow's sobriquet "the vast wasteland" but little known and not remembered is something else he said in that same speech: "I know the problems networks face in trying to clear some of their best programs—the informational programs that exemplify public service. They are your finest hours, whether sustaining or commercial, whether regularly scheduled or special; these are the signs that broadcasting knows the way to leadership. They make the public's trust in you a wise choice."

For years, special broadcasts and regularly scheduled programs of the type Minow described were tucked away at unwanted hours. Many of these were Sunday morning or afternoon broadcasts and they were soon termed the "Sunday ghetto." A brilliant exception for many years was the prime time evening hour or half-hour set aside by CBS-TV for "See It Now," "CBS Reports," the "CBS News Hour" and ultimately

"Sixty Minutes." ABC and NBC have had less regular reservation of special time during mid-week. Criticism of the Sunday ghetto, along with the emergence of heavy weekend sports schedules, led to its diminution. With less on Sunday and apart from the period of reaction to the 1959 quiz-program scandal which touched off a spurt of informational programming, there has been less informational programming regularly scheduled. At the same time, however, far more irregularly scheduled broadcasts have come into being.

Today the networks have dozens of such special broadcasts each season, carefully prepared documentaries that are not of a series but "preempt" entertainment programs. In addition, and of great importance, are the non-scheduled "instant" specials. Robert Kintner, having moved on to the Presidency of NBC, and to a lesser extent, his peers at CBS, were responsible for this development. Today an event of major consequence, be it a natural disaster, a world crisis, flights into space, racial disturbances of size, or even the death of a great man, are sure to touch off at least one instant special at one or more networks. While news departments at all networks still would like more time for straight news and documentaries, today they know that should an event of magnitude take place, pre-emption of prime time is the usual, not the unusual thing. Few newspapers would dream of adding a major insert of many pages to handle such an event and few are capable of doing so.

In addition to instant pre-emption, there is planned pre-emption of an entire evening's time. Few newspapers would devote an entire issue to a single topic, no matter how important (though the *Louisville Times* turns over all but a smidgeon of its space to the Kentucky Derby on that first Saturday in May). Television did exactly that, however, when NBC gave an entire evening's coverage to a single topic.

On September 2, 1963, NBC News devoted the entire evening to an examination of civil rights. It was called "The American Revolution of '63" and ran three full hours, produced by Robert "Shad" Northshield and Chet Hagan. Mixing live and film, it covered the full spectrum of the Negro Revolution, including reports on seventy-five different areas of the country and dividing the topic into five main areas: public accommodation, housing, voting, jobs and education. The guest list included virtually everybody who was pertinent to the topic—from Martin Luther King to George Wallace.

Critical acclaim was great (Jack Gould, in the *New York Times* called it "a turning point in TV's journalistic evolution") and two years later, NBC tried again with a three-and-a-half "White Paper" produced by Fred Freed and dealing with U.S. Foreign Policy. Dealing largely with Vietnam, this production was divided in three, the parts dealing with our relations with Russia, with the emerging nations and with Communist China. Critical acclaim came again though the inherent subject matter was not as exciting. Kay Gardella of the *New York Daily News* called it "an absorbing, if not belated, course in American foreign policy" and mused that "we should, we suppose, applaud it" for pre-empting one million dollars worth of prime time but, she noted, "the effort does become watered down when one considers that the shows bumped were all summer repeats." John Horn, in the *New York Herald Tribune* admired the "remarkable organization, smooth editing and skillful blend of words and pictures. But," he added, "it was too long . . . The reviews of events ground on one after another."

Undaunted, NBC came bouncing back a year later with another three-and-a-half hour broadcast. Plenty sexy this topic, it was "Organized Crime in the United States." Air date: August 25, 1966. Still summer re-run time but NBC was most pleased—the audience exceeded thirty-five million viewers (the average viewer in that vast audience watched one hour and thirty-two minutes according to NBC estimates).

ABC entered the field of all-evening documentary with its four-hour presentation on Africa in September of 1967. Brilliantly filmed with narration by actor Gregory Peck, it was the most successful of all such attempts. Where others might tend to run to slow spots, ABC's broadcast had the opportunity to show some of the most magnificent film footage ever shot, the colorful people, scenery and, most of all, animals of Africa. James Fleming had produced a superb broadcast which was later divided into four one-hour films for viewing by school children.

There is some serious question of how much value these one night extravaganzas have. In many ways they are journalistic stunts, a flexing of electronic muscles. How much audience can be retained through a full evening, how much continuity of idea can be maintained through so long a period, are questions to explore.

A somewhat different approach to the long, long television study was undertaken by CBS News in June of 1967 when it did a four-part, four hour study of the Warren Commission Report, devoting the 10 p.m. hour to that project on each of four consecutive days. Though this might be expected to hold an audience better than a broadcast lasting through a full evening, it has the disadvantage of expecting that audience to be available on each of four consecutive nights.

Incidentally, exercises in longevity need not be limited to networks. On December 28, 1968 a local station in Chicago, WMAQ-TV, presented its year-end review. The program lasted eight and a half hours! 1968 was quite a year for news but one suspects that only a few, stone-bottomed fanatics felt strongly enough to sit through over eight hours reviewing it all.

Television's more typical excursions into in-depth reporting have been in the form of the traditional documentary, thirty, sixty or ninety minutes long. The television documentary can't really be discussed without noting the work of Edward R. Murrow and Fred W. Friendly.

Murrow, Friendly and Joseph McCarthy.

Ed Murrow was one of the greatest journalists in history, certainly the finest produced by television, probably the finest in the 20th century. He was one of the few broadcasters without newspaper experience (Bob Trout and John Charles Daly were others) and once noted, "It is an ancient and sad fact that most people in network television and radio have an exaggerated regard for what appears in print." In 1935, Murrow joined CBS as Director of Talks and Education. Two years later he was sent to London as European Director of CBS. It was from there that Murrow's voice, on CBS radio, became the spirit of the war against Hitler. "This is London," he would begin and that magnificent voice would weave word pictures of bombing raids, children being evacuated to the country, Churchill in his finest hour, and all the rest.

In addition to his newscasts, he brought "Hear It Now" and "This I Believe" to CBS Radio. His partnership with Fred W. Friendly began in 1948 with a series of records "I Can Hear It Now" which led to the radio series "Hear It Now." Handsome, urbane Ed Murrow was matched with disheveled, disorganized Fred Friendly who Carl Sandburg once characterized as a man who "always looks as if he had just got off a foam-flecked horse."

Together they began to put new meaning to radio documentary and, ultimately, moved to television with a version of "Hear It Now." On November 18, 1951, "See It Now" opened with Mr. Murrow's laconic comment, "This is an old team trying to learn a new trade." From that opening broadcast which showed live pick-ups of both the Atlantic and Pacific oceans (talk of electronic muscle-flexing!), the "See It Now" team presented a dazzling display of virtuosity ranging from reports on segregation in South Africa to Christmas in Korea to land scandals in Texas.

None was more memorable nor more important than that of March 9, 1954 when "See It Now" dealt with Senator Joseph R. McCarthy of Wisconsin.

Joe McCarthy came as close as any man could to intimidating the American nation. He not only had developed the Red scare to a fine art but at one point in the winter of 1953-54, public polls showed that half the American people approved of his investigations. Further, McCarthyism had seeped into the networks and there were blacklists keeping suspected communists off the air. Friendly was later to write, "Ed and I knew that the timing on this broadcast was crucial. If we waited much longer, history or McCarthy—or both—might run us down."

Murrow was not the first to point out the excesses of the Wisconsin demagogue. Elmer Davis had been doing it right along but that was on radio. To have America's most popular television journalist do so on television was still another matter. "If the Senator believes we have done violence to his words or pictures and desires to speak, to answer himself," Murrow began, "an opportunity will be afforded him . . ."

He then said that his working thesis was this question: "If this fight against Communism is made a fight against America's two great political parties, the American people know that one of these parties will be destroyed and the Republic cannot endure very long as a one-party system." After a pause, Murrow continued, "We applaud that statement and we think Senator McCarthy ought to. He said it, seventeen months ago in Milwaukee."

With that, the broadcast turned to film clips of McCarthy. They made up most of the half-hour. There was McCarthy talking about "twenty years of treason." There was McCarthy disagreeing with President Eisenhower on whether Communism was an issue. There was McCarthy in pursuit of "the scalp of a pink Army dentist." There was McCarthy attacking mud slinging by the left wing press. There was McCarthy talking of Stevenson and saying "Alger—I mean Adlai" as he tried to tie Governor Stevenson to the Alger Hiss case.

Finally, there was McCarthy badgering Reed Harris of the State Department for a book he had written twenty-one years ago while at Columbia, asking him if he knew that the Civil Liberties Union which supplied him with an attorney had been listed as a Communist front.

Then there was this exchange:

McCARTHY: You wrote a book in 1932. I'm going to ask you again at the time you wrote this book, did you feel that professors should be given the right to teach sophomores that marriage "should be cast off of our civilization as antiquated and stupid religious phenomena?" Was that your feeling at the time?

HARRIS: My feeling was that professors should have the right to express their considered opinions on any subject whatever they were, sir.

McCARTHY: I'm going to ask you this question again.

HARRIS: That includes that quotation, they should have the right to teach anything that came to their mind as being a proper thing to teach.

McCARTHY: I'm going to make you answer this.

HARRIS: I'll answer yes, but you put an implication on it and you feature this particular point out of the book which of course is quite out of context, does not give a proper impression of the book as a whole. The American public doesn't get an honest impression of even that book, bad as it is, from what you are quoting from it.

McCARTHY: Then let's continue to read your own writings.

HARRIS: Twenty-one years ago again.

McCARTHY: Yes, we shall try to bring you down to date if we can.

HARRIS: Mr. Chairman, two weeks ago Senator Taft took the position that I taught twenty-one years ago, that Communists and Socialists should be allowed to teach in the schools. It so happens nowadays I don't agree with Senator Taft as far as Communist teachers in the schools is concerned because I think Communists are in effect a plainclothes auxiliary of the Red Army, the Soviet Red Army, and I don't want to see them in any of our schools teaching.

McCARTHY: I don't recall Senator Taft ever having any of the background that you have got.

HARRIS: I resent the tone of this inquiry very much, Mr. Chairman. I resent it not only because it is my neck, my public neck that you are, I think, very skillfully trying to wring, but I say it because there are thousands of able and loyal employees in the Federal government of the United States who have been properly cleared according to the laws and the security practices of their agencies as I was, unless the new regime says no.

After this last film exchange, Murrow came on camera to note that McCarthy had succeeded in proving that Harris had written a bad book and "As for Reed Harris, his resignation was accepted a month later with a letter of commendation. McCarthy claimed it was a victory. The Reed Harris hearing demonstrates one of the Senator's techniques. Twice he said the American Civil Liberties Union was listed as a subversive front. The Attorney General's list does not and has never listed the ACLU as subversive nor does the FBI or any other government agency. And the American Civil Liberties Union holds in its files letters of commendation from President Eisenhower, President Truman and General MacArthur."

Said Murrow in concluding:

"No one familiar with the history of this country can deny that Congressional committees are useful. It is necessary to investigate before legislating, but the line between investigation and persecuting is a very fine one and the junior Senator from Wisconsin has stepped over it repeatedly. His primary achievement has been in confusing the public mind as between internal and external threat of Communism. We must not confuse dissent with disloyalty. We must remember that accusation is not proof and that conviction depends on evidence and due process of law. We must not walk in fear . . ."

The documentary was a devastating expose of the McCarthy technique. There were over 10,000 phone calls and telegrams, ultimately 100,000 letters. Ten to one the viewers supported Murrow. Press reaction was equally favorable though not universally so. The *New York Journal's* critic called it a "hate McCarthy telecast."

McCarthy was to accept the offer for time and just one week later, on March 16, Murrow opened "See It Now" with word that the Senator would appear on April 6. Murrow then turned to what he called "the little picture"—the story of Annie Lee Moss before the McCarthy Committee.

The Senator had talked of a woman employed by the Army in its Code Room who was and might still be an active Communist. Annie Lee Moss appeared before the committee on March 11th. During the course of the hearing it became clear that McCarthy might have made a mistake and the Senator left early, his chief counsel Roy Cohn taking over the interrogation. The closing segment of film played like a Hollywood movie.

ROY COHN: I have no further questions of this witness at this time. We have the testimony of Mrs. Markward, the undercover agent of the FBI, stating that Annie Lee Moss was a member—a dues-paying member of the Communist Party—ah—the Northeast Club of the Communist Party. We have corroboration of that testimony by another witness who was called before the Committee and gave a sworn statement to the effect that she also knew Mrs. Moss as a member of the Northeast Club of the Communist Party.

SEN. JOHN MCCLELLAN: Mr. Chairman, I would like to make this point: We are making statements against a witness who has come and submitted to cross-examination. Now, if we—She has already lost her job; she's been suspended because of this action. I am not defending her. If she is a Communist, I want her exposed but to make these statements that we have got corroborating evidence that she is a Communist, under these circumstances I think she is entitled to have it produced here in her presence and let the public know about it—and let her know about it. (APPLAUSE.) I don't like to try people by hearsay evidence. (APPLAUSE.) I like to get the witnesses here and try 'em by testimony under oath.

SENATOR KARL MUNDT: The Chair will rule that the comments of Mr. Cohn be stricken from the record.

SENATOR MCCLELLAN: I didn't ask that. I didn't ask that, Mr. Chairman.

SENATOR MUNDT: (first inaudible) . . . try to produce a witness in public because the FBI may have her under cover. We don't want to . . .

SENATOR MCCLELLAN: You can't strike these statements made by counsel here as to evidence that we are having and withholding— you cannot strike that from the press or the public mind, once it's planted there. That is—that is the—evil of it. Well, I don't think it's fair to a witness—to a citizen of this country to bring them up here and cross-examine them, and then, when they get through, say, "We have something—the FBI's got something on you that condemns you."

SENATOR MUNDT: The Chair agrees . . .

SENATOR MCCLELLAN: It's not sworn testimony. It's convicting people by rumor, and hearsay, and innuendo . . . (APPLAUSE.)

SENATOR STUART SYMINGTON: Do you know anybody named Mrs. Mary Markward?

MRS. MOSS: No, sir, I do not.

SENATOR SYMINGTON: I think the record ought to show that Mrs. Markward says that she has never seen Mrs. Annie Lee Moss at any Communist meeting, but it is her recollection that Mrs. Moss paid her dues and was a member in good standing. Do you know anybody else in this town named Moss? Have you ever looked up a telephone number? Are there any other Mosses in Washington besides you?

MRS. MOSS: Yes, sir. There are three Annie Lee Mosses.

SENATOR HENRY JACKSON: What was that? Will you state that again?

MRS. MOSS: There were three Annie Lee Mosses. And when I went to get a real-estate license I had an awful lot of trouble then . . .

SENATOR SYMINGTON: I want—I want to say something to you—and I may be sticking my neck out, and I may be wrong—but I have been listening to you testify this afternoon, and I think you are telling the truth.

MRS. MOSS: I certainly am.

SENATOR SYMINGTON: If you are not taken back in the Army, you come around and see me, and I am going to see that you get a job.

MRS. MOSS: Well, thanks a lot. (APPLAUSE.)

The picture of the quiet, little Negro lady sitting in the Senate hearing room, first being quizzed heavily by McCarthy and then being defended by McClellan and Symington was far more telling than the original McCarthy broadcast. If giving McCarthy enough rope was the purpose of the first, it was better accomplished in the second.

There was a dispute over who would provide for the filming of McCarthy's April 6th reply. It was filmed on a Fox Movietone set and the bill of just under $6,400 was paid for by CBS.

The Senator Replies.

The Senator began with sneering reference to Murrow who he called "educational director" of CBS and who "had made repeated attacks upon me and those fighting Communists."

The Senator continued, "Now, ordinarily, I would not take time out from the important work at hand to answer Murrow. However, in this case I feel justified in doing so because Murrow is a symbol, the leader and the cleverest of the jackal pack which is always found at the throat of anyone who dares to expose individual Communists and traitors." In the orginal Murrow broadcast, said McCarthy, Murrow "followed implicitly the Communist line . . . laid down not only by the Communist *Daily Worker*, but the Communist magazine *Political Affairs* and by the National Conference of the Communist Party of the United States of America."

That was the tone of the Senator's reply. It was typical of Joe McCarthy on the attack; it made little reference to the actual Murrow broadcast, it made numerous comments trying to link Murrow with Communists and "Communist-line propagandists," and it ended with a promise not to be deterred by the attacks. "In complete humility, I do ask you and every American who loves this country to join with me."

Technically, the film was poor, the technique stagnant, and the effect weak. Friendly thought it a "vicious self-portrait."

The mail to CBS still ran in Murrow's favor but now by two to one, not ten to one.

"To say that the Murrow broadcast of March 9, 1954 was the decisive blow against Senator McCarthy's power is as inaccurate," wrote Friendly later, "as it is to say that Joseph R. McCarthy, Republican, Wisconsin, single-handedly gave birth to McCarthyism. The disease was here long before he exploited it. Elmer Davis compared it to malaria and prescribed courage as the only antidote."

If it is inaccurate to call the Murrow broadcast the "decisive" blow to McCarthyism, it is improper to underestimate its influence. If courage is the only antidote to McCarthyism, then Murrow-Friendly had more than enough of the serum, enough to share with the American public. Murrow's impact was tremendous. First, he was the single most popular newsman on the air. Match that with another characteristic of broadcasting and you understand why McCarthy would be hard put to answer effectively.

Television, as radio before it, imparts a certain respectability, a certain acceptability upon its product. Advertisers have found that their stature is enhanced because they are on television. This doesn't mean that they sell more of their product necessarily but it does mean that people accept it more readily, say to themselves that this must be something acceptable for it is on television. Even if it is a brand new name to the consumer, they feel it must have somehow met special approval or why else would it be on television.

So did the most respectable of newscasters, in attacking the most powerful of demagogues, have the nature of the medium working for him. Surely if Edward R. Murrow speaks so boldly about the Wisconsin Senator then there must be something wrong with Mr. McCarthy. Surely these reports about McCarthy carelessly attacking the innocent must have some substance—look at Murrow's report, look at Reed Harris, at Annie Lee Moss.

Others, notably Elmer Davis on radio, had spoken up but none carried the weight of this man, Murrow, and this medium, television. Two times thirty minutes of television had turned the tide. Opposition to McCarthy had new respectability, the courageous could now speak louder, the meek could speak for the first time, the fearful could at least listen and perhaps learn. The other side had surfaced.

The half hour between 10:30 and 11 p.m. Eastern time, March 9, 1954 must rank as one of the most socially significant broadcasts of all time. Yet, in one real sense, it was terribly unfair. It was unfair, in deference to the Fairness Doctrine, when it purported to give an equal amount of time to McCarthy. It "purported" to do so because all it really gave was an equal period on air to McCarthy. He could never match the production skill of Murrow and Friendly and his "reply" was doomed before it began.

This argument irritated both Murrow and Friendly. Murrow said later he was uncomfortable about the broadcast, hoped such powerful use of television would not be required again, but emphasized that he never regretted the broadcast. He and Friendly both were disturbed by a Gilbert Seldes column in the *Saturday Review* which talked of "the giant Murrow . . . fighting a pygmy" and called McCarthy's reply "a feebly handled newsreel talk . . . about as weak a television program as you could devise."

Friendly felt that Seldes' criticism smacked of "intellectual fastidiousness . . . abstract morality . . . pristine isolation." Seldes' own editors were obviously troubled; they ran a disclaimer to the column, praised their critic but noted that the critique had caused much debate among the staff. McCarthy was hardly a pygmy—even in this inept television performance. A private survey commissioned by CBS from Elmo Roper showed that fully one-third of McCarthy's audience (and it was immense) believed that McCarthy had raised serious doubts about Murrow or that he had proven Murrow to be pro-Communist.

It might also be argued that McCarthy need not have chosen the route of a "feebly handled newsreel talk." Even that early in the history of television, there were able advisors around to provide proper expertise.

What no one could provide, however, was the respectability, the reputation of Murrow and Friendly. This was the dilemma for McCarthy, for anyone answering charges. If the original source is highly regarded, especially qualified, and effectively sincere, the answer to accusation is extremely difficult to bring off. He might have improved the technique but he could not easily change the atmosphere. On the other hand, the miracle of that week in March was the ability of one broadcast or two to change the atmosphere which McCarthy had imposed upon a nation.

Seldes had called the exchange of broadcasts "a brilliant demonstration of the fallacy" of equal time. William S. Paley, founder and board chairman of CBS, who issued a defense of Murrow, noted that fairness cannot be reduced to mathematical formula. Equal time does not mean equal treatment. On the other hand, said Paley, "It must be recognized that there is a difference between men, ideas and institutions: some are good and some are bad, and it is up to us to know the difference—to know what will hold up democracy and what will undermine it—and then not to do the latter."

TV's Courage and Lack of Courage.

If equal time is fallacious, then the fallacy has two sides—that of the problem of the aggrieved having trouble in his reply but equally significant, the acceptance by the broadcaster of the notion that giving the time ends his responsibility. Broadcasting, when a Timid Giant, offers journalism forever saying "on the other hand, there is this argument"— and not taking to the issue firmly. In its finest hours, it has. On March 9, 1954 it did.

Such courage, in production and in defense of production, was rare in those days. Friendly's own examination of what happened, as expressed in his memoirs *Due to Circumstances Beyond Our Control . . .*, indicates that not everyone at CBS was happy about the broadcast, nor were all eager to defend it later.

Broadcasting has a mixed record of courage. Sometimes it is remarkably bold in presentation and defending its right to present controversy. Sometimes it seeks safer roads to travel.

In his book *The People Machine*, former NBC correspondent Robert MacNeil bitterly tells of his work on a documentary dealing with gun controls. Having commissioned a Gallup poll which showed that a vast majority of Americans wanted stricter laws concerning guns, producer Fred Freed and correspondent MacNeil planned to spell out the nature of the gun problem in a one hour program called "Whose Right To Bear Arms?" The title should indicate the editorial thrust of the hour.

MacNeil wrote that the 1966 broadcast included a searching interview with Franklin Orth, Executive Director of the National Rifle Association which "was designed to bring out very clearly the inconsistencies —in fact, the hypocrisy—of the NRA position." MacNeil was to follow this with a brief summary on camera noting that an interested minority was pressuring Congress with success. He called for the Congress to overthrow these pressures and pass a bill.

Word got around, says MacNeil, and NBC received a letter from Democratic Congressman John Dingell of Michigan. Dingell, a member of the Commerce Committee which oversees broadcasting, said that if the broadcast planned to actively press for a particular legislative position, he felt the opponents of legislation restricting guns should be given full opportunity on the broadcast. He was willing, the Congressman wrote, to go to the FCC and the Chairman of the Commerce Committee to express those views.

Of course the Fairness Doctrine does not insist that the "other view" be heard in the same broadcast but NBC, according to MacNeil, moved to soften the impact of the broadcast. The Orth interview was watered down and the closing essay was changed, made, says MacNeil, exceedingly tame. *Variety* called it a "cream puff" ending. MacNeil says that the late William R. McAndrew, President of NBC News, fought the pressures of the lawyers and the network brass but finally permitted re-editing. McAndrew's successor, Reuven Frank, says MacNeil is wrong about his facts, that McAndrew felt the broadcast needed more balance, that he ordered the changes "irrespective" of Dingell's letter.

As for Dingell, he later said he was "delighted" with the changes. He said he considers it proper for a Congressman to ask that NBC "behave properly."

The full weight of the U. S. State Department was thrust against network documentaries about Germans tunnelling under the Berlin Wall. In 1962, both NBC and CBS began work on such broadcasts. Word got to State and pressures against the productions were strongly felt. Robert Kintner, President of NBC, called it his network's "worst encounter with the government," called the pressure unremitting.

CBS News had particularly bad luck. In addition to the pressures from State, police in West Berlin blocked off "their" tunnel. There were other complications. Eventually, CBS abandoned its project. The network could hardly be pleased with the accolade from State Department Press Officer Lincoln White: "When apprised of the Department's view that involvement of American television personnel in clandestine tunnel operations was both dangerous and irresponsible, the Columbia Broadcasting System promptly and laudably withdrew from a tunnel project. This was greatly appreciated."

That October 19, 1962 statement continued, "NBC was made equally aware of the Department's view that such involvement was risky, irresponsible, undesirable, and not in the best interests of the United States. NBC chose to continue . . ." Actually, NBC did not show its documentary as scheduled on October 31st for the Cuban missile crisis had erupted. Kintner and McAndrew decided to hold it until international tensions had ceased. It was shown on December 10th.

The 90-minute documentary was a remarkable picture story of courageous Berliners fighting their way out of the Communist side of that divided city. The tunnel was completed on September 14th and fifty-nine East Germans, the largest single group since the wall had gone up, escaped. NBC had a complete film record of the affair. Kintner was to write, "I consider 'The Tunnel' to be one of the great achievements of broadcasting journalism."

It was produced and written by Reuven Frank with Piers Anderton as the correspondent. It was presented after high level State Department visits to New York which included a warning, incorrect as it turned out, that East Germans had discovered the tunnel and further work would be dangerous. NBC was certain that showing the film would not compromise the escapees or the family they left behind but that it would tell the flight-to-freedom story cogently.

As Kintner later put it, "Eventually, at least one branch of the United States government agreed: the U. S. Information Agency edited our hour-long (sic) program down to half an hour, and distributed prints overseas."

This situation is the reverse of that in 1961 when the USIA tried to stop an American documentary from a showing overseas. The head of USIA at the time was Edward R. Murrow. The documentary was his own, "Harvest of Shame."

The broadcast, which aired November 25, 1960, was a burning indictment of the plight of migrant workers in the United States. It was a non-fiction equivalent of John Steinbeck's best depression prose. The late David Lowe was the producer under the Murrow-Friendly aegis. Lowe's cameras followed the migrants as they picked their way through Florida oranges and tomatoes, Georgia peaches, beans in the Carolinas, corn in Virginia and on to potato fields in Long Island. Coming the day after Thanksgiving, it shocked millions of Americans and touched off a flood of protests by big agriculture interests.

The American Farm Bureau Federation was particularly distressed and flooded newsmen and Congressmen with letters and pamphlets calling the broadcast a "gross distortion, highly-colored propaganda, a rigged documentary." It wrote an "open letter" to broadcasters suggesting that the distortions, "the just plain dishonest reporting," could undermine public confidence in television.

Five months after it appeared, the BBC announced plans to show the CBS documentary. Murrow by that time had gone into government and was head of the USIA. He called the BBC and asked them to cancel their showing. The BBC refused. Murrow said his action was based on the fact that the broadcast was a description of a national blemish and not intended for export. The Farm Bureau, which also asked the BBC to withhold the broadcast unless the American farmer could tell his side of the story, claimed that after the CBS production Murrow had perhaps been exposed to subsequent disclosures which "may have caused him to seriously question whether it really was the 'truth'."

The story became public. Murrow was embarrassed, took full blame, insisting that he acted on his own for fear that British audiences consider the broadcast to have government support. Others were not willing to let Murrow hold the bag alone. It became apparent that there was much agricultural and Congressional pressure on the White House. The White House later admitted as much, saying it had encouraged Murrow since the State Department feared that "Harvest of Shame" would be considered an official American Government document, narrated by a top government official.

It was an unfortunate touch of tarnish on Murrow's great reputation. He himself called his actions "both foolish and futile." For him it was a bitter harvest.

If television documentaries can stir up such heat, it is a credit to broadcasting that despite lapses under pressure, such broadcasts continue to this day. It is a credit to broadcasting and a boon to the need to know in a democracy.

Sponsors and Controversy.

As a general rule over the years, sponsors seem less enthusiastic about controversy. There have been some remarkable examples of sponsor courage and some dreadful examples of sponsor fear.

In 1962, ABC News did a broadcast on Richard M. Nixon after he was defeated for Governor of California. Howard K. Smith included a number of figures, both pro- and anti-Nixon in the half-hour program. The most controversial was Alger Hiss who was convicted of perjury after appearing before a House Un-American Activities Committee hearing on Communist espionage. Hiss accused Nixon of being politically motivated in his pursuit of Hiss.

The appearance of Hiss at all on a broadcast involving Nixon touched off a flood of protests when word got out. Some of ABC's affiliates said they would not carry the program. The Schick Razor Company said it would cancel a million dollars worth of advertising with ABC. The Kemper Insurance Company threatened to drop another show. The network refused to honor the withdrawals, said it would hold these sponsors to their contracts.

James Hagerty, once the Eisenhower Press Secretary and at that time ABC's vice president in charge of news, came out with fighting words. "The issue deals with the basic American principle of freedom of the press, of exchange of ideas, free speech, free assent and dissent . . . pressure in advance to force cancellation of a program and pressure after it by economic means to punish or intimidate . . . threatens not only the very existence of freedom of the press, but enterprise itself. It must be resisted."

A hearty "amen" came from Newton Minow, then Chairman of the FCC. Ironically, Minow had been severely critical of ABC for its entertainment programming. On this issue he was most emphatic in support of Hagerty's position.

Re-examination of Kennedy's Assassination.

Television's involvement in longer broadcasts, its pursuits into in-depth reporting have touched on a number of controversies. As interesting as any was the CBS excursion into the debate over John F. Kennedy's assassination.

One of the most brilliant and meticulous, most thorough and most careful of CBS News producers is Leslie Midgley. When the Warren Commission was formed to investigate the killing of John Kennedy, Midgley formed a unit to follow that investigation. Every time a witness was called by the Commission, Midgley's people tried to interview that witness. In most cases, they got their interview.

Fred Friendly, by then President of CBS News, was determined to offer a complete documentary on the report at the time of its issue. The Midgley unit was gathering the raw data for television step by step as the Commission gathered its data for the report. It soon became apparent that the Commission was being thorough enough that the report would not come quickly. Even as it did its work, there was an outpouring of theories about conspiracies to kill Kennedy. In late September, the Commission would issue its conclusions.

George Reedy, then Presidential Press Secretary, invited the top Washington bureau chiefs—newspapers, news magazines, wire services, broadcasting—to a secret meeting at the White House. He made it clear that the report would be voluminous and so he wanted to issue it in advance to the media. They must have time to study it carefully, he said. A Sunday night release time would be arranged.

Friendly had received permission for a two-hour presentation on that Sunday night and urged this writer to encourage Reedy to set the release time to match. This was done successfully but suddenly CBS discovered a conflict and Friendly was asked to present his broadcast earlier, 5:00 to 7:00 p.m. Eastern Time. Friendly called in despair. He could not get the time changed and the Warren Commission release time was 6:30 p.m. What could be done? Midgley had a superb compilation of eye-witness interviews. To cut it to thirty minutes and match the release time would be disastrous. He went back to his colleagues at CBS headquarters but they would not budge—it would have to be 5:00 p.m. to 7:00 p.m.

Friendly called Washington again. Could Reedy change the release time? An inquiry was made. Reedy turned down the request; it was too late, too many things were in the works. Then came an inspiration from the Washington bureau chief: why not present the CBS News material from 5:00 to 6:30 p.m.—ending each examination with questions, note that at 6:30 p.m. the Warren report is made public and we would then give the Commission's answers to these questions. This was the answer!

Midgley started reworking his material into this new form—a 90-minute CBS News summary which raised a series of questions; then, once we received advance copies of the Commission report, a 30-minute climax giving the Commission answers. As it turned out, this format dictated by necessity had the virtue of building suspense. To assure Reedy that there would be no "cheating" by CBS News, he was invited to come to New York and view the first ninety minutes *before* the advance copies of the report were issued. Reedy said he had no concern about CBS News breaking the release time.

And so the Commission report came out on that late September day. With Walter Cronkite (who had carried the burden of four days of CBS News coverage during the post-assassination period) and Dan Rather (White House correspondent and covering in Dallas during the same four days) as moderators, it was a thorough report on what was known at the time and what the Warren Commission had reported.

It was not an answer to the multitude of alternative theories.

It was not a critical review of the Commission, nor could it be in the limited time available.

It could no more quiet those who questioned official explanation than could the Commission report.

The things it was not remained to haunt many at CBS News. In the summer of '66, with the many critics firing buckshot at the Warren Report, some at CBS News began to wonder if there wasn't more to be done.

Many members of the staff had doubts about the Warren Commission Report. They had read the alternate theories, they had seen the criticisms of the Commission approach. Gordon Manning, Vice President for News, suggested that CBS News embark on its own independent investigation. Richard Salant, his boss, was skeptical. Without legal power and the resources that the Warren Commission had, could CBS do a really significant examination? The debate swirled within high circles of CBS News.

The network did have one major advantage over the Commission— the passage of time had made not only the Commission Report public but had touched off a flurry of books and articles attacking it. There were those who felt that success by CBS News in discrediting the official report would be traumatic to the country but would be a most important public service. However, they reasoned, failure to show error in the Warren Report would be a wasted exercise. Some of us counseled differently. If CBS News embarked on a careful, objective study overtly probing weakness in the Warren Commission study, then the results would be extremely valuable, even if they changed not a word nor a thought of the official probe. The atmosphere of disbelief had flourished so, it would be a genuine public service to support the report—if our conclusions, independently and carefully derived, did reach the same position.

Midgley began preliminary work. Enthusiasm began to grow. It became apparent that CBS News could do that which the now defunct Commission could not: it could explore every significant attack on the Commission findings.

Much of the anti-Warren theory rested on the timing of the shots fired by Oswald and, eventually, Midgley set up a more valid test of the firings and showed them; tests from the right height, distance and angle involving a moving target. The FBI tests of Oswald's rifle were fired at a stationary target from a distance shorter than that between Oswald's perch and the President's auto. The CBS tests had shown that Oswald could have squeezed off three shots in the time span mentioned in the Warren report, something critics had strongly questioned. More important, CBS tests showed that the time span itself could have been longer.

The official timing of the shots was "clocked" by the only good film of the assassination, that taken by an amateur photographer, Abraham Zapruder. Zapruder's film was purchased and is still owned by *Life* magazine and in November, 1966 that magazine published a series of stills from his film. One of America's greatest physicists, later to win the Nobel prize, was Professor Luis Alvarez of the University of California. The *Life* photos piqued his curiosity. He developed a theory that photo analysis might reveal evidence of shock waves and in turn, help determine the number and timing of the shots.

Mr. Salant, now growing excited about the project, sent CBS News people to talk to Alvarez. The good doctor later decided his theory would not hold up and Alvarez dropped the shock wave approach. However, he opened many new vistas for the CBS News detectives to explore and Salant was now firmly wedded to the project.

It was too much for an hour, too much for two. Salant proposed a series of three one-hour broadcasts in prime time, the same time on successive nights. Ultimately this was expanded to four, the last serving as a summary and to explore fully the question of why there was so much public suspicion of the Warren Report conclusions.

At 10 p.m. Sunday, June 25, 1967 the first hour was presented, followed by Part Two on Monday, Three on Tuesday and the final Part Four on Wednesday, June 28th. A measure of public interest was the audience, some thirty million viewers for Part One alone—a top audience for any program and one of the top ten ratings for that week. Other audiences were almost as large.

An old friend of Midgley's who had worked on many previous Midgley projects came aboard on this one—Stephen White, Director of Special Projects at the Salk Institute for Biological Studies. White was later to write a book about the broadcasts (*Should we now Believe the Warren Report*, MacMillan, 1968) in which he said of the Commission:

> To the easier of its tasks, it was completely adequate. It did not turn out to be at all difficult to ascertain what happened that day in Dallas, and the Commission has nailed it all down as tightly as anyone could have hoped to see it done. The more difficult task, that of persuading the American people, escaped it.

That of course was not the approach of the four broadcasts but became its conclusion. The approach was to begin with skepticism, to prove the Commission wrong. The Commission errors uncovered by CBS News turned out to be minor, its virtues were confirmed. But no single fact was accepted without thorough questioning, doubting. As White put it:

> The people who wrote, filmed, produced and appeared on these broadcasts would have been the happiest journalists of this or almost any other century if they could have come up with a sensational "solution" to the Kennedy murder.

But it didn't happen. Witnesses and participants in the autopsy and Commission members who had never talked to the press before, did so for these broadcasts. The independent CBS News studies of ballistics, time of movements, angles of trajectories, etc. were remarkable. Walter

Cronkite felt that apart from the four days following the assassination itself, American television had never mounted such a massive single effort. The broadcasts were nine months in preparation, involved thousands of man hours, hundreds of thousands of feet of film, and a budget of half a million dollars.

Cronkite's conclusion at the end of the last broadcast said, "We have found that most objections to the Report—and certainly all objections that go to the heart of the Report—vanish when they are exposed to the light of honest inquiry. It is a strange kind of tribute to the Warren Report that every objection that can be raised against it is to be found in the Report itself. It is true that some of the answers to some questions leave us restless. The theory that a single bullet struck down both the President and the Governor, for example, has too much of the long arm of coincidence about it for us to be entirely comfortable. But would we be more comfortable believing that a shot was fired by a second assassin who materialized out of thin air for the purpose, fired a shot, and then vanished again into thin air, leaving behind no trace of himself, his rifle, his bullet, or any other sign of existence.

"Measured against the alternatives, the Warren Commission Report is the easiest to believe, and that is all the Report claims. But we have found also that there has been a loss of morale, a loss of confidence among the American people toward their own government and the men who serve it. And that is perhaps more wounding than the assassination itself."

It was to these points that Eric Sevareid addressed himself in Part Four:

What fed the conspiracy notion about the Kennedy assassination among many Americans was the sheer incongruity of the affair. All that power and majesty wiped out in an instant by one skinny, weak-chinned, little character. It was like believing that the Queen Mary had sunk without a trace, because of a log floating somewhere in the Atlantic, or that AT&T's stock had fallen to zero because a drunk somewhere tore out his telephone wires.

But this almost unbelievable incongruity has characterized nearly every one of the assassinations and attempted assassinations of American Presidents. Deranged little men killed Lincoln, Garfield, McKinley, tried to kill Presidents Theodore and Franklin Roosevelt. Only the Puerto Rican attempt on President Truman represented a real conspiracy.

There are still people who think Adolph Hitler is alive, people who think the so-called learned Elders of Zion are engaged in a Jewish plot to control the world. The passage of years, the failure of anybody anywhere to come up with respectable evidence does not shake the people who cling to these illusions.

And so, three and a half years later, there are people who still think some group of men are living somewhere, carrying in their breasts the most explosive secret conceivable, knowledge of a plot to kill Mr. Kennedy. These imagined men supposedly go about their lives under iron self-discipline, never falling out with each other, never giving out a hint of suspicion to anyone else.

And nearly three years after the Warren inquiry finished its painful and onerous work, there are not only the serious critics who point to the various mistakes of commission or omission, mistakes of a consequence one can only guess at, and of a kind that has probably plagued every lengthy, voluminous official investigation ever staged; there are also people who think the Commission itself was a conspiracy to cover up something.

In the first place it would be utterly impossible in the American arena of a fierce and free press and politics to conceal a conspiracy among so many individuals who live in the public eye. In the second place the deepest allegiance of men like Chief Justice Warren, or of John McCloy, does not lie with any President, political party, or current cause—it lies with history, their name and place in history. That is all they live for in their later years. If they knowingly suppressed or distorted decisive evidence about such an event as a Presidential murder, their descendants would bear accursed names forever. The notion that they would do such a thing is idiotic.

Public reaction to the broadcast series was highly favorable, about three out of four letters were in praise. Most critics were friendly. But the undercurrent of advocates of the conspiracy theory is strong. *Variety's* reviewer was a skeptic, noted that one reporter had observed that the Kennedy windshield had been shattered. He may have believed he observed that but the windshield in question still exists, it is at the National Archives, available for all to examine. It is unbroken. The criticism is typical of the kind of thread that is woven into the conspiracy legends.

As White said in his book, "CBS News failed to cover every issue which a dozen critics managed to raise, but it could not have done that in four hours or two hours or twenty hours, and in any case it was not worth doing. Every important issue was covered, and most of the rest are merely frivolous."

It was a remarkable series that those thirty million viewers shared. In addition to White's book, another dealing largely with the CBS News inquiry was later published. Mark Lane, the most vocal of the conspiracy theorists, attacked the series in *A Citizen's Dissent—Mark Lane Replies.*

Ironically his publisher was Holt, Rinehart and Winston—a publishing house owned by CBS, Inc.

Network Documentaries in the 60's.

The documentaries of television in the 1960's are an impressive anthology of alert journalism dealing with every known social ill of our society, with every major political and international crisis. It is easy to criticize the general output of the mass media, it is easy to complain of the relatively small air time devoted to the real world but conversely it is important to acknowledge the use to which that time is put.

This was a decade in which ABC-TV, least productive of the three networks, gave us "Walk In My Shoes," a brilliant examination of the Negro problem produced in September of 1961. ABC also provided a home for Robert L. Drew to produce his "Crisis: Behind A Presidential Commitment," "Yanqui No!" and "The Children Were Watching." John Secondari, most prolific of the ABC producers and his wife Helen Jean Rogers gave us the series "The Saga of Western Man" and the ABC-TV was home for the first television treatment of the Theodore H. White studies of Presidential campaigns: "The Making of the President, 1960."

NBC during the decade of the '60's and under the direction of Executive Producer Irving Gitlin offered its White Papers which included "The U-2 Affair," "The Battle of Newburgh" (one of the most telling examinations of the controversy over Welfare programs), the "Business of Gambling," "Cuba: Bay of Pigs" and "Cuba: the Missile Crisis."

That series also produced "The Death of Stalin" and "The Rise of Khrushchev"—two broadcasts that irritated the Russians so that NBC was ordered to close its Moscow bureau. In a rare gesture of network friendship, Richard Salant—head of CBS News—offered NBC full use of its Moscow bureau and correspondents. McAndrew of NBC declined because NBC feared that the Russions would throw CBS out, too (they did, at other times, for other broadcasts). It took direct intervention by Secretary of State Dean Rusk, who negotiated personally with Foreign Minister Gromyko, to get NBC back into Moscow.

NBC also produced "Same Mud, Same Blood"—one of the finest documentaries done on Vietnam. Frank McGee magnificently did the story of the Negro soldier and his contribution to our efforts in Vietnam, his problems being a Black.

CBS News produced Fred Friendly's fascinating study (two broadcasts) "Storm Over the Supreme Court," "The Business of Heroin," "Case History of a Rumor" (which infuriated right wing extremists), "Murder and the Right to Bear Arms," and "Gideon's Trumpet—the Poor Man and the Law." It even did a documentary on television ratings in 1965 and that same year, David Lowe's biting study "Ku Klux Klan—The Invisible Empire."

One of the most impressive CBS News efforts came in 1968 with "Hunger in America," a moving hour that evoked memories of "Harvest of Shame." Produced by Martin Carr, reported by David Culhane and moderated by Charles Kuralt, the hour opened with film of a baby actually dying as the camera took its picture.

The broadcast had tremendous impact, especially on the Secretary of Agriculture, Orville Freeman, who bitterly attacked it and demanded equal time. He called it "shoddy journalism" that blackened the name of the Agriculture Department. Even as Freeman attacked, he was taking official steps that CBS interpreted as conceding the broadcast's main points: the Department abandoned its ceiling on food stamp programs, sharply expanded the number of counties with such programs, enlarged the quantity and variety of surplus food and sought (and won) Senate approval for an additional $200 to $300 million for food programs.

Despite the movements in the directions suggested by the broadcast, Freeman remained vehement and kept demanding time on the network. CBS President Frank Stanton turned him down. CBS broadcast the documentary again with mention of Freeman's criticism. A number of Congressmen whose districts were portrayed were furious. Later, a Senate investigation into the subject was set and Senator Philip Hart of Michigan said the CBS broadcast had more to do with creation of the Senate inquiry than anything else. "Yet," he said, "CBS caught hell because they put on that show. But I welcome a chance to thank them for doing it."

Further vindication, if it were needed, came from the President of the United States. Mr. Nixon, speaking at the Department of Agriculture said:

> I noted the tremendous interest and I think it is encouraging that such an interest finally is developing among the people at large —the interest in the problem of hunger in the U.S. It was a CBS Television program a few months ago in which millions of Americans, for the first time, living in what is really the best fed, best housed, best clothed nation in the world—millions of Americans saw on television that in this rich land there is hunger.

Sometimes television does its thing best simply by presenting long, well-edited interviews with wise, old men. Best of the lot, perhaps, was the series with Walter Lippmann talking to different CBS News correspondents (Howard K. Smith, Cronkite, Schoenbrun, Collingwood and Sevareid). Fred Friendly was the creator of that happy idea. He and

Lippmann share an anecdote concerning Friendly convincing the distinguished journalist to go on television, telling him he'll get him away from the little-read editorial page. "Friendly," Mr. Lippmann is said to have replied, "I give you respectability!"

In December of 1968, CBS News presented an hour with Justice Hugo Black. Strikingly edited by producer Burton Benjamin (the genius behind the "Twentieth Century" series and its sparkling son, "Twenty-first Century"), the hour was the first time a member of the Supreme Court discussed the nature of that body on television. The interview was handled by Eric Sevareid and Martin Agronsky. The competition, on NBC, was an hour with French sex-star Bridgit Bardot. The Bardot audience was many times that of CBS that evening but a quiet offer to send one copy of the U.S. Constitution to anyone who wrote in resulted in 125,000 letters.

Such programs prove that good talk, in that "picture medium" television, can often suffice. A good picture isn't always needed. The much abused "talking heads" approach can be excellent if they are talking sense.

Ed Murrow once said, "The fact that your voice is amplified to the degree where it reaches from one end of the country to the other does not confer upon you greater wisdom or understanding than you possessed when your voice reached only one end of the bar to the other." On the other hand, greater wisdom and understanding, talking from one end of the country to the other, can be exhilarating.

But do the documentarians and great interviews reach from one end to the other? Unfortunately not always. Traditionally, CBS News got spotty acceptance of its regularly scheduled news hour because a number of affiliates tend to prefer passing the hour in favor of something more saleable or more attractive to mass audiences. The situation greatly improved in recent years. NBC often does better because its special programs are scheduled irregularly and stations cannot regularly by-pass them with a local series.

ABC has had the saddest experience of all with its "Scope" series of documentaries (many dealing with the Vietnam war). At one point, less than fifty of the 170 or so ABC affiliates carried it live, another two dozen carried it delayed, often at the poorest of air times. In time, even this sad record deteriorated and "Scope" went off the air.

CHAPTER 3

TELEVISION AND
THE BLACK REVOLUTION

THERE IS AN ancient Swahili proverb that says, "The hungry man does not hear."

This could be the slogan of the Black Revolution of the 1960's, or most any other revolution for that matter. The hungry do not hear the drum beats that others do. The poor do not read the lessons of the law. The oppressed do not hear the sermons of the righteous. The frustrated cannot learn the lyrics of national anthems.

As progress is made in identifying disease, salving symptoms and even curing causes, the hungry and the deaf and the frustrated seem angrier and more troublesome, not less. This is the nature of Revolution. Sometimes first victories, first successes don't appease; they agitate. In the case of the Black Revolution, it is whites who can't understand the pattern. The initial rebellion catches them by surprise. Their conscience twinged, their tranquility disturbed, the white establishment grants concessions. Astoundingly, the Blacks seem to agitate all the more.

"Why can't they be like us?" the whites ask. "Why can't they work their way up as our immigrant fathers did? Why can't they follow the manners, the mores of our upward motivated society? Why can't they obey the laws? Are not the laws for all?" Anatole France slyly reminded us that "The law, in its majestic equality, forbids the rich as well as the poor to sleep under bridges, to beg in the streets and to steal bread."

The Black Revolution may be no different than other revolutions, in the general nature of what social revolution is and how it comes to be. It is considerably different in its impact, the speed in which its ideas are transmitted within and without the Black culture, and the manner in which those ideas are transmitted. It is, in short, a revolution with television. It is a "first."

To associate the Negro drive of the 60's with television may seem parochial. It reminds one of the story that received currency at the turn of the century when outsiders would tour the areas of the South still smarting from the Civil War. There was a melancholy tendency to date every event with the War.

"How beautiful the moon is tonight," the visitor would observe.

"Yes," the native would reply, "But you should have seen it before the War."

Before television, Black may have been beautiful but it was a quiet beauty. Though there were fifty years or more of Negro protest, the only real victory and the most important spark of public attention came in 1954 when nine white men, dressed in black, ruled that school segregation was unconstitutional. In those fifty years, according to the U. S. Crime Commission, over 4,500 persons were lynched. How conscious of this was America? In contrast, the television coverage that grew in the 60's served as companion to demonstrations. Unlike those of other years, attention was now paid. With success, the demonstration grew, the coverage increased, and the Revolution spun on with frenzied momentum.

It was untidy. Revolutions are. There were "civil insurrections." We tend to call them riots but riots, "race" riots, are different. These were not whites against Blacks; they were Blacks against their environment.

Historian Theodore H. White noting the emergence of both the Blacks and the rebelling young, said early in 1969: "In 1960 we still lived in the old environment... During the past eight years we've had the Black revolt and the student revolt, which could take place only on the stage that TV provided. We have become accustomed to the new rhetoric of confrontation which Martin Luther King first devised..."

He first used it in 1955 in Montgomery, Alabama. Rosa Parks, a Negro seamstress, was fined ten dollars for refusing to give up a seat on a public bus. The Black community of Montgomery started a bus boycott and a young preacher named Martin Luther King took over its leadership. The boycott lasted 381 days, ending in November of 1956 when a Federal court injunction prohibited bus segregation. During that year, Dr. King was arrested, his home was bombed, and his name became nationally known. Television. There was plenty of coverage in the print media but television brought home the picture of quiet eloquence, of determined righteousness.

The following year was the year of Little Rock. President Eisenhower sends in 1,000 paratroopers to escort nine Negro students into Central High School. Plenty of print coverage but none to match the scenes on television: armed guards walking next to teen-age Blacks, angry white mothers shouting scurrilously into the cameras, white officialdom saying "never."

Then came the 60's. On February 1st, 1960 a small group of Negroes began a sit-in at the Woolworth dime store lunch counter in Greensboro, North Carolina. Before the year was out, it had spread across the South (and some in the North) with sit-ins at lunch counters, hotels, movie theatres, libraries, supermarkets, amusement parks, bus depots.

On television, with its rapidly growing audience and rapidly increased news coverage, there was a college of vivid scenes: young Negroes dragged out of buildings, grim-jawed sit-ins surrounded by angry whites, hoodlums pouring mustard on the heads of Blacks at a lunch counter, police moving in with brutal swiftness.

The chief Washington representative of the National Association for the Advancement of Colored People, Clarence Mitchell, wrote this author that: "People who did not bother to read newspaper stories of civil rights violations saw such violations dramatically produced on the screens in their homes . . . this had a profoundly constructive effect on many persons. In addition, some of those who perpetrated violence against persons exercising their civil rights seemed to have second thoughts when they viewed themselves on television. For example, I heard one restaurant proprietor on a program almost pitifully reproaching himself after he had seen a tape of his attack on some Negroes. I believe he put a messy mixture of flour, eggs or some other gooey combination on the heads of the demonstrators. His act came through on the screen as malevolently childish . . ."

It is doubtful that many such acts of contrition or repentance resulted from viewing one's own actions on television. But millions of less committed viewers share the viewings. What impact there? Abe Lincoln, exactly one hundred years earlier said that public discussion is helping doom slavery: "What kills a skunk is the publicity it gives itself."

The publicity in 1960 culminated at New Orleans in November. Two elementary schools were desegregated and there was wild white reaction: a boycott of the integrated schools, picketing and violence. The spring of 1961 saw the beginning of the "Freedom Rides." On the 4th of May the first left Washington, D. C. with New Orleans as a goal. Ten days later, the bus was stoned and burned in Anniston, Alabama. The smoke lingered on in every television news program. Riders were attacked in Birmingham, Montgomery (where martial law had to be declared) and in Jackson, Mississippi.

The following summer, in Albany, Georgia, there was an unsuccessful attempt to desegregate all public facilities. Martin Luther King was arrested. The charge: "parading without a permit." All of this now becoming daily fare on television. On September 30th, James Meredith tried to enter "Ole Miss" and riots broke out on the Oxford, Mississippi campus. Governor Ross Barnett had blocked the 29-year old Air Force veteran at the school doorway. President Kennedy federalized the National Guard and sent in troops as the campus was torn up—two dead, many injured.

Targets at "Ole Miss" included newsmen. Angry whites turned on reporters and television cameramen. Nicholas Katzenbach, Deputy Attorney General when he stood at another schoolhouse door confronting Governor George Wallace at the University of Alabama, wrote:

> Newsmen have been the occasion of violence in the South in large measure because segregationists realize an unquestionable truth: that press coverage is an essential part of the civil-rights movement. Exposure, after all, is a central means of making a private moral conviction public, of impelling people all over to see and confront ideas they otherwise would turn away from.
>
> The bitter segregationists' view of this is that the demonstrators are following the cameras, not visa-versa. To them, it is the Northern press and the television networks which seem to be the motive force in the civil-rights movement. This idea apparently motivated many of the toughs during the 1961 Freedom rides in Selma and elsewhere. Almost their first moves were against the camera.
>
> Yet news coverage has been a powerful deterrent to racial violence in the South. For every assault on newsmen, many more incidents have been defused by their presence. Reporters and cameras, particularly the network television cameras, which symbolize the national focus on Southern violence, have had a tempering as well as instructional effect. Even more basically, the importance of full coverage has been demonstrated by its recording of fact. Only because of the extensive reporting and film evidence on the University of Mississippi rioting in September, 1962, was it possible to show how absurd were the persistent claims that the United States marshals had started it all.

A black man, Clarence Mitchell of the NAACP, echoes this when he says, "I believe that even though there was a great deal of brutality against persons staging sit-ins, etc., it would have been worse if cameramen had not been on the scene making a record. Knowing the tactics of some law enforcement officers of that period, I believe that if there had been no pictorial record a great many people would have been shot 'while attempting to escape' or for 'assaulting an officer'."

At this stage in the civil rights movement, the violence was still "racial" in the sense of whites versus Blacks, unlike later stages in which Blacks burned down the ghettoes they lived in. The number of deaths and injuries, widely publicized as they were, compared badly with the victims of earlier race riots. In East St. Louis, Illinois in July of 1917 there was rioting following the hiring of Negroes by an aluminum plant that had been struck by an all-white union. Before it ended, thirty-nine Negroes and nine whites were dead, hundred of people injured and 300 buildings destroyed. Chicago in 1919 was tense because of Negro housing. In a period of just a few years, fifty-eight Negro homes had been bombed. An incident at adjoining white and Negro beaches led to several days of rioting, some three dozen deaths, hundreds of injuries, vast property damage. Detroit in 1943 saw a riot that killed twenty-five Negroes, nine whites and caused two million dollars damage. In Harlem that year, six died and 500 were injured.

At "Ole Miss", in 1962, two died.

Television had another effect. Newspapers which had treated the stories lightly (some did so even when it was in their own city) began to give the civil rights movement more attention. Local radio and television, in some places as protective of The Establishment as the local newspaper, were shamed into coverage because it was there, on the network newscasts.

Spring of 1963 saw one of the most dramatic displays of local, white authority in confrontation with demonstrators—the fire hoses and police dogs of Birmingham Police Commissioner "Bull" Connor. The 16 mm. film record of marchers, including school children buffeted to the curb under tremendous water pressure was seen across the country, across the world.

Then, in rapid order, came the flood of new impressions: Birmingham Negroes rioting after Dr. King's motel room and his younger brother's home are bombed; George Wallace at the University's "schoolhouse door" in Alabama reading his long statement on "oppression of State's Rights" as Katzenbach stands by ready to deliver a Presidential proclamation calling for the registration of two Negroes (all of this on the television); Mississippi NAACP State Chairman Medgar Evans murdered as he entered his home in Jackson; demonstrations and riots in Cambridge, Maryland and finally—the March on Washington.

August 28, 1963: the culmination of non-violence in the civil rights movement. A quarter of a million people, over one out of five are white, fill the Mall from the Lincoln Memorial to the Washington Monument. Live, network television carries much of the day; the networks coming in and out of live coverage of the program. It is the largest, most dramatic and most peaceful of all civil rights demonstrations and culminates with Dr. King's magnificent "I have a dream . . ." speech.

And less than three weeks later, a Birmingham church is bombed during Bible class and four little girls are killed, many other Negro children injured. President Kennedy expresses the "deep sense of outrage and grief" of the nation; Negroes express anger and frustration and the calls of "Freedom now" are louder. Many young Negroes begin to reject the non-violent rhetoric that has prevailed. Especially vocal are members of the Student Nonviolent Coordinating Committee (SNCC). They were the creation of a call to Raleigh, North Carolina by Dr. Martin Luther King in 1960 but already had moved away from his more cautious approach.

The pattern of protest changes in the mid- and late 60's. There is much more violence—riots in the cities begin, in Harlem, Rochester, Jersey City, Philadelphia; Malcolm X is murdered in the Audubon Ballroom in New York and Black Muslim headquarters are burned in that and other cities; Mrs. Viola Liuzzo is murdered on an Alabama highway and four Klan members are arrested for the shooting of this white civil rights worker from Detroit; James Meredith is shot as he begins his "March Against Fear" from Memphis to Jackson.

Emergence of Black Militants.

The more militant Negro leaders begin to emerge. Television coverage makes them nationally known in a matter of weeks. Stokely Carmichael became head of SNCC in May of 1966. One month later, during the Meredith march, he first enunciates the phrase "Black Power." Within days, the phrase and the man become the symbol of Black militancy. H. Rap Brown succeeded Carmichael as chairman of SNCC exactly one year later and within a matter of months is equally well-known, is author of the suggestion that "Violence is as American as apple pie."

William B. Monroe, Jr., who cut his teeth on the race story as news director of a New Orleans television station and later went on to head the NBC News Washington bureau, calls television the chosen instrument of the Black revolution.

> Television is their chosen instrument—not because television set out to integrate the nation or even to improve the South, but because when the Negroes got ready for their revolution, television was there. Television was coming of age as a journalistic medium. It was, unlike the newspapers, a national medium; it had the courage—in most cases, a courage drawn from the old tradition of the American press— not to shrink from the fierce and often ugly scenes growing out of the Negro struggle; and it conveyed the emotional values of a basically emotional contest with a richness and fidelity never before achieved in mass communications . . .
>
> Negroes looked to television to tell their story not only because of its communicative power as a medium, but also out of necessity. In the South, most of the local news media and the local authorities were deaf to their pleas and blind to their demonstrations . . .
>
> Ten or fifteen years ago, with few exceptions, Southern news-

papers and Southern radio and TV stations carried very little news about Negroes and paid almost *no* attention to news involving racial issues ... the first time many Southern whites saw Southern Negroes standing up and talking about their rights was on network television. They just plain did not believe it. Some of them still don't. Some of them are still convinced that the networks are manufacturing these unbelievable Negroes ...

At the same time it was bringing new ideas to Southern Negroes, network television was also bringing the outside world to Southern whites. But there was a difference. Southern Negroes realized they were looking at the real world when they watched national newscasts. Most Southern whites did not. They had no consciousness of living in what a Mississippi historian has called a "closed society."

The elements of racial coverage in an atmosphere of contention can be rejected by the white (or Black) mind, in the South (or North) because the events in this coverage are polarized. It is "Bull" Conner versus Martin Luther King, George Wallace versus Nicholas Katzenbach, Stokely Carmichael versus Negro moderates.

Emergence of the Black TV Image.

There is a great deal more to television than these moments of confrontation. The newscasts and, increasingly, the entertainment programs (and most significantly, the commercials) show more and more Negroes in the stream of American life. Once fearful that a Black face would hurt sales, many advertisers now seemed eager to show Black. It established credentials, it could open new markets, it might help protect against the embarrassment of boycott or picketing or worse.

The "tactile promptings" of television, as MacLuhan put it so well, are touching Americans almost every hour as they watch. It is touching low-income Americans most of all. This includes most Blacks and many low-income whites who, with their lower middle-class brothers, are the heart of "white backlash." Adults in middle-class America watch television a few hours a day. Low-income adults watch it five hours a day. Low-income Blacks watch six hours a day. Their children watch more.

Think of eight hours as a typical workday and you are stunned to learn that one-fourth of low-income adults spend eight hours a day watching television (according to testimony before the President's Violence Commission). While 7% of middle-class teenagers might spend eight hours a day watching television on Sunday, twice that number of lower class whites and five times as many low-income Black teenagers do. It is said that 40% of the general public gets most of its news from television but 70% of low-income Americans say TV is their main source. The majority of Americans say they believe television more than newspapers; an even larger majority of the lower class does.

In the words of Bradley Greenberg of Michigan State University, "For the low-income American, television is the preponderant, if not quite the sole, source of mass media stimulation. It is his critical link to the outside world of the 'haves.' He is far less likely than the middle-class citizen to have done any magazine reading lately, he reads the newspaper less frequently, and when he does read it, he reads it less intensively (focussing on the 'headlines' and ads) . . . this pattern of adult differences in media usage is reflected almost identically in the media usage patterns of their teenage children."

The comments of sociologists who examine the effect of all this television include phrases like "frustration aggression"—you see a beautiful world that is not yours and tension mounts to a breaking point. Television, they tell us, feeds frustrations and angers in the Black masses by exposing them to a world that can never be theirs. Television, they add, is a remorseless reminder of affluence to those who live the barren, sterile life.

It might also serve as a goad to seeking some of that affluence, either through traditional, legitimate channels or through others. The psychiatrist Bruno Bettleheim says we are reaching a crisis brought on by the availability of goods, "The mass media portray everything as easy . . . so our poor feel that all of these goods should be made immediately available to them without work." It has even been suggested by Dr. S. I. Hayakawa that looting by Blacks (and whites) during riots may be a response to the materialistic world of television and its depiction of violence "as a way of life."

Many social observers are concerned that while television may titillate the aspirations of the Black community (for good or bad) and television may report momentous conflict, it tends to ignore the daily life of the ghetto. The Kerner Commission which investigated the riots of the summer of '67 said its major concern with the media was "not in riot reporting as such, but in the failure to report adequately on race relations and ghetto problems . . ."

> They have not communicated to the majority of their audience—which is white—a sense of the degradation, misery, and hopelessness of living in the ghetto. They have not communicated to whites a feeling for the difficulties and frustrations of being a Negro in the United States. They have not shown understanding or appreciation of—and thus have not communicated—a sense of Negro culture, thought, or history.

Says the Commission, "The world that television and newspapers offer to their Black audience is almost totally white, in both appearance and attitude."

The Commission would have television devote large segments of time to the lot of the ghetto dweller. Unfortunately, in newscasts at least, there is serious question of how much time can *properly* be devoted to the topic, no matter how serious. To impose it upon newscasts for social "good" is to distort the pattern of the news. It is akin to those who say there is not enough good news on the air, too much doom and disaster, so why not artificially seek out "good" news?

David Ginsburg, the articulate Washington lawyer who served as staff director of the Kerner Commission, faults television for its failure to cover the events that precede or follow a riot:

> The urban problem, the Negro problem, the poverty problem ... this is generally regarded as the most important domestic crisis today. But if one listens to television throughout the country one would never guess it. Somehow it's not a matter of excitement. Unless the media dig into the problem and help educate the electorate to their responsibilities, then I find it very difficult to see how the crisis can be overcome.

The major network newscasts have been focussing on racial stories but there is a limitation; it is imposed by the restrictions of the time available and the need to present other material as well. "Shad" Northshield, then producer of the "Huntley-Brinkley Report," said, "I agree with Ginsburg that the Negro Revolution, or whatever you want to call it, is the most important story of our time, more important than Viet Nam, and we're trying to cover it. But what does Ginsburg want? After the commercials are lopped off, I've got only twenty-two minutes of news time, and within that time, I've got to put on the significant national and international news of the day."

Northshield's Washington bureau chief, Bill Monroe, complemented the argument about space limitation with the moral question: "There's a limit to how far the media can go in agreeing with the Riots Commission or anyone else that a certain kind of information ought to be emphasized on newscasts. If you assume, because the commission says it's so, that certain material ought to be seen by the country for the country's good, well it would be like brainwashing the country, and it would be a little frightening."

There is always a basic conflict of interest between do-gooders and journalists. As anywhere else where such a conflict exists, there was first a great attraction. Most journalists do have a sense of social purpose but the best realize that this is best fulfilled hewing to a sense of journalistic purpose, of covering the news as they see it.

Seeing it objectively presented the varied images that enhanced the Negro Revolution and those that might embarrass it. They ranged from the dignity of the little colored girl escorted to school by soldiers while a white housewife spat at her to the vulgarism of a Black militant shouting "Burn, baby, burn." Showing both was and is important.

Showing in itself has made the difference. David Brinkley notes that "These same things had been happening for years, certainly since the Supreme Court decision of '54. But until the last few years there wasn't any national television of any importance. I think television has made a great difference to the Negroes themselves. They look at news a great deal because they are in it."

TV's In-Depth-Treatment of Blacks.

To seek contrived means to make the Negro attractive or artificial ways to dramatize his plight—either in content or in the aggregate devoted to the subject—is to distort. Television must evolve its more involved treatment outside the daily newscast—if it feels deeper involvement is called for. NBC did that on Labor Day, 1963 when it devoted a full evening to "The American Revolution of '63." That creation of Robert Kintner devoted three full hours to all facets of the Black Revolution and all participants, including the Southern bloc in the Senate as well as the Black advocates.

As Kintner himself noted, "We didn't spare NBC itself. We showed Negro pickets marching outside our own studio entrance to demand jobs in television, and we carried a comment by Herbert Hill of the NAACP that television people were 'frightened little men' on the race issue."

Kintner's innovation, however, did not come in the abstract simply because someone thought it would do some good. It came at the end of a summer that saw the riots in Birmingham, the cattle prods in Louisiana, the March on Washington, the Wallace stand at the school-house door, and the murder of Medgar Evers.

Similarly, in 1967, as the Kerner Commission was preparing its report it held a conference with top members of the mass media in Poughkeepsie, New York. This was at the end of a year that saw riots in Detroit, Newark, Tampa, Boston, Cincinnati, and Milwaukee—in all there were 164 disorders during a nine-month period.

In attendance was Richard Salant, President of CBS News. He came from the meetings with a determination to do a series of broadcasts on the Negro in America. The series was produced under the supervision of Perry Wolff, one of CBS News' most talented producers.

⌐"Skee" Wolff was inspired to open the series of seven broadcasts (all in prime time, the first aired on July 2 and the last on September 2, 1968) with "Black History: Lost, Stolen or Strayed." It was an inspired hour, narrated by Negro comedian Bill Cosby, and was as candid a presentation as commercial television had yet seen.

The theme was the Black man that white society overlooked in its classrooms, its history books, its movies, its stage, and even in its language. Cosby's opening words included, "What's the whitest thing you know? Whiter than the driven snow, whiter than the whites of your eyes? Sugar. Non-integrated, non-black, sweet sugar. But you see there is a Black man in your sugar. His name is Norbert Rillieux. Norbert Rillieux in 1846 invented a vacuum pan that revolutionized the sugar refining industry. You have to dig to find that fact. I mean, it's not much history, but it's still history."

From Rillieux, the narrator went on to talk about some other Blacks that history forgot: Jan Ernst Mateliger who invented the machine that made mass-produced shoes possible, Jean Baptiste duSable who founded Chicago, the Black who helped open the West with Lewis and Clark, 5,000 Black cowboys, 186,000 Blacks who fought with the Union Army, four Black regiments that went up San Juan Hill with Teddy Roosevelt, Matthew Henson who was navigator to Admiral Peary and first man to reach the North Pole, Daniel Hale Williams who first performed open-heart surgery successfully. "This list could go on forever," says the narrator, "Blacks who made it, Blacks who made history, but who didn't get into the history texts at all. And the strange thing is, how little there is about us in the textbooks. Napoleon once said, 'History is a fable agreed upon.' And the fable agreed upon up to now is that American history is white on white."

Cosby then goes into the treatment of slavery and says, ". . . if you want to look history right straight in the eye, you're going to get a black eye. Because it isn't important whether a few Black heroes got lost or stolen or strayed in America's history textbooks. What's important is why they got left out. Now this country has got a psychological history: there was a master race and there was a slave race, and though there isn't any political slavery any more, those same old attitudes have hung around."

This first broadcast in the "Of Black America" series ends with a powerful bit of film to illustrate Cosby's point that "if you can't wash white, even if you have the money, if you can't wash white 'cause you're basically black, what you do is react, sometimes radically." Then comes a chillingly, simple sequence: the classroom of a young Black named John Churchville in Philadelphia. Put together and financed by Churchville, it is to give pre-school children "a Black preparation" before they enter the city's schools.

CHURCHVILLE: Are you going to be scared of me?
VOICE: No.
CHURCHVILLE: Are you going to be scared of some—President of the United States?
VOICE: No.
CHURCHVILLE: Some Mayor?
VOICE: No.
CHURCHVILLE: Some policeman?
VOICE: No.
CHURCHVILLE: All right. You're a Negro . . . You're a Negro, Eric.
ERIC: No.
CHURCHVILLE: Somebody pass me my stick. I said you're a Negro, boy.
ERIC: No.
CHURCHVILLE: You're getting mighty soft. You're a Negro!
ERIC: No.
CHURCHVILLE: Very good, sit down. You, young man, come here. Your nationality is American Negro. Yes.
BOY: No.
CHURCHVILLE: Your nationality—look, don't play with me. You're a Negro.
LEON: No.
CHURCHVILLE: I am your teacher. You are a Negro.
LEON: No.
CHURCHVILLE: Suppose I threaten to beat you, what would you say? Aren't you a Negro now?
LEON: No.
CHURCHVILLE: What are you?
LEON: I'm black and beautiful.
CHURCHVILLE: What is your nationality?
LEON: My nationality is Afro-American.
CHURCHVILLE: Suppose I had some money in my pocket, suppose I gave you a dollar to say that you're an American Negro. This is money, now. Money talks, money talks. This dollar—and if you don't say it you don't get it. You're an American Negro, aren't you?
LEON: No.
CHURCHVILLE: You won't have any money. You know you need money, don't you?
LEON: Yes.
CHURCHVILLE: You need money to live, don't you?
LEON: Yes.
CHURCHVILLE: All right, all you have to say, Leon, is that you're an

American Negro. Aren't you an American Negro? Are you an American Negro?

LEON: No.

CHURCHVILLE: What are you?

LEON: I'm black and beautiful.

CHURCHVILLE: What's your nationality?

LEON: My nationality is Afro-American.

CHURCHVILLE: Very good, man, keep it up. Go sit down. You had to think about that a minute, didn't you?

LEON: Yes.

CHURCHVILLE: All right. All right everybody, what is your nationality?

CLASS: My nationality is Afro-American.

CHURCHVILLE: Very good. All right, what I did is what people are going to do to you in different ways when you get out of this school. They're not going to just right up to you and give you a dollar or say if you say that you're an Afro—if you say you're an American Negro I'll give you a dollar. But they're going to be very nice to you some of them, and they're going to try to, you know, get you not to love black people. They're going to try to get you to, you know, be something other than you are. They're going to try to make you—make it seem as though you're different from the masses of black people. And they want you to be—"Go away, I'll tell you . . . I'll give you special things if you'll just come along with me and do what I say." But you must reject that. Now, do you know what that means? That means you're not going to have the money you'd like to have. The money is not important. We need money, you know, we have to buy things with it, but money is not the thing we're living for. The only thing that makes a person worth living is being a man and being a woman, being strong in character, seeing straight, telling the truth and living in the truth and doing the right thing. You understand that?

CLASS: Yes.

CHURCHVILLE: So no matter what happens, I want you all to always tell the what?

CLASS: Truth.

CHURCHVILLE: You may not get the marks you're supposed to get in school. You may be doing the work, but because the teacher doesn't like your attitude and she'll always tell you, "I don't like you attitude" because you're independent. But you're not going to school for grades. You're going for what?

VOICE: Learn.

CHURCHVILLE: All right, and what kind of people is everybody in

this room going to be? Tell me the kind of people you're going to be.
CLASS: Black and beautiful.
The sequence ends and narrator Cosby concludes:
COSBY: It's kind of like brainwashing. Or is it? Can you blame us
for overcompensating?

I mean when you take the way black history got lost, stolen or
strayed, when you think about the kids drawing themselves without
faces and when you remember the fine actors who had to play
baboons to make a buck, I guess you've got to give us the sin of
pride. Pride. "Hubris" in the original Greek.

Three hundred years we've been in this American melting pot
and we haven't been able to melt in yet. That's a long wait. Listen,
we've been trying all kinds of parts to make the American scene.
We've been trying to play it straight and white, but it's been just bit
parts. From now on, we're going to play it black and American.
We're proud of both. Hubris.

I'm Bill Cosby. And you take care of yourself.

Pretty strong fare for television but pretty good reflection of the
feeling of Blacks, young ones in particular. The series went on to explore
Blacks in entertainment, in sports, in our military during wars as well as
the attitudes of Black leaders and African leaders towards the growing
Afro-Americanism of the Negro young. One broadcast took a group of
American teenage Blacks to Africa to get their reactions.

The final broadcast was devoted to a CBS News Public Opinion Survey conducted by the Opinion Research Corporation of Princeton, New
Jersey. The survey was entitled "White and Negro Attitudes Towards
Race Related Issues and Activities." As reported on the September broadcast, the survey showed that the white racism which the Kerner Commission called the key to the Black problem is a characteristic of a minority
"but a dangerously large minority" of whites and that it is receding, especially among younger people.

The survey asked if Black extremists were the people to whom the
Negro looks for leadership and the answer was "no." "Black people are
listening harder to the extremes, but they haven't joined in numbers of
dangerous consequence."

Fascinating was the study of awareness and support for Negro leadership. The second best-known Negro (after Dr. Ralph Abernathy, successor to Dr. King and much in the news at the time of the survey) was
militant Stokely Carmichael, third was militant H. Rap Brown. About
three-fourths of both Blacks and whites knew them (indeed, Carmichael
was the single best-known figure among whites; 84% had heard of him)
yet only about five or six per cent of the Blacks and one per cent or so of

the whites "feel the same way" as Carmichael and Brown, far fewer would give them "active support." Over one-third of the Blacks and 44% of the whites said they disagreed with Carmichael and Brown. Being well known and being supported are obviously two different things in the world of Black leadership. Only Abernathy and Roy Wilkins of the NAACP showed impressive signs of personal following, of active support.

By the way, as a pollster's device to check the honesty of respondents, CBS News producer Perry Wolff's name was added to the long list of Negroes. Some 4% of the Black respondents said they knew him, 2% of the whites said they had also heard of him but none would indicate they agreed, or disagreed with him or would give him active support.

The 1,000 persons surveyed were asked about mass media treatment of the race relations problem. Ten per cent of the Blacks and a full 64% of the whites felt too much attention was paid to the question. Almost half the Blacks but only 8% of the whites felt there wasn't enough coverage. Was the Negro story treated fairly? Yes, said 47% of the whites but less than 30% of the Blacks; No, said over half (52%) of the Blacks and one-third of the whites.

Despite the dichotomy on this and most questions, despite some disturbing results (one-third of adult whites are "racist by dictionary definition" and there are "two-thirds of a million Black people willing to resign from the United States of America"), most Americans are somewhere in the middle.

The broadcast, and the series, concluded:

> The danger is that a group of white and Black extremists are seizing the debate for themselves. The advantage of the CBS News poll is that, perhaps for the first time, we counted the center, and discovered the center overwhelms the extremes. Revolutionists and racists believe that the masses have to be led. Most Americans believe that the people lead. You have heard the people speak. There is commonality, there is hope, and there is still time. It is not yet five minutes to midnight, but it is clearly late in the day.

The series, admirable as it was, received some criticism for the small number of Negroes involved in its preparation. CBS News, in addition to Cosby, used its only two Black reporters, Hal Walker and George Foster. There were few Negroes on the production staff.

Negroes in Television.

A continuing problem for the Negro is this, the small number of Negroes actively employed in the mass media. The Kerner Commission makes special note and called for an increase in the number of Black journalists. Virtually every major station in every big city is seeking Black reporters as are most newspapers, magazines, local broadcasters and the networks. You don't even have to have all those qualities as long as you have one: that you are Black.

Journalism schools are trying to encourage Black enrollment. Still there is very limited history of Blacks in journalism and it will be quite a while before the number approaches anything like the proportion of Blacks in the population, longer still before they achieve a measurable share of top management positions. One unhappy result is that Blacks now in journalism tend to change jobs frequently; there is always a good offer waiting.

Black ownership in the mass media is an even gloomier picture. In broadcasting, Negroes own only six of some 7,350 stations says FCC Commissioner Nick Johnson. He calls it a kind of "corporate censorship."

On the other hand, there is a growing amount of air time being devoted to programs dealing with the urban crisis. A poll by *Television* magazine in the summer of 1968, indicated that most local television stations have devoted programs to the problem. Of approximately one hundred stations replying, some ninety-five had aired programs dealing with civil unrest, only two had not. The quality of these local efforts vary widely and while the growing attention paid to the ghetto problems is significant, it is hardly enough to fit the needs described by the Kerner Commission's staff director.

One radical move is suggested by Roy Innis, head of the Congress of Racial Equality, who brands the mass media as racist and calls for an allocation of free network broadcast time to Black leaders on a regular basis. How much time? Ten per cent of all air time.

Even if this were possible—or if the networks granted any small portion of time to Black "leaders"—who would decide who they are? The emergence of the militant who, like Stokely Carmichael, becomes instantly famous with television exposure has irritated many other Blacks. Whitney Young, head of the Urban League, is fond of characterizing Carmichael as having a following of "about fifty Negroes and about 5,000 white reporters, newspaper, television and radio reporters. They have created him."

Clarence Mitchell of the NAACP says, "I believe that television has over-emphasized the inflammatory and irresponsible statements of Negroes. It is my opinion that this has helped to spread such activity because those who seek coverage have learned that the surest way to be on camera is to say or do something which is sensational and blood curling."

James Farmer of CORE once noted, "The press assumes that anything that is shocking is appealing. A fellow by the name of Isaiah Brunson called for the stall-in (at the opening of the New York's World's Fair).

All of a sudden, Brunson found himself a great militant Negro leader with an audience of millions."

How does one determine who a "leader" is? How does television cope with exposure of Negroes who might, because of the very nature of television's impact, instantly become famous? These are not easy questions to answer.

The heavy exposure early in their emergence on the national scene has been regretted by some Black leaders. It is common for them to ban white reporters and cameramen from their meetings. One winter night in Oakland, California a rally featuring Stokely Carmichael was closed to television networks unless they were willing to pay $1,000 each. Educational television and four local radio stations were to be permitted in without charge "because they have been friendly to us." It is quite possible that television treatment of "leaders" who have no real following might deflate them soon after making them "famous." In any case, it is safer in a democracy to allow dissident voices to be heard, even if they represent a very small, minority view rather than risk the chance of stopping a single voice of consequence, a single view of importance.

In the touchy atmosphere of the Black Revolution's second stage, that of emerging militancy, it is difficult for viewers to accept exposure of strident voices. The resentment toward television for doing so is a growing resentment. It probably has already resulted in considerable bending over backwards.

Over sixty years ago, however, Woodrow Wilson wrote, "We have learned that it is pent-up feelings that are dangerous, whispered purposes that are revolutionary, covert follies that warp and poison the mind; that the wisest thing to do with a fool is to encourage him to hire a hall and discourse to his fellow citizens. Nothing chills nonsense like exposure to air; nothing dispels folly like its publication; nothing so eases the machine as the safety valve."

This is advice that might be hard to take in a day when nothing irritates the majority public more than the strident words of the militant. But if it is "pent-up feelings that are dangerous" then perhaps we should be more tolerant of public discussion, on television or otherwise. The pent-up feelings we didn't know about were responsible for 239 civil disturbances in five years, from 1963 to 1968, and they occurred in every city in America.

These disturbances are the subject of the next chapter.

CHAPTER 4

TELEVISION AND
THE BLACK RIOTS

AN URBAN RIOT is rather good at attracting attention and rather bad at solving problems.

That doesn't mean much to the Black ghetto dweller. Without attention, his problems remained not simply unsolved but unknown to the mainstream of America. Help began to come with the demonstrations of the late '50's and early '60's but "Whitey" really became sensitive when the cities started to burn.

The rioting in the Watts section of Los Angeles in August of 1965 stunned an entire nation.

In the few years leading to the riots of early 1968, after the shooting of Martin Luther King, there were civil disorders and riots in every major city in the nation. Over 200,000 participants in almost 250 violent outbursts reflected the frustrations of the ghetto. Hundreds of millions of dollars in property damage, almost 200 deaths and some 8,000 reported injuries.

The riots in the streets were the second stage of the Black Revolution.

Joseph Conrad said, "The real signifiance of crime is in its being a breach of faith with the community of mankind." From Watts on, you could substitute "riot" for "crime" in that epigram.

It is interesting that the CBS News survey conducted for the broadcasts "Of Black America" showed that 88% of Negroes (and 98% of whites) said they would not engage in demonstrations that might lead to violence. Only 3% of the Negroes flatly said they would. But in the cities, more than that have. In that same survey, in another question asked of whites only, 15% admitted that they probably would join a riot if they were Negro.

Watts exploded on August 12, 1965. The *Los Angeles Times* said, "There are no words to express the shock, the sick horror that a civilized city feels at a moment like this." White America first realized the explosiveness of pent-up feelings without safety valve. Quickly, in a matter of just hours really, over 200 business buildings were destroyed and the business loss alone was $44,000,000, almost three dozen persons were killed, over 750 others injured and over 2,500 persons arrested. It scared the hell out of White America. The first concern, probably, was that an explosion in the Negro ghetto might spread the next time to White areas. The second concern, surely, was "how could it happen here?".

It could happen, as the next few years illustrated, anywhere. The pious Establishment spokesmen in other cities forgot Montaigne's observation that "an untempted woman cannot boast of her chastity." Their cities, too, had riots or civil disorder or demonstrations—depending on your definition. Some cities handled it fairly well or luckily; others handled it badly or were cursed with bad luck.

Television, local or network, had no better luck in reporting the riots. Wise and careful handling were not always the hallmark of TV reporting. Television treatment of the rioting instinctively reached for the dramatic and found it in abundance. But the implications of its treatment, the awareness that the medium itself might be part of some message, the thought that television might be accused of exacerbating the disorder, all worked to restrain first impulses. In time, and a very short time, television in cities across the country as well as at the networks learned the problems that their coverage entails. These often are questions without clear-cut answers or even answers at all. They involve the very presence of cameras on the scene (do they stir up more trouble?), the pattern of reportage (should you treat it fully and frighten a community?), the timing of the first bulletins (should they be delayed to give local authorities more time?), the use of lights at night (does it encourage more demonstrators to come to the scene?), the rhetoric of rioting (how much restraint—even in using the very word "riot"—and how much can you permit participants to be heard, especially those screaming "Burn, baby burn"?), and, most haunting of all, the validity of the report (is television's eye unable to see anything but that directly ahead, is it devoid of peripheral vision?).

What Was the Lesson of Watts?

Watts, being what it is and where it is, was studied more carefully than most communities. Watts being among the first and most shocking, was ready-made for the social scientist. Watts could tell America something about the "who" and "why" of riots. It also had some things to say about the rule of television in the "why" of riots. Later, the Kerner Commissioner had much more to say about television as the reporter of the riot and its shortcomings in reporting the "who" and "why."

A profile of the participants in the Watts rioting emerges from data prepared at UCLA. About 15% of the adult population actively participated, another 31% were "active" spectators. Heaviest participation was by young men and women. It is said that the rising class rebels more readily—this could be the key to the violent, second stage of the Black revolt. In Watts, though, there was a high level of discontent generally. Blacks holding jobs felt more discriminated against than the unemployed and were more sensitive to discriminatory practices. Educational level seemed of little significance. Point of origin meant little: Southern emigrants were no more frustrated than California residents (over half the people of Watts have lived in the area for ten years or more).

Elements common to most involved living conditions, the major point of complaint, and mistreatment by whites. White merchants and police were the major targets of physical violence, the main object of protest. Almost four out of five Blacks in Watts accused police of lack of respect for Negroes. Three out of four believe police used unnecessary force in making arrests. This attitude toward police is shared by Blacks in most major cities. A study in Detroit in 1967 showed 82% of Negroes believed that police used brutality. A 1965 Gallup poll said this feeling was shared by 35% of all Negro males. A 1964 *New York Times* study showed that 43% of Harlem agreed on the existence of police maltreatment of Blacks. The CBS News survey in 1968 showed 59% of Negroes feel that police have been brutal. In contrast, only 6% of whites felt that way, 58% of the whites feeling the police had been "fair."

Even more telling, 70% of the whites felt police *should* get tougher. Later that same year, public reaction to television's treatment of police tactics at the Democratic convention in Chicago echoed this white reading of the Cop. Negroes, it was said, chuckled at those whites discovering in Grant and Lincoln Park police brutality for the first time.

Pepperdine College did a study of about one hundred Blacks in the Watts area, a study that showed some 85% of the men and 77% of the women believed Negroes would never get what they needed without riots. Some 70% of the men and 44% of the women indicated they were ready to participate in a riot if another took place. Nineteen out of twenty felt the merchants whose stores were looted and burned, got what they deserved.

Only a third of these Watts residents subscribed to a daily newspaper, less than half took magazines (Negro publications like *Ebony* and *Jet* were most commonly named) but 92% had access to television and watched it several hours a day.

Fred L. Casmir of Pepperdine summarized the study thusly:

> . . . it can be stated that television is the major source of informa-
> tion and entertainment for Negroes. The medium presents an image
> of American society which is different from that familiar to minority
> groups and it is frequently out of their reach. The same may be said
> of many members of the white majority. However, less frustration
> among whites is the result of their general status which makes im-
> provement of living conditions at least a realistic possibility. Negroes
> do not feel that they have the same chance. Thus property destruc-
> tion and looting, a common feature in all racial disturbances, could
> be interpreted as one means of "balancing" the existing situation.
> Findings . . . strongly suggest that many of the racial disturbances
> may very likely be much less racial and much more economic in na-
> ture, the racial part being vital only because of the disadvantaged
> position in which the Negro finds himself as a group. Evidence would
> appear overwhelmingly in favor of a more determined self-study by
> the television industry dealing with the part it plays in developing
> and furthering civil disturbances not as its prime purpose, but as a
> direct result of the images it has created and continues to develop
> in the minds of our Negro citizens.

This study of Blacks reflected other studies regarding television as
a source of information. Asked what source they would check to discover
the truth about something happening in Los Angeles, 46% said they
would turn to television. Only 6% said radio and another 6% said newspapers. About 43% said they would check none of these. Fully half the
Negroes questioned by the Pepperdine pollsters said they had no confidence in any of these to be fair in reporting Negro affairs. Of the other
half, two out of five chose television as the fairest medium.

The Kerner Commission, too, was critical of the media's reporting
of the ills of the ghetto. "Slights and indignities are part of the Negro's
daily life, and many of them come from what he now calls 'the White
press'—a press that repeatedly, if unconsciously, reflects the biases, the
paternalism, the indifference of white America. This may be understandable, but it is not excusable in an institution that has the mission to inform and educate the whole of our society."

The Longest, Hottest summers: 1967.

The summer of '67 was the roughest season of discontent of all and
the worst of it came during a two-week period in July, first in Newark and
then in Detroit. On July 28, President Johnson established the National

Advisory Commission on Civil Disorders to answer three basic questions: what happened, why did it happen, what can be done to prevent it from happening again. Chairman of the Commission was Governor Otto Kerner of Illinois and the Vice-chairman was Mayor John Lindsay of New York.

Its report, in the words of Tom Wicker of the *New York Times*, was "a picture of one nation, divided."

Many myths were nullified. There was little evidence of Negro snipers in the '67 rioting—most of the shooting came from scared Guardsmen and policemen. There was no organized conspiracy; the militant Blacks had no plan of incitement but largely relied on oratory. The cliché that Negroes could work themselves "up" as turn-of-the-century immigrants did was shown to be a hollow analogy; it was not the unemployed, undereducated, immigrants from the South but the young, native ghetto dwellers who verbalized and demonstrated the greatest hostility.

As Wicker summed it up: "The rioters were mistrustful of white politics, they hated the police, they were proud of their race, and acutely conscious of the discrimination they suffered. They were and they are a time-bomb ticking in the heart of the richest nation in the history of the world . . . They will not go away."

Chapter 15 of the Kerner report dealt with the news media and tried to answer a specific question put forth in the President's charge to the Commission: "What effect do the mass media have on the riots?"

The question itself was reflective of a growing uneasiness in the country. Did the media, television in particular, serve to stimulate or spread riots? Do the media set the stage for discontent? Is there some kind of social dynamite inherent to the reporting of civil disorder, or urban restlessness?

The Kerner Commission said despite incidents of sensationalism, distortion and inaccuracy, the media—on the whole—made real effort to give a balanced, factual account of the 1967 disorders. There was exaggeration of "both mood and event." Original impressions and beliefs formed by commission members were not supported by their inquiry. Did millions retain incorrect impressions? For example, reports of property damage were exaggerated. In Detroit, at the height of the riot, reports called it half a billion dollars damage. Months later, an AP dispatch referred to Detroit saying "Damage exceeded one billion dollars." Investigation by the Michigan State Insurance Commission placed damages at $40 to $45 million.

The most significant commission conclusion, "ultimately most important" they called it, was media failure to report adequately on the causes and consequences of civil disorder, to report the underlying problems of race relations. "By failing to portray the Negro as a matter of routine and in the context of the total society, the news media have, we believe, contributed to the Black-white schism in this country." The commission charged the media with just plain ignorance of ghetto life. There has been no serious reporting of the Negro community, there are few real race experts in journalism, there are few Black reporters, and when the media go to the ghetto, they are greeted with suspicion.

During the rioting, however, the media rated better. The Kerner staff examined 955 television sequences of riot and racial news and classified 494 of these as "calm" treatment, only 262 as emotional. There was a small proportion of scenes showing actual mob action, people looting, sniping, setting fires or coming into physical contact. Moderate leaders were shown far more often than militants, three times as often. "Overall, both network and local television coverage was cautious and restrained."

Television, however, was faulted because it tended to give the impression of Black-White confrontation, a "race riot" in the traditional sense. The impression was false, the riots were Negroes doing damage to Negro neighborhoods because of resentment, frustration and rejection of slum conditions. Since most of the police, troops, public officials and local proprietors were white, there was a tendency to show an unbalanced ratio of white male adults—one white to each two Negro male adults.

Does television coverage intensify a riot? The commission thought not. In fact, after the first day, television coverage tends to decline. The only exception in 1967 was Detroit where the riot reached its climax forty-eight hours after its start and it was two days before television coverage declined.

As for live coverage (as opposed to film), television representatives told commission members that they thought live coverage via helicopter during the Watts riot was inflammatory. Network news executives expressed doubt that live coverage would ever be repeated. The broadcasters prefer the opportunity to view and edit taped or filmed sequences.

Caution, by television, can distort, however. The Kerner study says that leaning over too far backward to seek balance and restraint, television emphasized control scenes rather than riotous action and "may have given a distorted picture."

In that regard, after noting that this story is projected against a background of anxieties and apprehension, the commission warns:

> This does not mean that the media should manage the news or tell less than the truth. Indeed, we believe that it would be imprudent and even dangerous to downplay coverage in the hope that censored reporting of inflammatory incidents somehow will diminish violence. Once a disturbance occurs, the word will spread independently of newspapers and television. To attempt to ignore these events or portray them as something other than what they are, can only diminish

confidence in the media and increase the effectiveness of those who
monger rumors and the fears of those who listen.

Eric Sevareid once noted, "The worst, truly race riots of this century
occurred before there was television, or radio. The chief medium of communication was the oldest, the most irresponsible of all, word of mouth."

How is TV to Treat Riots?

In a number of communities the news media have created codes
dealing with the manner of reporting racial disturbances and setting a
period (generally very brief, just thirty minutes) during which there is no
reporting of the incidents. This is to allow local authorities to bring disturbances under control. The commission said it might have been effective
in some cases. Witnesses, however, noted that a voluntary news blackout
in Detroit for part of the first day—apparently at the request of local officials and civil rights groups—failed to de-fuse the situation. The city
"blew" anyway.

Newsmen told the commission that far better than any code was
experience in covering disorders. Wire service reporters on the local scene
tend to do badly since they have had almost no experience in covering
riots; improvement comes as more experienced reporters fly in. The
Kerner report concluded that codes are seldom harmful, often useful,
but no panacea.

The distinguished journalism critic, Ben Bagdikian, has noted that it
is not just the news system that tells us of violence. There is the telephone,
there is word of mouth: "To silence the news is not to silence the fact; it
merely surrounds the fact with uncertainty and rumor." A study of seven
cities with disorders in 1967 showed that 79% of the ghetto residents
first heard of the outbreak in their own city by word of mouth.

On the day the President issued the Executive Order creating the
Kerner commission, Senator Hugh Scott (GOP, Pennsylvania) wrote the
networks and the wire service chiefs and called for a conference to "draw
up a code of emergency procedure to be followed in reporting riots and
incidents or speeches which could spark disturbances or permit militants
to signal opportunities for disturbances in other areas." He said the media
must report the news but in a manner that will "help dampen the fires
burning in our cities."

The heads of NBC and CBS were particularly strong in rejecting
Scott's call for a code. Julian Goodman, President of NBC, wrote "a code
cannot exercise judgment. It cannot foresee all the variables in the fast-
breaking events with which newsmen must deal."

Dr. Frank Stanton of CBS was equally strong and gave a definitive position for opposing voluntary codes:

> We are not going to make subjective value judgments that the American people are capable of hearing and evaluating some spokesmen for some points of view and that others are unsafe or too dangerous for them to hear. Such a course would be a denial of the basic principles of self-government and a defiance of the fundamental purposes of a free press.
>
> Nor can we enter any compact with other news organizations, on either an intra-medium or an inter-media basis, to restrict or present the news in any predetermined way whatsoever. One of the primary safeguards against excesses in a free press is a diversity of reporting and of news judgments. Any proposal, however high its purpose, to get the press to decide in concert what it will report, and how it will do it, would establish a precedent of the most hazardous implications. With the possible exception of wartime, such a practice not only is abhorrent in principle but also would cast doubt on the validity and thoroughness of all news. As a result, speculation of the wildest sort would arise as to what was being suppressed, or handled by prearranged agreement, or "managed" on the grounds that the people cannot be trusted.
>
> The suggestion that a "code of emergency procedure" is the answer to the coverage of thorny situations is not new in either our national experience or the history of the news media. CBS has always objected to such stratagems because they amount to censorship by voluntary agreement and, no less importantly, to the abandonment of our individual responsibilities as reporters and editors to a consortium that will furnish an automatic yardstick by which uniform news judgments and reportorial procedures will be imposed upon all constituent publications and stations. Such a device that aims at the suppression or conditioning of the news, by agreement of editors and publishers, on the grounds that it may be dangerous for the people to hear some of it, strikes me as no less hazardous, and possibly more so, than suppression or conditioning the reporting of news by government edict. The people can at least remove government officials in the next election; they have much less defense against a monolithic code arrived at in private by private parties entrusted by our institutions with a public responsibility.
>
> The practical difficulties inherent in such a code must also be considered. How is it to be enforced? What of the news organizations which refuse to become a part of it? Who is to adjudicate disputed

or borderline cases? Who is to be responsible for decisions? And to whom are they answerable? I do not believe that any self-constituted code authority could reach effective answers to such questions without permanently weakening the news media and setting up a concentration of private power that would give rise to crises far more serious than it was established to cure.

Codes have been tried in a number of cities. In Toledo, Omaha, Buffalo and other cities there is a voluntary thirty-minute "hold" on inflammatory stories. One of the earliest codes and one of the most controversial was adopted in Chicago in 1955. It calls for voluntary embargo until police say it's all right to run it. The code resulted in much criticism of Chicago stations during some racial outbreaks and was gradually eroded. One Chicago news director who broadcast news of a disturbance before police ended their request to hold off, noted that there is a danger to innocent citizens passing through the area. He felt they deserved to be informed.

In Detroit, where news of the July, 1967 riot was withheld for most of the first day (at the request of the Michigan Civil Rights Commission) it was said that this tended to keep it from spreading more quickly than it did. However, Richard Marks who was director of the city's Community Relations Commission felt it was wrong to impose a blackout. "When there is an honest-to-God problem, you must inform the public," he said, adding that the Black community gets the word anyway via the grapevine. "Without the media giving them the full story, there was a distorted belief that the police weren't even trying to stop looters." This was the kind of rumor common to almost all urban disorders: looting was running unabated. There are many others. The accepted means of news dissemination are the only way to squelch rumors and even they might be ineffective. To ignore rumors is to encourage them.

Lyndon Johnson had appointed a second major commission, this one after the assassinations of Senator Robert Kennedy and Dr. Martin Luther King. It was before this Commission on Violence, that the following exchange took place between CBS President Stanton, the witness, and Dr. W. Walter Menninger, a member of the commission.

DR. MENNINGER: You sometimes wonder about where can the media be tied in as clearly a precipitating influence in bringing about a riot. The example that seems most specific to me was in effect what happened after the death of Martin Luther King, because while the media was not responsible in the sense of causing it, as other specific incidents or as the incident itself might be considered a cause, it was the immediate communication of that incident that was followed throughout this country in many localities by violence of an entirely different sort.

Riots that police couldn't cope with because they were all over the place, of disturbed citizens who then had had their emotions built up and responded to them.

Now, I'm not asking that the TV or radio should not report the news. The question I ask is when mass communications instantaneously can prompt such a reaction, one can't deny that the communications has had something to do with what takes place, and therefore, what do you think is the media's responsibility? What can the media do in the public good for the social order in trying to cope better with that kind of problem?

DR. STANTON: If we had the experience to live through again, God forbid that we do, as far as I'm concerned I wouldn't do anything different than we did at the time.

DR. MENNINGER: Have you really examined what took place at the time, Dr. Stanton? Has there been a careful assessment of anybody, by saying this is what happened, so that, as you say, if you lived through it again, your—

DR. STANTON: Dr. Menninger, are you asking me, has there been an assessment of reactions?

DR. MENNINGER: No, you said if you would do it again, you would do it the same. As you make that statement, is that based on the fact you carefully examined what was done by the network and—

DR. STANTON: I saw every minute of it. It seems to me that the response to the—that what you're describing isn't a response to the media. The media was simply a means of transmission. If you hadn't had this means of transmission, you would have had some other means of transmission, and unless you were prepared to wipe out all means of communication from one part of the country to another, I don't see how you could achieve the thing I think is implicit in your question.

It seems to me whenever you have a problem such as you had at that time or for that matter, in connection with any news event, the most important thing to do is get the word out as widespread and as fast as possible. If you don't, you will have something else happening. You will have rumors. You will have leaks. You don't know where to stop this thing.

So the only policy that has guided me as my North Star in my job is to have as much information as possible. I think this is the only solution in an open society. I don't think you can begin to hold back.

The problem that created the conditions that you described in my opinion came about because of what happened to Martin Luther King, not because television or newspapers or radio reported what happened.

It is interesting to examine the outbreak of riots that followed Dr. King's death. It was the second worst month of rioting in history. It was the first time—the only time—that disorders in different cities were touched off by a single, national event.

Broadcasting had learned the lessons of Watts, of '67 and offered mature coverage, both network and local, as ghettos in scores of cities burned. From the first bulletins of the shooting of Dr. King during the evening of April 4, 1968 to the funeral service on Tuesday (which captured much of the daytime schedule of all three networks) through the coverage of disorders in over 100 cities, television was almost everywhere. CBS News devoted almost twenty hours to the story, NBC television seventeen hours and ABC about thirteen hours. Lost revenues because of the network and local pre-emptions cost broadcasting about five million dollars.

Camera crews moved about in unmarked autos, used only available light and not their usual bright lights. On the air, restraint in editing and in language was used, guidelines based on the experience of earlier years were brought into play.

In scores of cities, television played an additional role—it was used to get the message out: "Cool it." In Washington, D. C. the local stations set up "pool" coverage at police headquarters where live cameras were used to carry messages from Mayor Walter Washington, Presidential trouble-shooter Cyrus Vance, the chief of police and others. The facilities also permitted local newsmen to reject rumors almost as soon as authorities could confirm that such reports were false.

There were 6,000 arrests in the Nation's Capitol, widespread looting and burning and 12,000 army troops to supplement local police. Washington police do better than most in community relations but even in the Capitol there is suspicion and hostility. One Black resident welcomed the troopers, saying, "Thank God, they're here. They'll protect us from the police!"

Despite the scope of the outbreak, it might have been worse and Mayor Washington praised the media for reporting accurately, well and fast. Some TV stations stayed on throughout the night, an all-night vigil to keep the public informed.

One of these most effective uses of the local "pool" was an appearance by James Brown, one of the nation's most popular Black singers, who gave an eloquent plea to "cool it." His remarks were played again and again. "Don't terrorize. Organize," he implored. "Don't burn. Give the kids a chance to learn. Go home. Look at TV. Listen to the radio. Listen to some James Brown records . . . When I was a boy I used to shine shoes in front of a radio station in Augusta, Georgia. Today I own that station. *That's* black power!"

Brown made a similar plea in Boston. In effect, he worked to minimize his own audience at a concert that had been scheduled for weeks. At the request of the Mayor, Brown permitted the local educational station to televise the two-hour show at the Boston Garden. It is estimated that over 12,000 of an anticipated audience of 15,000 young Negroes stayed home that night, the night after the assassination. Brown's message was the same: cool it.

In Detroit, WXYZ had athletes taking phone calls from youngsters to quiet a nervous city. It was part of a full day's telethon designed to keep school children at home (schools were closed in respect for King) and all other programming was dropped except network coverage of Dr. King's funeral. In Baltimore, WJZ-TV dropped commercials from a baseball game and instead carried appeals from Baltimore players: "Baltimore's my home, too; let's not burn it down."

The networks carried much special programming as tributes to Dr. King, many of these broadcasts designed to calm the country. The most moving single broadcast was carried on educational television. The Public Broadcast Laboratory carried a two-hour "unfinished documentary" on Sunday night, April 7th. PBL had been filming Dr. King for three months for a special broadcast scheduled originally for April 21. It included some magnificent, candid footage. It also included a sequence with Associate Producer Joseph Luow who was near Dr. King as he was felled in that Memphis motel. Luow took still pictures seconds after the shooting, later shown in *Life* and around the world. He narrated his own stills and told what it was like at the time of the assassination. The documentary was much praised and won first prize at the Venice Film Festival later in the year.

Broadcasting magazine talked of "TV-radio maturity" and said the coverage "was widely hailed as an important element in keeping the violence from getting further out of hand and in gradually restoring calm." It noted that coverage of violence "was generally carried in regularly scheduled newscasts in an effort not to exacerbate already tense situations in numerous ghetto areas."

Broadcasting is, of course, a publication very friendly towards the industry; it has been called the voice of broadcast management. On the whole, however, it would appear that television had learned the bitter lessons of those bitter summer days of earlier years.

Special Problems for TV.

Some things, however, are beyond the cure of experience. Television's equipment is often bulky, usually obvious, and therefore runs the risk of exaggerating an incident by its very presence. The Kerner Commission made note of this:

> Most newsmen appear to be aware and concerned that their very physical presence can exacerbate a small disturbance, but some have conducted themselves with a startling lack of common sense. News organizations, particularly television networks, have taken substantial steps to minimize the effect of the physical presence of their employees at a news event. Networks have issued internal instructions calling for use of unmarked cars and small cameras and tape recorders, and most stations instruct their cameramen to film without artificial light whenever possible. Still, some newsmen have done things "for the sake of the story" that could have contributed to tension.
>
> Reports have come to the Commission's attention of individual newsmen staging events, coaxing youths to throw rocks and interrupt traffic, and otherwise acting irresponsibly at the incipient stages of a disturbance. Such acts are the responsibility of the news organization as well as of its individual reporter.

There has been much searching, self-examination by the networks on these very themes. As early as 1963, one network warned its staff to beware of "the unsettling effect on a stimulated crowd that the presence of cameras may have."

Television, fearful perhaps of official censure or regulation, has tended to publicly downplay the effect of the camera on the scene while privately urging its people to caution. The matter did come into public view when Senator Philip Hart raised the point at a hearing of the Violence Commission—first with ABC News President Elmer Lower and then, with Commission Counsel Philip Tone joining, with CBS News President Richard Salant:

> SENATOR HART: Why in heaven's name does television dance around and suggest that there is some uncertainty as to whether the presence of a television camera has any effect on the scene and the story and the action?
>
> To me, my own experience leads me inescapably to the conclu-

sion that when those things move in, everybody acts differently—beginning with me, not just because I am a politician and want to look as good as I can, but because I am a human being, and it is to me ridiculous to hem and haw about this. I sit up and I try and sound my G's and I hope I resist the temptation to ask curved ball questions when the cameras are here but ignore them when they are not. I am not sure I always resist that temptation, but I know—and I think I am normal—that that camera influences me enormously. Why don't you admit it? It doesn't follow that you shouldn't take the camera to a riot in order to enable you more effectively and wisely to plan what you are doing.

MR. LOWER: Senator, if I may reply to that. Often the people who ask the question single out television. I would tend to agree if you would enlarge—or those who speak to this would say the presence of all the mass media have effect on people who are doing something.

SENATOR HART: That doesn't support television's reluctance to acknowledge the influence that the camera has. I accept the proposition that the print media influence is enormous—the still camera also. If we lived without any neighbors, our conduct probably would be different if there wasn't a neighbor. I mean just to me, I would be more comfortable if I heard the television people say, "Sure, we know that this thing is dynamite"—because it is—instead of saying, "Well, we are not sure whether it affects this thing, but in case it does we now move in unmarked cars."

❋   ❋   ❋   ❋   ❋   ❋   ❋   ❋

MR. TONE: I have a particular question addressed particularly to Mr. Salant.

You have stated in at least to CBS news personnel that disturbing events like demonstrations and riots may be shaped to some extent or another by the mass medium, including television. That is a simple fact of journalistic life.

Would you tell the Commission what you believe, in view of that fact, what you believe to be the obligation of journalism in covering events, and particularly television journalism, in covering events in which the presence of the camera may make a difference?

MR. SALANT: Let me back up on that and perhaps kill two birds with one stone, which is the wrong image here and say that you won't find a hem or haw out of me on the question of the effect in one way or another of the presence of cameras.

As Senator Hart said, I think it is also true of the print media to a lesser extent because they are more conspicuous about the presence of reporters. I behave myself. Everybody behaves themselves, differently when somebody is around taking down what they are saying when—you have the same influence on me. This is a fact you must live with.

The important thing in our end of the business is to realize this. It is something that we have talked about, we have written about. When we have time late in the evening we debate among ourselves and we worry about it.

I have written a number of times and I made public statements, I have written to my staff, that we have to be as inconspicuous as possible. We have a budget. We are working on new devices, lights and smaller cameras—I don't know how much good that will do. But our people must be aware that there is this effect in reporting. They must take it into account.

As early as 1963, when I first came across the problem concretely, I issued a memorandum which has been re-issued in several forms since, including just before Chicago, that any time a correspondent in the field who is in charge feels that the presence of the camera is creating or aggravating or continuing disorder, which but for the presence would die down or disappear, his job is to cap the camera and get out of there. We have done that.

MR. TONE: I might say that memorandum was furnished to the Commission by CBS counsel.

MR. SALANT: This goes all the way back to 1963 because this is one that worries us. The answer isn't don't cover these things, as Senator Hart said, because otherwise if we didn't cover all things or people in one way or another we affect, you would have a diet of natural disasters.

SENATOR HART: If I could interrupt first to thank you for what you said—I agree with your last point because I don't want to be misunderstood. All I am suggesting is that we deal with dynamite in a certain way. We don't outlaw it. We recognize the enormous potential for good and bad. We treat it. We plan to treat it with respect, acknowledging that potential.

The reason I was speaking as I did was that if the cameras were treated by you who control them against the acknowledgement that they can do this, then that is the best we can hope for. That is good.

Much has been said about the camera's presence; Senator Hart has been one of the few men to demand that television acknowledge that the camera does have effect, but with that he insists that this is no reason to avoid coverage. As he said to a different television executive at a different time, "If you were to concede that by being on the scene you cause trouble, it does not mean you are surrendering your rights to be there."

Nevertheless, television continually strives to be as unobtrusive as possible. In an internal memo, CBS laid down the following guidelines for use during disorders:

> *Guidelines.* There are precautions that we can take . . . to keep from spilling more fuel on the flames. To this end, both CBS News and news department of the CBS Owned stations have instructed their news personnel to: (1) use unmarked cars, with very few exceptions, when carrying equipment and personnel to riot scenes, (2) avoid using lights when shooting pictures, since lights only attract crowds, (3) obey all police instructions instantly and without question—even in the occasional cases where their orders may seem unreasonably harsh, (4) exercise extreme caution in estimating the size, intensity and mood of a crowd, (5) check out all rumors and eyewitness reports before using them, (6) balance all statements by rioters or their supporters with others by responsible officials, and (7) play the news straight, without emotion, and avoid catch-words or phrases —such as "police brutality," "angry mob," etc.—that may antagonize or inflame an already incendiary situation. The important thing is to convey to the viewer that he is seeing only the impression of an event, not an event itself.

Guidelines, however, are just that: lines to guide one. There are occasions when CBS News personnel must make exceptions. Just as a code could be too restrictive, so must guidelines be measured by the situation.

In that context, there was internal debate at CBS News as to whether lights should have been used during the 1968 Chicago convention demonstrations since the guidelines for racial disorders would preclude their use. Following is one rationale for departing from guidelines as written by a CBS News bureau chief:

> In a racial disturbance—or *any* kind of riot—if those lights create unusual disturbance, attract more to the scene, or place our crews and others in physical danger, they should be doused; our cameras should be capped. Yet, is there not an argument to be made that on *some* occasions to do so would be a disservice greater than any effect we have on the event?
>
> *If,* in Chicago, we used no lights, we capped our cameras, we stepped away from the story, then we certainly avoided encouraging some demonstrators to shout louder for our benefit. We also avoided telling the American people that a significant expression of dissent was taking place in downtown Chicago.
>
> Without lights, we could *tell* of police using clubs on protesters,

reporters, bystanders, etc. with brutal abandon. With them we could *show* scenes so searing that few Americans will forget them soon.

It is often said, in Civil Rights demonstrations, that our presence is a protection against police brutality at its worst, that state troopers in Alabama are more careful in the presence of cameras. Could it be said that Chicago's police would be even rougher? Or, perhaps, Chicago's police had lost all restraint and this is what we showed best.

One can argue that lights should have been held in reserve until the roughing-up started. Would any newsman worth his salt "pass" on what *then* happened, even though his lights might cause more disturbance?

One can argue that the others, other networks and local stations, did not hesitate to use lights and we could "ride" on their illumination. This is the poorest argument of all. We should not "ride" on their mistakes, if this *was* a mistake.

Just as Dr. Stanton offers eloquent arguments against codes which would make rigid the television coverage of social disturbances, so can one argue against inflexible guidelines. Despite the apparent public sympathy for Mayor Daley and his police, one can argue that the social consequences of their actions needed the full light of publicity.

To argue otherwise is to say that good television manners take precedent over good reportage. There are times when the story must come first. If there had been fuller light, fuller publicity of the event of the '30's in Germany, Munich might never have been permitted; a free world might have known Hitler better. Mayor Daley, let me make it clear, is no Adolph Hitler but the victims (including the provocateurs) of his police have a right to have their story reported. Our errors might be in degree, in treatment, in style but certainly not in our right and our duty to report the events of late August on Michigan Avenue.

The defensive tone of television people as they justify their medium is partially a result of pressures from public officials. Frustrated with the helplessness in stemming civil disorder, they question whether or not television might not be the cause of it all. Get the medium is their message.

In Detroit, Newark, and Toledo there were charges that television inflamed the riots. The Kerner studies disprove this. In Cleveland there were similar charges and it took an official inquiry to exonerate television. The coverage of the Democratic convention in Chicago touched off a whole series of investigations.

Though the Kerner Commission could uncover no signs of television either causing riots or encouraging their spread, there are those still not satisfied. They talk darkly of staff members of the commission who felt the topic hadn't been fully probed.

Eric Sevareid addressed himself to the topic one summer evening in August, 1967:

Ever since the forefathers' forefathers gathered in their first gatherings on the rocky shores of this country, it has been an unquestioned article of faith that every American is equally expert on politics, religion, and the weather, and in this generation a fourth field has been added: television. This is probably fair enough, because television is almost as all-pervasive, if not all-persuasive an element as weather, religion or politics.

One of the natural hazards for a universal element is that it will become the universal whipping boy from time to time, depending on the national mood. So right now an assumption is prevalent among many, including Congressmen, that television causes city riots. The evidence for this seems tenuous so far, but there are already proposals that broadcast news people should get together and agree on procedures for withholding or delaying or managing news of riots in some degree or other.

There seem to be two parts to this concern: one, that a riot in a given spot may have started because cameras were present at the spot: two, that pictures of rioting in one city stimulate the irresponsible to riot in some other city. It is certainly true that some controlled demonstrations did not start until cameras arrived, which is also true of many press conferences, parades, or ribbon-cutting ceremonies. It is true that some demonstrations never occurred because editors refused to send cameras, judging the affair to be only a publicity stunt. Demonstrators, of course, want their pictures taken, but it's highly doubtful that criminal rioters do.

On the second point, there is certainly a contagion about the riots. All contagions occur through communication, word of mouth, printed press, or broadcast, and whether the contagion is toward violence or sobriety, confusion or clarity. Wreckers require communication, but so do those who prevent wreckage. Because television does have an exceptional immediacy, many of its news people take certain precautions where riots are concerned. They try not to use camera lights at night; they use unmarked camera cars; they avoid emotional tones; they check and correct unfounded rumors, one of the most immediate and inflammatory causes of violence. They can blunder and do, like policemen or Guardsmen or city officials, but no general agreement or code for managing riot news is going to prevent this. It would almost certainly make things worse, because people would immediately distrust the news they do receive, and the rumor-mongers would have a bigger and more fertile field than ever.

Black Suspicion of the Media.

As for the Black audience, it has a general distrust of the "white press," of all the media. It distrusts television less than the others, not because TV is more honest in the eyes of the Blacks, but because ghetto residents believe that it lets them see the actual events for themselves.

The Kerner report gives three reasons for Black distrust. One, they look upon the media as an instrument of the white power structure, defending with enthusiasm and dedication white officials, white police, white store owners. Secondly, they feel that newsmen rely on police for most of their information about what is happening during a disorder and rarely report what Blacks are doing and saying. Thirdly, the ghetto resident feels the media is basically unfair and, in the Kerner report, they cite the failure of the media:

> To report many examples of Negroes helping law enforcement officers and assisting in the treatment of the wounded during disorders;
> To report adequately about false arrests;
> To report instances of excessive force by the National Guard;
> To explore and interpret the background conditions leading to disturbances:
> To expose, except in Detroit, what they regarded as instances of police brutality;
> To report on white vigilante groups which allegedly came into some disorder areas and molested innocent Negro residents.

The Kerner group recommends several means of restoring trust in the Black community. They call for better training in the field of urban affairs, improved police-press relations, regular review of media performance on riots and racial issues, and a news service to supply special material on urban affairs. Most of all, the commission urges the hiring of Negroes in journalism.

It is estimated that fewer than five percent of all editorial employees in the news business are Negroes. Less than one percent of editors and supervisors are Negroes and almost all of these work for Negro publications.

"If the media," says the Kerner report, "are to report with understanding, wisdom and sympathy on the problems of the city and the problems of the Black man—for the two are increasingly intertwined—they must employ, promote and listen to Negro journalists."

CHAPTER 5

THE VIOLENT AMERICAN

IT WAS CHRISTMAS, 1968 at Long Binh, Vietnam and Bob Hope was making his annual overseas trip to entertain servicemen. "I'd planned to spend Christmas in the States," Hope said, "but I can't stand the violence."

There were 30,000 soldiers in the audience and they laughed heartily.

Violence is not new in the United States. When still an agrarian country, the U.S. saw protests and uprisings. There was Shay's Rebellion in Massachusetts (1786), Fries' Rebellion in Pennsylvania (1799) and so on. There were the Grangers, the Greenbackers, the Farmers' Alliance and, during World War I, the Green Corn Rebellion in Oklahoma. The last one hundred years saw the actions of the Bald Knobbers in the Ozarks, the White Cap Vigilantes, the Ku Klux Klan. There was labor strife—the bitter railroad strike of 1877, the Colorado mining strikes of 1913, the Haymarket riots in Chicago—all violent.

This kind of "group" violence has been and is much a part of America. In the 1960's, about 220 Americans died and another 9,500 were injured during a five year period. These were the result of protest, however, not rebellion. The death rate due to group violence was 1.1 per million population. It was far less than the world-wide average of 238 per million.

Individual violence, as opposed to that resulting from group protest, has worried Americans more. The FBI's annual report always seems much worse than its report of a year earlier. The island of Manhattan (New York City) has more homicides with its population of less than two million than does all of England and Wales, population forty-nine million. In cities of over 100,000 population the incident of violent crime rose to well over fifty per cent over the 1960 figure in just half a dozen years. There are almost a quarter million aggravated assaults and almost as many robberies every year.

Firearms are part of America's involution with violence. The emergence of Black militancy and the Vietnam protests caused the sale of guns to zoom, in a five year period during the '60's, from 2,700,000 to over 6,000,000 guns sold in one year. Almost 40% of American homes have firearms "for self-defense" (about 60% of accidental deaths from guns, about 2,500 a year, occur in the home).

"Violence," said Black Militant H. Rap Brown, "is as American as apple pie." The statistics are sobering but apple pie may not be as popular as it seems. Less than ore per cent of the population engages in crimes of violence. Those who do, and their victims, are found in ghetto areas primarily. The upper middle class American, living in the suburbs, is not likely to be physically assaulted. A study in Chicago places the odds against this as 1 in 10,000. In white, middle class areas of the city, the odds drop to 1 in 2,000 but are still pretty "safe." In the Black ghetto, the odds are 1 in 77 that you will be the victim of criminal assaut. Watts, apart from the period of the riots, accounted for 60% of all criminal arrests in the entire Los Angeles area. The Watts population is only 15% of the overall population.

The rise in violent crime is sobering but less so in a comparison with the rise in population. Arrests in New York City, on a per-population basis are far fewer than they were a century ago. Dr. Karl Menninger, in 1968, noted, "A hundred years ago, violence was much worse than it is today. You say it isn't safe to walk down the streets today. It was never safe to walk down some streets."

Whatever the safety factor in city streets is, whatever the validity of crime statistics, whatever the role of status and neighborhood, violence is one of America's favorite obsessions. It is in the fabric of our history, the heart of our literature, the color of our rhetoric. Americans may not engage in violence to the degree that they like apple pie but they engage in preoccupation with the topic to that extent or more. They love to read about it, talk about it, study it, complain, lament, bewail, censor, forebode, decry, and secretly relish it.

One recalls the words of Alfred North Whitehead: "In England, if something goes wrong—say, if one finds a skunk in the garden—he writes to the family solicitor, who proceeds to take the proper measures; whereas in America, you telephone the fire department. Each satisfies a characteristic need; in the English, love of order and legalistic procedure; and here in America, what you like is something vivid, and red, and swift."

Examination of our literature, popular or lasting, indicates that our best and our worst writers have sought the "vivid and red and swift."

It is in our daily newspaper, our daily broadcasts, everything but our daily bread. Maybe it is there, too—a sort of staff of everyday life.

Popular obsessions always bring out reformers. The obsession with violence is particularly vulnerable to reform. While there is much we know about fascination with the matter, there is little we know about consequences of that fascination. Does the media portrayal of violence breed violence? In the 1930's, reformers aroused and mobilized the public against violence in the movies. In the 1940's and 1950's, it was the comic books. In the 1960's, television was the prime target.

TV Treatment of Violence.

Violence on television comes in two forms—there is violence in the real world (i.e the war in Vietnam) which may or may not be "real" in experience and there is the "fantasy" violence in television entertainment. Both could be ritualized and basically artificial to the viewer. Television remains a surrogate instrument, it is not the real thing but rather an impression of reality. Seeing it on television is not living it. The reformers ask, however, does seeing it on television plant the seed for living it?

There is no lack of violence to be seen. Numerous quick studies show this. In October, 1968 the *Christian Science Monitor* reported that its staff had viewed almost 75 hours of prime time programming during the first week of the new season. They calculated 254 incidents of violence including 71 murders, killings and suicides. This was done after the networks, following the assassinations of Martin Luther King and Robert Kennedy, had promised a review of the violence content of entertainment programming. The violence content was no different in a similar survey by the newspaper in July of 1967 (210 violent incidents and 81 killings in 78¼ hours of television).

The National Association of Better Broadcasting monitored television stations in Los Angeles during the second week of July, 1968— one month after Robert Kennedy was assassinated in that city. On the seven VHF stations in Los Angeles, July 6 to July 12, there were 390 murder attempts.

ABC was most criticized in the study. In one evening alone, on ABC, you could view 46 acts of violence including 11 killings. Some 56% of NBC's schedule during that period had programs with violent incidents, one every 14.2 minutes on the average and a killing every 45 minutes. The staff of the National Commission on the Causes and Prevention of Violence reported that the average number of violent encounters per hour on ABC had declined in 1968 after reaching 8.5 per hour the year before. It was now a mere 6.3 violent encounters per hour

—more than one every ten minutes. The percentage of programming containing violence increased however—where 88% the year before, it was now 91% of all ABC evening programming.

On Saturday mornings, when animated cartoons for children are the ABC fare, the Violence Commission study showed 100% of them in 1967 *and* 1968, contained acts of violence, increasing from 15.6 violent encounters per hour to 17.3 per hour in 1968. Cartoons were providing a violent incident every three and a half minutes; no long waits.

ABC's President Leonard Goldenson, on the defensive, told of ABC plans to reduce the content, to "change that concept." There were, he said, plans to do a series on Smokey the Bear. Perhaps because television is usually on the defensive at such sessions with government investigators, no one raised the question: what is the ratio of violent encounters in fairy tales? How non-violent are Aesop's fables? Who counts the violent incidents in the Old Testament? In the history of America's west?

There is, of course, a second plane of criticism: is television, by its nature, more damaging when it portrays violence than other means of communication?

There is no scientific answer. Perhaps there cannot be. The Violence Commission, in an interim report spelling out its problems, raised questions about this.

Most persons will not kill after seeing a single violent television program. However, it is possible that many persons learn some of their attitudes and values about violence from years of exposure to television, and that they might be more likely to engage in violence as an indirect result of that learning. We need to learn the probable effect of daily exposure to media portrayals of violence from infancy to and through adulthood. Just as the family is not the only factor which shapes the attitudes and behavior of children but instead contributes to the molding of individuals along with the churches, schools, friends and other sources of learning and socialization, so the effects of years of exposure to media violence may be more important than the short-run effects of exposure to one or twenty violent media programs.

TV Violence and The Young.

For over a decade, the Senate's Juvenile Delinquency Subcommittee under the chairmanship of Senator Thomas Dodd (Dem., Conn.) has probed television as it affects young people. This is particularly pertinent, since some studies show the increase in violent crime in recent years is directly related to minors as offenders. As the percentage of the young in our society grows, an increase of over 22% in the '60's, so does the increase in juvenile arrests, an increase of about 100% in the '60's. The Violence Commission said in the interim report, "Minors account for nearly all of the increase in arrests for serious crimes in this decade."

The Dodd staff, in 1965, said that it is clear that television, more than any other medium, affects the behavior pattern of the young. "It is the subcommittee's view that the excessive amount of televised crime, violence and brutality can and does contribute to the development of attitudes and actions in many young people which pave the way for delinquent behavior."

During the Dodd inquiry, a number of producers of network entertainment programs offered terrible indictments of the industry. One said he was ordered to put sex and violence in his show. Another said, "I like the idea of sadism." There was a spectacular memorandum asking for "broads, bosoms, and fun." The subcommittee concluded that networks "clearly pursued a deliberate policy of emphasizing sex, violence and brutality on dramatic shows."

Robert MacNeil, who left NBC News and wrote a book critical of television (*The People Machine*), addressed the nature and not the amount of violence on television when he said, "Much attention has been devoted to the quantity of violence on television. What seems even more important is the moral context in which it occurs. It is often violence approved and respected as a solution to human problems. The adventure serials, the police serials, the westerns, sometimes seem like one commercial for violence. Like cigarette commercials they say violence is fun, violence is a deeply satisfying outlet for your frustrations, violence is manly, violence gets you girls. One measure of human progress is the extent to which aggression and violence have been civilized out of us; the extent to which we are conditioned from childhood to behave civilly without dangerous aggression with each other. In that sense these programs may be decivilizing, particularly when one considers the other important ingredient in their moral climate: the gun cult. The networks may be cutting down the number of blanks fired per episode but the cherishing of guns goes on."

MacNeil refers to Americans as having "prolonged exposure to a seductively pleasant world in which it is not only manly but downright heroic to cut through the obstacles of life with fist and gun." In the early '60's, one study stated that the average American child will, between the ages of five and fourteen, witness the violent destruction of 13,000 human beings on television.

In his testimony before the Violence Commission, FCC Commissioner Nicholas Johnson quoted Dr. Wilbur Schramm, one of the most prolific contributors to the study of television and children as saying, "We are taking a needless chance with our children's welfare by permitting them to see such a parade of violence across our picture tubes. It is a chance we need not take. It is a danger to which we need not expose our children any more than we need expose them to tetanus, or bacteria from unpasteurized milk."

But Dr. Schramm, director of Stanford's Institute for Communication Research, also has said, "The roots of criminal behavior lie far deeper than television; they reach into the personality, the family experience, the relationships with others in the same age group as the delinquent or criminal individual. At most, television can be merely a contributory cause, and is likely to affect only the child who is already maladjusted and delinquency prone."

The fact of the matter is that facts which matter are yet to be confirmed by adequate research. What stimulates a child? What incites him to aggression? What compels criminal acts? If we insist that the answer to all questions is in television's current fare, we run the risk that the remedy will be wrong because the diagnosis was faulty.

There is no shortage of strong feelings on the matter. J. Edgar Hoover, head of the FBI, has flatly stated that "The explosive danger to society from excessive television violence is obvious. Concerned authorities feel that brutality and violence are becoming accepted as normal behavior by young impressionable minds." Reformers should be more cautious in their passion for cleansing television. Until it has scientific base, it is their greatest weakness and ultimate arrogance. It is just too early to purge television; too much is needed in the way of knowledge.

Pinpointing TV's Responsibility.

Program reform can be argued for many reasons—the present fare is popular but poor drama, the violence is not needed for audience or effect, the writing could be improved, the subject matter can be varied. Program reform is possible—but beginning with the premise that present programs lead directly to violence is premature assumption at best.

Not that the average American doesn't feel that there is too much violence. The Violence Commission had the Louis Harris pollsters do a survey which Congressman Hale Boggs revealed at the December 20, 1968 hearing. It showed that 59% of male adults and 63% of female adults feel that there was too much violence on television. Representative Boggs went on to quote the survey as showing that 32% of the population felt it likely that television makes people insensitive to real acts of violence; another 28% thought it possible that TV had this effect. Over half (52%) felt it likely that television triggered violent acts from people who are maladjusted or mentally unstable; another third (34%) felt it possible that TV had this effect.

Dramatically, Mr. Boggs turned to another commission member— Dr. W. Walter Menninger, the noted psychiatrist:

REP. BOGGS: Now, Dr. Menninger, can you tell me the number of people who are maladjusted and mentally unstable?

DR. MENNINGER: You are getting into an area of much controversy, whether you take it . . .

REP. BOGGS: Well, just a guess.

DR. MENNINGER: I would say the potential is, if you take people who need to go into a hospital, is 10%.

REP. BOGGS: So this could have the effect of 86%, according to this survey, upon 10% of the population and 10% of 200 million is 20 million people.

That conclusion is staggering. Imagine—20 million people sit poised before television waiting for the right program, "Gunsmoke," or "The Avengers," or "Bonanza," to trigger them into violent acts. And that invokes just those unstable enough to require hospitalization. Is there not a larger group of the maladjusted, a kind of *petit mal*, not requiring hospitalization and thus not ready for the big violence but ready to be triggered for mini-acts of mini-violence?

Before the millions are dispatched into action by television, one should examine Boggs' premise. No one has *proven* that television has this effect—Louis Harris has just said that most Americans *think* it does. President Goldenson of ABC tried to correct the record when he noted that "I don't think there has been any conclusive evidence adduced from all of the research that has been available so far" and offered ABC support to such research:

REP. BOGGS: May I ask you a question? What research are you doing? Have you hired an independent, non-biased, objective organization like the Gallop organization or the one that we hired (a committee aide told him it was Harris a moment later) to make research for the American Broadcasting Company? I am not talking about sales.

MR. GOLDENSON: You are talking about a poll of people. I am talking about research on audience reactions and impact of our programs on people.

REP. BOGGS: What do you think I gave you a minute ago?

Moments later the matter arose again and Goldenson tried again but Boggs did not see the distinction:

MR. GOLDENSON: That is purely a poll of individuals. But it does not get to the basic research that I am suggesting. That is merely a poll.
REP. BOGGS: We have had before this commission psychiatrists, journalists, and a host of others in the last several days, many of whom have spent many years doing research on this subject, as well as a representative of the government agency (FCC) directly responsible, none of whom have anything good to say for you.
MR. GOLDENSON: Well, I merely repeat what I said.

The matter arose once again when Dr. Frank Stanton, President of CBS, took the stand. Boggs had deftly led Stanton through a series of answers illustrating the impact of television as a sales medium and as a political soap-box. Then he asked:

REP. BOGGS: Well, now why is television effective in reaching people and advertising and political campaign and is not effective when it shows sadism, masochism, murder, mayhem, and rape?
DR. STANTON: I didn't say it wasn't.
REP. BOGGS: What do you say?
DR. STANTON: I said at this particular point in time we simply don't know.

Boggs noted that the networks have been promising studies since 1954 and pressed Stanton to explain why CBS wasn't engaged in such research at the moment. Stanton replied, "I am not proposing a study now. The reason I am not proposing a study now is I wouldn't know how to spend one million for it or ten million for it. Because we don't have the methodology. If you will tell me how to do it, I will make a commitment to you right now. I will go out and do it."

Boggs called this "an amazing admission" and "astounding."

Amazing as it may seem that a network chief (with a most distinguished background in research) should express inability to determine television's impact on its violence-prone constituents, there *is* no unanimity of belief. Research has been very limited. Conclusions have been carefully restrained. The social scientists with their usual passion for ifs, ands, and buts, remain especially careful not to be more declarative in this muddled area.

Gadfly Nick Johnson in prepared testimony for the Violence Commission offers his own, provocative suggestion: make the networks legally liable if anyone can prove damages done by television. Noting that this "has often proven to be an effective spur to reform" in other fields, Johnson explained his approach:

> Most products are warranted as safe for the purposes for which intended. Why not the televised product? A drug manufacturer must do sufficient experimentation ;o prove the efficacy and harmless nature of his product before offe.'ng it to the public. Why not the television company? Why shouldn't the broadcaster bear a measure of any tobacco manufacturer's liability to the widow of a lung cancer victim for failing to tell her husband the whole truth about the impact of cigarette smoking? Many states recognize "psychic" or emotional injury. (For example, bill collectors may be liable for harassing innocent debtors.) Why shouldn't a television network be liable for the psychic harm it does millions of young children who watch the Saturday morning "children's programs"? The television set manufacturer is legally liable for physical damage done by radiation from the set. Why should the network be free of responsibility for the psychic harm done by what it radiates from the set? To state the extreme case, suppose a psychiatrist would testify that a child's mental illness was directly traceable to a particular show watched regularly. And suppose, further, that numerous other children were affected in this way—and that the network knew the program would likely produce that result. Is legal liability out of the question? If there is not legal liability for the fate of millions, is there not at least a moral responsibility that is even greater? Legal liability has been an effective instrument of reform in the past, and is at least worth examination as a means of improving the most extreme instances of injurious programming.

This brought strong comment from a leading conservative spokesman, columnist David Lawrence, who took strong issue with the logic or consistency of "so-called" liberals. If Johnson and government could dictate the course of television drama, "officials could do the same for every theater in the country, and could tell every newspaper that the printing of stories of crime is psychologically injurious and must be suppressed . . . Many of the criticisms on the handling of violence on the air and in the press are superficial, and not based upon a thorough study of the psychological as well as criminal phases . . . If the whole nation is to be aroused to the necessity of getting to the heart of the problem of incitement to violence, this will not be accomplished by telling the news media to say less and not more about such things or not to picture just what really is happening in this country."

In Commissioner Johnson's testimony before the commission, he was asked to expand on his proposal and did so thusly:

> There is no question in my mind if a drug manufacturer has the responsibility to know about the impact of his product on the user before he is permitted to market it, that the television manufacturer obviously it seems to me has the same responsibility. This is most clearly illustrated with those people walking along holding transistor radios with the ear plug in the ear. Everybody else is sitting with their eyes focused on this screen.
>
> If someone would propose that every evening you wanted to put electrodes upon the skulls of half of the American population and feed electronic energy into the brain that would realign the brain cells and affect the thinking and imagery and sense of values and so forth of the American people, I think it would be a long time approving that proposal. Yet that is precisely what is happening every evening. I think that that does carry with it an extraordinarily high responsibility and I think the network executive simply can't come in here and say gee, we don't know what the impact is any more than a drug manufacturer can come in and say I didn't know what the impact of that drug would be. It is your business to know. If you don't know you are responsible in dollar damages to the harm you did to the fellow. Punitive damages as well. I think at least as high a standard and I would say a higher standard ought to be imposed upon television people.

Commission members picked up the drug analogy and pressed it with representatives of the networks. CBS' Stanton argued that "you have the long sweep of history in which you had violence in many other art forms before you had television . . . as against drugs and application of some of the more sophisticated drugs that have come into our society in a relatively recent time, we have grown up with violence. We haven't grown up with drugs to the same extent, if you will."

ABC's Goldenson promised support to research but noted that should ABC do it, as Johnson suggests the drug industry does its own research, then it would be suspect. He promised cooperation with any such research conducted by the commission or similarly responsible groups.

Violence in News Coverage.

Earlier, we noted that violence on television comes in two forms—the fantasy violence of entertainment programs and the violence of reality in news coverage. This last is not "real" violence. Real violence is performing or being victim of or witnessing the act. The violence in news coverage is doing that vicariously.

TV Guide, a mini-magazine with brief articles and tiny editorials (and often the most perceptive of criticism), made concise comment on the Violence Commission hearings when it said it was difficult to separate the effects of violence in entertainment from that in the news but every effort should be made to do so. "Let the Government—in this case the FCC and Congress—abide by the First Amendment to the Constitution and leave the coverage of news to journalists."

TV Guide implies that the FCC and Congress should, however, consider entertainment programs fair game. But does not the First Amendment apply equally to fiction? Is freedom of speech limited to those who talk of or write non-fiction? Are the fiction writers, including the poets and philosophers of truth, unprotected from Government control? The answer must be "no"; all are protected within the limits of First Amendment interpretation.

The Violence Commission, of course, did not limit its concern to fiction; it was extremely interested in news on TV. The thirteen members of the commission included college professors (Dr. Milton S. Eisenhower was chairman), lawyers, judges, Congressmen, clergy, psychiatrists and a longshoreman-author-philosopher (Eric Hoffer). They all became students of journalism. Their staff conducted a weekend seminar with leading journalists, surveys of the literature of journalism were conducted and a number of witnesses from the field including the head of each network's news operation was quizzed.

In addition, the Violence Commission issued a massive subpoena for each network. It asked for many things including a breakdown of personnel in each news department, all documents relating to news policy and behavior, all documents relating to public statements regarding violence or public disorder, copies of specific broadcasts, and everything relating to the October, 1967 March on the Pentagon, the July 23, 1968 Cleveland riot, and both the Republican and Democratic conventions in 1968. Other than those relating to a specific event, all documents from January 1, 1963 to late 1968 were to be submitted.

They also subpoenaed all film relating to the Chicago convention disturbances. This meant *all*, not just the film used on air. Network news departments bitterly oppose distribution of any film other than that which has been aired.

The aired material is, in effect, the published record. The "outs" or "trims," the unused film, is more like a reporter's note pad—material gathered but not used. Julian Goodman, a newsman who became president of NBC, called it reviewing the television reporter's work product and stated: "This unusual intrusion into a journalist's working materials has raised the gravest doubts in our minds and has given us the uneasy feeling that there has been an infringement of the basic rights that are guaranteed all free Americans by the First Amendment."

Defensive as network heads might have been concerning violence in entertainment, they were forthright and strong on the question of news. *Variety* called it "Statesmanship on News Issue."

At least one network news chief was determined to risk contempt and refuse to answer questions on the basis of the First Amendment should the commission attempt to probe into matters of news judgment. It never got to that; the commission was curious but not hostile on the news front. Congressman Boggs was bitter over the alleged "bugging" of the closed session of the Democratic Party Platform Committee which he chaired but since the accused, NBC, faced legal investigation on that matter, he did not press it.

Dr. Stanton spoke for CBS and said: "While we are open to questions concerning the techniques of news gathering, we believe it inappropriate for this commission or any other goevrnmental body to raise questions involving news judgment." ABC's Goldenson said: "We reject any attempt to abridge the freedom of our news department to report the news as we see it." NBC's Goodman said: "We do not believe that suppression of information is the answer to anything."

The nature of the questioning was more of mild exploration than of challenging news judgments. One witness was John F. Dille, Jr. who heads the Communicana Group which operates newspapers, radio stations and television outlets in Indiana. He presented a newsman's concern that the way to treat violence is in the telling, not trying to control reporting or limit it:

> We can agree that violence is morally bad. But is it morally bad to expose violence? More precisely, is it morally bad to fail to expose it?
>
> It has been argued that our exposure of violence is germinal, that it creates more violence, that violence grows in the light we cast on it. Others argue that if we do not expose it, violence will grow—that, like fungus, its most hospitable environment is darkness.
>
> Who is right? Who will give us the undeniable and inevitable results of our exposure or nonexposure of violence? We of the media do not possess these divine qualities. We have yet to find who does.
>
> Our course must be to throw light on things good and bad. Often it will be on the bad. If we are to be an instrument of social change,

we must portray the bad which cries out for change. If the people or the government won't change, we have at least done our duty and history will make its judgments.

Violence, on television newscasts, has a strange and remarkable impact. A very tiny percentage of the time devoted to the Chicago convention dealt with violent actions or even discussion relating to that. At NBC and CBS, less than 3% of total airtime devoted to the Democratic convention dealt with the disturbances. At ABC, which ran condensed coverage of the convention, there was an even smaller percentage, 1.1%.

Just a trickle in the torrent of convention material—but the trickle is remembered, the rest of the stream pretty much forgotten except for the fact that a ticket was nominated. The violence is burned into memory. Violence is vivid (and red and swift?); the rest is vanilla.

This is not surprising. Spend two weeks on vacation and it is placid and calm. But punch a neighbor in the nose or have him punch you and the memory of a single moment is real, it remains. Few Americans believe they saw so little violence during those four days of August, 1968. They remember a lot; it was real, it remains.

Similarly with newscasts in less troubled times, remembrance is not based on how much was shown but on what was shown. Elmer Lower, President of ABC News, did a survey of an entire year's news coverage— a year that included the 1968 Democratic convention. It showed that only 9% of the news was even remotely associated with violence. "Even within that 9%, the actual presentation of violent acts on the air was very rare."

If Lower's statistics apply to all networks, they still beg the issue. Even if one were inclined to agree that quantitatively there is comparatively little attention to violence in TV news, what about the quality of its impact, little or not? Is the cliche true that support for the Vietnam War was doomed from the start because people could see the killing in their living rooms? Allowing for striking impact, however, is it therefore true that depiction of violence in the news leads to emulation of that violence? And if it does, is even that enough to curtail, to censor the news?

Leon Jaworski, a member of the Violence Commission, put it this way while questioning Richard Salant, President of CBS News: "Suppose it was determined as an actual fact that the constant depiction of violence in news gathering was inimical to the public interest because it had actually been shown that it spawned crime and violence in large proportions, would you still invoke the First Amendment and say we don't need to go into this issue and don't want to get into it?"

Salant said he was prepared to answer though advice from his counsel (a lady member of the Commission was smiling and shaking her head) was that he shouldn't. He did so, he said, because the question was "purely hypothetical" and put so pleasantly. "I think the First Amendment has put a priority on the importance of the right of the people to know, and if you exclude from your normal news judgment a whole area of legitimate news happenings because reporting the truth is likely to cause some effects, then you are in serious trouble. I would say then as a hypothetical academic issue, I would argue most vigorously that there never should be anything excluded from news if it is legitimate news."

Jaworski was not satisfied. The First Amendment, he noted, does not permit one to get up in a theater and "holler fire" as the classic exception was put. The testimony, said Jaworski, talked of an effect that television has and there was no distinction drawn between a news story and a fictional play. What, he repeated, if it were absolutely shown that reporting of such news is "an actual spawning ground for crime and violence"?

"I think the societal values," said Salant, "of telling what is happening overrides concern—if, for example, someone should contend, with a great deal of persuasion that reporting on riots is contagious and causes riots—a thing which the Kerner Commission backed away from, it didn't say that, but suppose it had been something like that—I think it is important to tell it because if it isn't told this nation will not get to work on solving the problems. Nothing is happening."

An interesting contention, that. Even if proven that news of violence spawns violence, the nation has a right to know what's going on. Otherwise, nothing happens.

Does the nation want to know? The years 1967–68, with racial uproars and anti-war disorders, were years when the nation really didn't want to know. The turmoil of racial discord, political assassination, the rebellion of the young, and the defiance of the Vietnam protestors was not pleasant fare for the American viewer. "We," said the president of ABC, "are presently reaping the harvest of having laid it on a line at a time when many Americans are reluctant to accept the images reflected by the mirror we have held up to our society."

"It," said the president of NBC, "has long been a fact of life, for the journalist, that those who do not like what they read or hear or see are apt to condemn him and his medium for distorting truth. And it is an easy step from there to suggesting that the reporter and the medium contribute to problems by reporting them. In short, the medium is blamed for the message."

In that kind of an atmosphere, it is no wonder that governmental agencies and commissions and committees of the Congress probe into the nature of news on television. The people are concerned. The news is uncomfortable, it makes you twitch. It makes you itch (which would please Ed Murrow).

A professor of radio and television at Northwestern University,

Martin Maloney, has called the crusade against violence on television pointless and dangerous. "It is a crusade without risk, pain or hard decision; and if we join it, we may very well never find out where the social action really is."

A reformer's zeal is not wrong; it sounds the first notes of social change. That note sours only when it is used to shut off other notes, when it cuts off the flow of other sounds. Television news is not always accurate in its treatment of turbulent events. No man has a corner on truth. Ideas emerge from a diversity of believed fact. Limiting diversity is stifling, even if the limitation stems from righteousness, from a desire to do good. The First Amendment gives not only the right to report the news but, in the words of Frank Stanton, "the even more profound Constitutional right to be wrong."

Violence is not socially accepted (though some contend that it might be in the case of war) but reporting of violence must always be accepted or there is social damage. Diversity of reporting is a yeast from which opinions develop. Sometimes they run contrary to the *status quo*, to the Establishment, the party in power. They're supposed to do that, sometimes.

That brings us to Vietnam.

CHAPTER 6

TELEVISION'S FIRST WAR

IN JANUARY OF 1969, William Stringer wrote in the *Christian Science Monitor:* "The United States has experienced a communications revolution —so that every miserable or marvelous national or international problem or achievement is brought straight into the living room or parlor, via television . . . The war in Vietnam, for example, has got to end; too many people have been mentally anguished by what they've seen on TV."

At about the same time, the incoming President was greeted by a 620-page study, *Agenda for the Nation,* which was produced by the prestigious Brookings Institution as a guide to the problems he faced. It told Richard Nixon that his first order of busines is to settle the war and said so in a sentence beginning, "The brutality and horror of the war— made vivid as in no previous war by the immediacy of television . . ."

Everybody was saying it. The war was terrible because there was blood to be seen in the living room.

It was television's war. No other war had such coverage. No other war brought the shooting of sons before the eyes of mothers. No other war showed it as it really was. No other war had all its horror portrayed in living color.

Clichés. But like all clichés, the grain of truth there.

Even Marshall McLuhan agreed, using his own clichés: "The Vietnam War has taught Americans that they cannot have a *hot* war in a *cool,* or involved, age. When electric immediacy has got everybody involved in everybody all wars are world wars, under electric conditions. TV brings them into our homes, and some American parents have seen their own sons killed on TV news programs. Seeing them on TV, moreover, we experience all sons as our own."

In fact, not that much has been seen on television. The amount of war's gore on the tube has not been that extensive. But like so many things that television transmits, this is remembered because it is striking, burned into the memory. Observers of the media have always contended that it is the little picture that sears the mind, that scorches memory. The headlines dealing with thousands of injured, the television copy that tells us of the weekly dead and injured are facts that mean as little to the average man as the phrase "one billion dollars."

In contrast, the NBC film sequence which showed South Vietnamese Brigadier General Nguyen Ngoc Loan walk up to a captured Viet Cong officer, lift a pistol to his head and shoot him, is one that few will forget. The years of the War had their share of such incidents and they are remembered. It was television's first war. Korea had much simpler treatment in an early era of TV though Murrow's "Christmas in Korea" was a classic film treatment of the horror called war. In this chapter, we shall examine how the war was covered by television and in the next, how anti-war was covered by television.

TV News in Vietnam.

By the late '60's, Saigon had become the second largest news bureau, second only to Washington, in each of the three networks. Between them, the networks probably spent over five million dollars a year to cover the Vietnam war.

The day in Saigon begins with the network staff reviewing the cables that flowed in during the night from New York. A review of the wire service copy is also in order.

Somewhere in the provinces, one or several correspondents and their camera crews are in search of or involved in battle action. In Saigon or Danang, "local" stories will be covered. Tips flow in from staff members including Vietnamese employees, their friends and relatives. As the day progresses, the bureau begins to worry about getting film out, meeting flights heading for the United States or Tokyo. New York is now asleep and the cable traffic is heading the other way.

At the end of the afternoon, there is the daily military-political briefing—the so-called "Five O'clock Follies." Some fifty to one hundred reporters fill a small theater at the Joint U.S. Public Affairs office. They are given a cursory description of the day's action, of developments, political and military. The "Follies" are radioed to the Pentagon and reporters there will share the information later in the morning in Washington.

A few hours later, the radio circuit is "up" and the Saigon bureau has contact with New York where it is now 7 a.m. Radio stories are filed, some voice-over narration for film that is already en route to the U.S., and the newsmen chat with their editors back home. Hopefully, by this time, they are able to give progress reports on their correspondents out in the field

At the height of the Vietnam war, some 400 or so newsmen were accredited. Only one-fourth of these ever left the city for regular probes into the battle zones. Most of those who did, worked for television.

How do they go about covering battles? If there is a big, running confrontation it is easy to make the assignment. More commonly it works this way, as described by CBS News Correspondent Morley Safer:

> Well, most of the time it's really a question of sticking a pin in a map. If you're in Saigon and you say, "Well, I think I'll go out on an operation today," or "I think I'll cover it."
>
> It's a shooting war—try to find it. And really, you just sit around and say, "We haven't been up to Pleiku for a while," up in the Highlands; so you pick up a phone and you get yourself a place on a plane the next day to Pleiku, which means getting up around 3:30 in the morning to catch the plane and then you get off the plane and then you start working. And by starting to work, I mean you start trying to find somebody who's going to be nice enough to give you a ride in his jeep to one of the helicopter pads.
>
> You hang around the helicopter pads and have coffee or something with the pilots. You ask them what's happening. The men who know what's happening in Vietnam are the helicopter pilots. No one else may know but they know because they're in to resupply troops with weapons, they're in carrying troops, they're in running medical evacuations, they're pulling people out of this kind of thing and they've got a pretty good idea and they'll say, "Why don't you go out to the Third—Fourth of the 25th Division. I think they've got a little happening going on." So you wait around until someone's going and gives you a lift . . .
>
> Now, chances are, as you know, you can go jungle-bashing in Vietnam for a month with—all you get is the crud, which means that the skin starts falling off your feet, and tired and constipated usually from eating C-rations, and find nothing. Absolutely nothing. And the only movement you see is the flutter of government leaflets coming out of the skies calling the V.C. to defect. Just at the point where you've had it, something will happen . . .
>
> We went out on a thing with the 1st Division last August. We got a call from them saying there'd been a fairly heavy contact, would we like to come up and talk to some of the survivors. So we went up carrying three rolls of film. I didn't have so much as a canteen.

Got a lift out to where this fighting was and went in on an armed personnel carrier with the new battalion commander who was going in to look the place over. He'd been in the country two days. And, wham! You know, ran into one of the most extraordinary battles that I've ever—that I'd seen in eighteen months of—it just happened.

It was the moment that we got in, was the moment we realized that we were surrounded by a battalion of Vietcong. Spent the whole day in there, spent the whole night in there under continuous fire, realized that we were the perimeter. This is the only time that I've been in a situation in Vietnam in which people were getting hit— killed—behind us.

You know, that's when you sit there and wonder what in God's name am I doing here and you're no more than ten minutes away from the air-conditioned roof of the bar of the Caravelle Hotel.

I remember the last thing I was on, I was talking to "the old man," the company commander. The old man was twenty-four years old and he came up to me and said, "You fellows are a little bit old for this kind of stuff, aren't you?" And I said, kind of defensively, "What do you mean by that?" And he said, "Well, gee whiz, our light colonels, our battalion commanders, they won't let them go on any of these operations if they're older than thirty-four."

That was Safer's description of the daily regime, as he told it on "Debriefing," an informal CBS News radio series which interviewed correspondents as they returned from important assignments.

The pursuit of the big battle has been the heart of one of the great controversies involving television in Vietnam. Many correspondents and producers, despite disclaimers from New York, insist that the "name of the game" is to "shoot bloody," to get the good battle footage. Sometimes it is not that direct. Sometimes it is a cable saluting a good story on pacification or the upcoming election or refugee problems and there is the added note: "By the way, the competition got some great battle footage of the Marines near Hue."

Pentagon officials, many of them unhappy about television's treatment of the war, charge that the medium is far too engrossed with battle scenes or civil uprising. They say that television is in search of the violent, the dramatic and that this is often simplifying a complex war.

Another criticism is of the pattern: following small units, a platoon or even a squad. This is a "sampling" of battle action, says the Pentagon, it does not encompass the "big picture," the movements of battalions and brigades. CBS News Correspondent Peter Kalischer relates the time that General Douglas MacArthur upbraided him in Korea, threatened to throw him out, and when he finally relented to let Kalischer return, said:

"But don't report the war from the platoon level any more." Says Kalischer, "So this is a very old complaint. Wars always look better from division headquarters than they do in foxholes."

The heat and the wet and the mud of Vietnam makes the going tough for newsmen and lots of young correspondents get a crack at war coverage. This, too, is criticized by the military and even by White House spokesmen. Robert Fleming, when Assistant Presidential Press Secretary, told a public gathering that new, young, unsophisticated, "inexperienced" reporters were one of TV's weaknesses in Vietnam. Yet some of the most experienced hands at all three networks have spent their share of time there: Cronkite, Sevareid, Huntley, Howard K. Smith, Kalischer, Rather, Collingwood, Bernard Kalb, Cioffi, John Rich, Fromson, Frank McGee. The networks have tried to balance the young reporter with the older, more weathered correspondent.

Pentagon Concern Over TV.

In the first years of the war, there was much criticism over the showing of casualties. The networks developed a pattern of making sure that families were informed, wherever possible, before showing films of wounded and dead. Still, there was much criticism. Pentagon officials claimed that field commanders were getting emotional letters from their wives back home asking, "Why do you let TV show such pictures of your men?". It was said that General William Westmoreland, chief of our forces in Vietnam, at one point considered a ban on all filming in the field. Pentagon advisors talked him out of it.

Arthur Sylvester, Assistant Secretary of Defense for Public Affairs and some of his aides, visited the networks to resolve the problem. They could cite only one incident of a woman who saw a picture of her son wounded and that was in a local newspaper, but there had been reports of others. They cited instances of wounded men clearly identified and in a state of shock ("We have a duty to protect the privacy of men wounded," said Sylvester) but admitted that "we had to look through a lot of film to find such examples."

The networks were most sympathetic to the specific problem of protecting a mother or wife from the shock of seeing a loved one on the battlefield. They made it clear however that this was in no way to be construed as a policy of "easing up" on war coverage. "War is unpleasant, it is ugly," they said. "We plan to portray it as it is."

There was one occasion cited in which a man, in shock, was in very bad shape apparently and the network commentary implied that he had not survived. It turned out that he was suffering from little more than that shock and was back on the battle line a few days later. This sort of problem compelled Sylvester's successor, Phil Goulding, to write the networks at a later date and review the problem. He noted that some 85% of Americans wounded in Vietnam have been returned to duty. He expressed concern that the average viewer thought of "casualty" as one who is dead. To counteract this, he announced, Saigon would break down the wounded into those requiring hospital care and those not requiring such care.

Much earlier, the military had dispensed with actual casualty counts as they related to specific incidents. Instead, the vague terms "light," "moderate," or "heavy" were used to describe American casualties. Each briefing officer or field officer had his own concept of what light, moderate or heavy meant.

Much of the credibility gap derived from the disparity in figures given out in Vietnam. Reporters found the casualty count irregular, sometimes due to simple ignorance on the part of the military source. Sometimes it was an attempt to affect the reporting of the incident. Often the men in the field send in a casualty count that is inaccurate becuse it might please their superiors, especially their count of enemy dead. In Saigon this figure is released. Subsequently a reporter at the scene or one arriving just after the battle finds the figures highly irregular and credibility is damaged. A phrase was coined for these incidents: WAG. It stood for Wild Ass Guess.

As for enemy body count, that was tough to do. The enemy tried to carry off his dead. One result was that figures for enemy dead were extremely high, as reported by American (and more often South Vietnamese) military sources. Occasionally reporters wondered if there were any left to fight for the Vietcong. Newsmen became increasingly skeptical, cynical about the reports given them at the Five O'clock Follies. The claims of damage to North Vietnam due to bombing raids grew increasingly extravagant and at one point, after the Air Force sources listed hundreds of bridges destroyed during the course of several weeks, reporters asked, "Just how many bridges *are* there in North Vietnam?"

One network correspondent wrote his home office that "they have made it increasingly difficult to find the facts. They have ordered servicemen to refuse to comment to reporters, without prior approval by information officers. It has become such an effective method that, even without full censorship, the military succeeds in managing a substantial amount of news reports through the daily MACV briefings. There are suspicions, even, that occasional items are actually planted at these briefings in attempts to influence public opinion at home."

All of this resulted in increasing frustration for the public information people at the Pentagon, in Vietnam and at the White House. In no war had they tried to be more cooperative. There was no censorship.

Reporters were not removed from accreditation. An elaborate arrangement to keep information flowing was established.

Yet, the press resented the military. Suspicion flourished. The defenders of the faith soon grew equally suspicious. They ascribed all sorts of motives to newsmen. Many felt the newsmen were on the side of the enemy.

The Burning of the Huts at Cam Ne.

The frustration reached its peak, perhaps, in the single most famous bit of reporting in South Vietnam. On August 3, 1965, the "CBS Evening News with Walter Cronkite" led its broadcast with a cable from Morley Safer. It told of the burning of a village named Cam Ne by U.S. Marines with "orders to burn the hamlet to the ground, if they so much as received one round (of fire)" according to a Marine officer.

Two days later, that same newscast showed first films of the burning of the village including scenes of Marines using cigarette lighters to set fire to thatched huts. Safer was the only correspondent present and reported that 150 homes were levelled in retaliation for the burst of gunfire. His report concluded: "The day's operation . . . wounded three women, killed one baby, wounded one Marine and netted these four prisoners. Four old men who could not answer questions put to them in English. Four old men who had no idea what an I.D. card was. Today's operation is the frustration of Vietnam in miniature. There is little doubt that American fire power can win a military victory here. But to a Vietnamese peasant whose home is a—means a lifetime of back-breaking labor—it will take more than presidential promises to convince him that we are on his side."

The Establishment exploded in anger. In Saigon, a spokesman said, "Marines do not burn houses or villages unless those houses or villages are fortified."

The Department of Defense released an order by the Vietnam commander, General Westmoreland, on the importance of minimizing civilian casualties. A spokesman said it was 50, not 150 houses, that there was heavy, not light fire, that there was warning from U.S. helicopters prior to the ground attack.

Washington called the report "grossly distorted."

Policy instructions from Marine commander, General William Walt, were made public, instructions that cited "the primary importance of protecting and safeguarding civilians whenever possible," called for utmost discretion and restraint, and said: "The injury or killing of hapless civilians inevitably contributes to the Communist cause, and each incident of it will be used against us with telling effect."

If the Cam Ne story was "the frustration of Vietnam in miniature," then the over-reaction to the report was the frustration of the military in magnification. Fred Friendly, President of CBS News, issued a statement telling of several days checking on the story. He was convinced of the accuracy of the Safer report.

At the same time, Secretary Sylvester wrote Friendly (Safer's boss) with a copy to Dr. Stanton (Friendly's boss) and included a Marine Corps analysis of the Cam Ne affair (some of which was contradicted by Safer's film) plus other documentation showing the military's desire to protect civilians at all costs. In that letter, Sylvester added "some observations of my own"—an attack on Safer, who is Canadian. "Canadian military friends of mine who know Mr. Safer personally and have a high regard for his ability and integrity," Sylvester wrote, "nevertheless tell me he has long been known to them and others as a man with a strong anti-military bias." Sylvester cited stories "worthy" of coverage such as the medical dispensary set up there, a new marketplace and new bridge built for the villagers. "Maybe a Canadian has no interest in our efforts in Vietnam and no realization that the Vietnam conflict is not World War II or Korea, but a new type of political, economic military action."

Safer himself found things a bit rough at first but soon was back to normal reporting:

> Well, there were a couple of days or couple of weeks of uneasiness right after the event in which I found them less than candid and less than cooperative, less than keen in wanting to help us. That's about all. There was on direct threat which was kind of a bad moment where a Marine Colonel threatened the lives of myself and the cameraman, Ha Thuc Can, and said, we should—we'd never be allowed on another Marine operation because if we came he couldn't be responsible for what the troops would do to us, which was just absolute rubbish. We went right back and there was no problem at all. This guy is still there, still mad.

As for Sylvester, he did not forget the matter at all. He brought it up continually with CBS News and other news people. It irked him as Safer won a number of journalism awards for the story at Cam Ne.

Nine months later he was still smarting. Following is an excerpt from a memorandum of mine to my superiors following a luncheon at the Pentagon attended by network bureau chiefs, Sylvester and his aides and a number of top military Information people. It is dated May 13, 1966.

> Sylvester sat next to me and in private conversation expressed concern over relations between himself and CBS News. I told him that I was disturbed because many people we deal with at the

Pentagon, taking a lead from Sylvester's openly anti-CBS posture, assume a posture of anti-CBS themselves.

Arthur assured me that the public controversy over Safer didn't diminish his respect for me or for CBS and went on to note that we had McNamara on exclusively on more occasions than any other network. I agreed and thought the matter had been laid to rest.

However, as lunch proceeded, Sylvester, enriched by several Martinis, slipped back into his more familiar character. Bill Monroe of NBC said, "Arthur, I wish you wouldn't attack Morley Safer. As a result he has won every award in sight." Arthur expressed disbelief but several of his aides said that they agreed with the assumption that Sylvester's attacks had enhanced Safer's reputation.

Mr. Sylvester then proceeded to get most nasty, beginning with the observation that he didn't understand why CBS would hire a "cheap Canadian." I hoped to snuff out the trend of the conversation with a light joke and said, "Art, no matter what else, none of our correspondents come cheap."

This didn't deter Mr. Sylvester from making a proper sonofabitch of himself. He ranted at length about Safer doctoring the news and called upon several of the military people present to note the inaccuracies of the hut-burning story. It was time, finally, to leave and my last observation was to note—after one Pentagon officer observed that they did their best to clear this up quickly—"I assume you mean recalling all Zippo lighters."

On that unfriendly note we parted.

Arthur Sylvester is a perfectly charming man personally. He can be very good company, very pleasant—most of the time. His obsession with the Safer affair never left him.

The Question of Patriotism.

The feud continued in print that spring. Both Safer and Sylvester were asked to contribute articles to a special issue of *Dateline*, the Overseas Press Club of America magazine. In his article, Secretary Sylvester gave his views of the problems of television in Vietnam, comparing them with other war coverage, mildly complaining that television cameras see only part of the scene and don't tell what happened before or after.

In his article, Safer related an incident in Saigon which poured much more oil (or lighter fluid) on the fiery feud. It told of a Sylvester visit to Vietnam and a meeting at the home of USIA chief Barry Zorthian, the main spokesman for both the military and diplomatic authorities in Vietnam:

I was with Murray Fromson, CBS Southeast Asia correspondent. As we returned from our nightly broadcast to New York we looked forward to the cool drinks that are always available at Zorthian's villa.

Inside it was cool. The chairs had been arranged around a low settee where Zorthian usually holds court.

Zorthian opened by saying that this was not to be the usual briefing "for information," but a bull session. "Let's face it, you fellows have some problems covering this war," he said . . . "I want Arthur to hear what they are. Maybe we can get something done."

Zorthian was less relaxed than usual. He was anxious for Sylvester to get an idea of the mood of the news corps. There had been some annoying moments in previous weeks that had directly involved Sylvester's own office. In the first B-52 raids, Pentagon releases were in direct contradiction to what had actually happened on the ground in Vietnam.

Also, those of us involved in broadcasting were anxious to discuss the increasing problems of communication. There was general opening banter, which Sylvester quickly brushed aside. He seemed anxious to take a stand—to say something that would jar us. He did:

"I can't understand how you fellows can write what you do while American boys are dying out here," he began. Then he went on to the effect that American correspondents had a patriotic duty to disseminate only information that made the United States look good.

A network television correspondent said, "Surely, Arthur, you don't expect the American press to be the handmaidens of government."

"That's exactly what I expect," came the reply.

An agency man raised the problem that had preoccupied Ambassador Taylor and Barry Zorthian—about the credibility of American officials. Responded the Assistant Secretary of Defense for Public Affairs:

"Look, if you think any American official is going to tell you the truth, then you're stupid. Did you hear that?—*stupid*."

One of the most respected of all newsmen in Vietnam—a veteran of World War II, the Indochina War and Korea—suggested that Sylvester was being deliberately provocative. Sylvester replied:

"Look, I don't even have to talk to you people. I know how to deal with you through your editors and publishers back in the States."

At this point, the Hon. Arthur Sylvester put his thumbs in his ears, bulged his eyes, stuck out his tongue and wiggled his fingers.

Sylvester was furious, wrote angry letters to the editors of *Dateline* and to Victor Riesel, President of the Overseas Press Club ("Perhaps I shouldn't squawk when I consider the distortion of U.S. Marine activity Safer perpetrated on CBS, for which he won a prize and the undying contempt of the Marines."). He accused the editors of "editorial dishonesty" for billing his article as a reply "to an abusive piece in the same issue by Morley Safer." They had—in the sense that it was "in reply" to Safer that Sylvester discussed TV reporting.

The *Dateline* editors replied in print, accused Sylvester of ducking the questions they had posed in their invitation to do the article. As for the incident that Safer reported, the editors claimed that eight other correspondents present had confirmed it. Safer's article was reprinted in the *Congressional Record* and Sylvester was asked about it when he appeared before the Senate Foreign Relations Committee on August 31, 1966. Sylvester denied Safer's account and CBS News President Richard S. Salant issued a statement calling Sylvester "wholly mistaken," citing the Safer account as accurate, and noting that the Cam Ne story was not only accurate but had earned Safer five awards from his fellow journalists. "With all respect to Mr. Sylvester, he has his job to do, and responsible journalism has its job to do."

Arthur Sylvester, who ran the most controversial public information shop in Washington, retired in February, 1967. He had held the post since 1961, the longest any man had lasted in the job.

Sylvester's battle with Safer was a dramatic example, not the usual thing, of the problems between press and government in Vietnam coverage. Despite elaborate mechanism to keep information flowing, government figures still managed to be at odds with the press—perhaps it is always so when news is not always good.

In Arthur Sylvester's memoirs, or any other forthcoming books from officials who lived these troubled times, there are probably disturbing accounts of press shortcomings. Their motives were pure, on the side of the flag. They couldn't help but question the motives of reporters. But one remembers that Ambrose Bierce defined an infidel in New York as one who does not believe in the Christian religion; in Constantinople, one who does.

In correspondence with this author, George Christian—the Press Secretary to President Johnson—noted that "Television reporters in the field aren't going to make the news with dull stories; action makes the world go around. But maybe the action is the most important thing after all, since the most fascinating of all subjects is the story of life and death.

"The President did worry about the news coverage of the war, as did Secretary Rusk and other high officials. I never met a top military man from Vietnam who did not downgrade press coverage of the war."

For the establishment, the military or administrative establishment, the message is not the one they would convey. Television, the messenger, is easy to blame. Another opportunity came in late November, 1969 when horror stories came into circulation, stories of alleged mass killings of South Vietnamese civilians in My Lai hamlet in Quangngai Province over a year and a half earlier. The atrocity reports received wide circulation on radio and television as well as in print. A dramatic moment came on November 25, when Mike Wallace of CBS interviewed Paul Meadlo, a former member of the infantry unit charged with the killing of 109 to 370 civilians (depending on the report). Meadlo bluntly talked about the killings, including his own participation under orders.

The morning after the interview, Senator Peter H. Dominick of Colorado rose to the Senate floor and bitterly attacked CBS for carrying the interview which he said jeopardized the legal rights of both Meadlo and his commanding officer. Angrily, Dominick said Meadlo confessed that "he had personally participated in the murder of some of these men, some of these women and some of these children. He specifically mentioned the name of the man who is under indictment. What kind of a country have we got when this kind of garbage is put around?"

Senator Ernest Hollings of South Carolina associated himself with the Dominick attack on CBS calling Meadlo "obviously sick" and saying he "ought not to be exposed to the entire public." Hollings went on to ask whether every soldier who had committed "a mistake in judgment" during the heat of combat was "going to be tried as common criminals, as murderers?"

Anger at CBS, at the messenger, for carrying the story of the atrocity. One could sympathize with Senator Dominick's fear that news exposure can corrupt a trial (though a military trial would be before disciplined military officers as opposed to twelve civilan peers) but throughout his complaint and those of his fellow Senator was a thread of discomfort at television for delivering the news.

CHAPTER 7

TELEVISION AND ANTI-WAR

MONDAY, SEPTEMBER 2, 1963 was a most important day to television. The "CBS Evening News With Walter Cronkite" went to thirty minutes (NBC's Huntley-Brinkley Report was soon to follow) and the dream of a full half-hour evening newscast was realized.

An important day for electronic journalism. It called for something special on that first broadcast. What could be more special than an exclusive interview with the President of the United States? Done! John F. Kennedy agreed; Walter Cronkite taped an interview at Hyannis Port, the summer White House.

Vietnam wasn't even the lead. Civil rights and the 1964 election came first. Then the interview was interrupted for other stories. When Cronkite's news broadcast returned to the taped interview, Vietnam still wasn't touched. There was the unemployment question and taxes and the test ban treaty.

Finally, Vietnam.

Began the President, "Unless a greater effort is made by the South Vietnamese Government to win popular support that the war can be won there . . . I don't think the war can be won unless the people support the effort. In my opinion, in the last two months the Government has gotten out of touch with the people. The repressions against the Buddhists we felt were very unwise. All we can do is to make it very clear that we don't think this is the way to win . . .

"With changes in policy and perhaps with—in personnel . . . If (President Diem) doesn't change it, of course, that's his decision. He's been there ten years. And as I say, he has carried this burden when he's been counted out on a number of occasions. Our best judgment is that he can't be successful on this basis. We hope he comes to see it."

A candid evaluation, that. In Saigon, it was later said, this was considered the tip-off. Kennedy had "had it" with Diem. In his NBC interview a week later, the President was equally candid.

On November 1, a military coup moved swiftly—it caught the U.S. and Diem unaware. President Ngo Dinh Diem and his brother Ngo Dinh Nhu were mercilessly assassinated. A new crowd reigned in Saigon.

Pierre Salinger said it was CBS' fault. In editing the interview, some of the answers were tightened. Said Salinger in his book *With Kennedy*: "The result was a partial distortion of JFK's opinion of President Ngo Dinh Diem. In the actual interview, which was filmed, President Kennedy spoke of his respect and sympathy for the problems of President Diem. When the film was shown to the public, only the unfavorable Presidential remarks remained, and JFK's praise of Diem had been deleted.

"The impression was left that JFK had no confidence at all in Diem, and when he and his brother Ngo Dinh Nhu were later shot to death in a military coup, there were persistent charges from Madame Nhu and others that the President's statements had given aid and comfort to Diem's enemies. JFK was deeply hurt by the accusations."

Salinger may be right about the President's feelings, he was closer to him than most people. He was wrong about the editing.

An examination of the original text edited by Don Hewitt, producer of the newscast, shows that the omitted material included a reference to how long Vietnam has been at war, an assertion that we should not withdraw from Vietnam (which repeated a similar line that *was* broadcast), and a reference to Diem being counted out a number of times (also repeated on the air). These edits were done to avoid redundancy.

President Kennedy *did* say "I admire what the President has done" but he quickly coupled this with the need for Diem to re-establish popular support. Other than this one line, there was nothing omitted which would indicate Kennedy's "respect and sympathy for the problems of Diem."

There *was* a final exchange when Walter Cronkite asked, "Did that go all right from your standpoint?" and Kennedy replied, "Yeah, that was fine. Maybe just a little long on the answers. But I don't mind if they decide to edit any of this stuff."

Theodore Sorenson, Special Counsel to Kennedy and later his biographer, noted the CBS and NBC interviews as being "surprisingly candid." He makes no reference to distortions. He does mention a controversial cable which had gone out earlier indicating that the U.S. would not oppose a spontaneous military revolt against Diem.

The interview is cited because it sums up the kind of problems involving television and government over Vietnam. Government quick to blame television when the message isn't getting the result anticipated. Government mistaking the proper role of television (Salinger was even wrong on a technicality: it wasn't film, it was videotape). Government suspicious that television distorted the story.

So it was to be for the life of the war in Vietnam.

Anti-war Protest in America.

During the half-dozen years that followed, anti-war protests were to grow until something like 700,000 people took part in cities and on campuses across America. It began peacefully with "teach-ins" on campus and climaxed bloodily with the March on the Pentagon and the "Confrontation on Michigan Avenue" during the Democratic Convention in 1968.

In the beginning, there was disagreement over a television interview. Before it was over, many defenders of our Vietnam policy were to blame television for setting the climate for the most intense protest against war in the history of this nation.

Dissent in time of war is not new to America. Even before there was a nation, during the French and Indian War, Quakers protested and suffered severely for their opposition. Many of the heroes of the Revolution, as other patriots of otherwise pacifist bent, argued that England was the enemy of peace and the Revolution was a "war to end war" (Thomas Paine).

The War of 1812 was extremely unpopular. The Massachusetts legislature asked for formation of a peace party and one was formed which demanded that President Madison sue for peace. The Mexican War of 1846 saw as many as twenty peace petitions a day reach the House of Representatives and the American Peace Society condemned the war, blamed the U. S. Government for the conflict. A young Illinois Congressman named Lincoln voted for a resolution which referred to the war as illegal.

The Civil War was pockmarked with protests, to the point that Robert E. Lee wrote his wife in April of 1863 that all the South had to do was "resist manfully" until a new administration comes to Washington and bows to the peace pressures. A faction of the Democratic party in the North, known as Peace Democrats or Copperheads, called the war cruel and unnecessary and engaged in clandestine efforts to undermine the morale of soldiers. The Heroes of America and the Peace Society were two secret societies in the South, with an estimated membership of 100,000 Southerners, which encouraged desertion, gave information to the enemy, and weakened morale.

The Spanish-American War spawned the Anti-Imperialist League which included such distinguished officers as former President Grover Cleveland, Jane Addams, Andrew Carnegie and the President of the University of Michigan, James B. Angell. Woodrow Wilson, who had joined the American Peace Society four years earlier, named anti-imperialist William Jennings Bryan as Secretary of State. Bryan hastened to negotiate a galaxy of peace treaties (twenty-one of them were ratified), and to pass out souvenir paperweights showing a plowshare beaten out of a sword. When we entered World War I, it was—of course—a "war to make the world safe" (Woodrow Wilson).

World War II had little protest after initial efforts by pacifist groups to head off the growing conflict. It was America's most popular war. It was "a war to survive" (Franklin Delano Roosevelt).

Five years later, the U.S. was back at war in Korea. "We are trying to prevent a third world war" (Harry Truman). In the 1952 election campaign, Korea was the key issue: Republicans called it "Truman's War," their slogan was "Had enough?" and their candidate General Eisenhower dramatically promised to fly to Korea and personally see about a cease-fire. He was elected.

And then came Vietnam—"an attempt to prevent a larger war—a war almost certain to follow" (Lyndon Johnson).

When President Johnson took office, there were about 16,000 military "advisors" representing the U.S. in Vietnam. It is obvious that the Kennedy Administration did not anticipate the Vietnam situation approaching anything major, certainly it was not comparable to Cuba or Berlin or any serious crisis of the thousand days of John F. Kennedy.

A strange irony developed in 1964. The war situation did not change much (by year's end, only 5,000 more "advisors" were there and the number of U.S. dead came to 245). It was an election year and Vietnam became an issue, not with the party in power but with the opposition candidate, Barry Goldwater. He was quickly tagged "trigger happy" and never escaped the label. There was confusion over whether or not he would use atomic weapons to "defoliate" the jungles. There was no confusion over his calls for greater military effort in Vietnam.

On November 3, the Democrats scored their biggest victory since 1936: 61% of the vote in the Presidential race, two more seats in the Senate where they already had substantial majority and thirty-eight additional seats in the House. Goldwater had carried only six states.

There were other issues in the campaign but certainly Vietnam was an important factor in Goldwater's defeat. Why? The American public had sensed the dangers in that growing conflict and Goldwater was the more militant of the two candidates. In the campaign, Johnson ridiculed the pugnacious approach of Goldwater ("Some are eager to enlarge the conflict") and emphasized his own restraint ("We are not about to send American boys nine or ten thousand miles away from home to do what Asian boys ought to be doing to protect themselves").

Television and Anti-Vietnam Sentiment.

Things were to change. And television played an important role in the chronicle of events, the nature of impressions created by that chronicle and ultimately, the end of Lyndon Johnson's political career.

Let us examine the progress of the war and the role that television played in terms of one network, CBS, which the author knows best. Others played an equally significant role. NBC probably carried the most news about Vietnam in terms of actual hours on air, including one full year of "Vietnam Weekly Review," a series devoted only to the war, and ABC, in an even longer run of weekly reports, devoted 107 weekly half-hour documentaries ("Scope") to the story of Vietnam.

Yet CBS had special concerns with Vietnam and they are worth examination.

The CBS News coverage was at once typical of the networks generally but at the same time, it is a dramatic illustration of the nature of journalism within the framework of broadcasting. It was at CBS that a conflict over Vietnam coverage led to the resignation of the president of the News Division. It tells more about networks than about Vietnam but it is worth examining.

At the start, the coverage like the national temperament, was spotty and building slowly. In daily newscasts on all networks, the war received increasing coverage—the tactile prompting of television was repeating the messages.

Little in 1964 was of major significance. Even the Bay of Tonkin incident received little more than routine concern for a political campaign was underway. It happened the first week in August, 1964 when North Vietnamese PT boats attacked the U.S. Destroyer Maddox on patrol in the Bay of Tonkin. The Maddox and fighter planes off the carrier Ticonderoga repelled the attack. That was August 2. Two days later, the North Vietnamese PT boats attacked the Maddox and the C. Turner Joy.

Shortly before midnight, President Johnson went on television to announce that air action to reply was underway. U.S. planes hit North Vietnamese bases, naval craft and oil storage depots. The President sent a resolution to the Congress and within three days it was passed. The vote was 441 to nothing in the House, 88 to 2 in the Senate.

This joint resolution was Lyndon Johnson's blank check for Vietnam. It affirmed support of "all necessary measures to repel any armed attack

. . . to prevent further aggression . . . to assist any member or protocol state of the Southeast Asia Collective Defense Treaty requesting assistance."

Americans were angry over the Tonkin attacks but few realized the significance of House Joint Resolution 1145. The election campaign was underway.

War fever grew, early in 1965, when Viet Cong guerillas on February 6 attacked a U.S. military compound at Pleiku, killing eight Americans and wounding 126 others. In retaliation, 49 U.S. planes swept in from the sea, bombed and strafed Dong Hoi, North Vietnam. The bombing came just a few hours after Soviet Premier Alexei Kosygin had arrived in Hanoi, reportedly on a peace mission. Three days later, the Viet Cong attacked an American billet at Quinhon, killing twenty-three Americans.

Escalation was underway. Advisors became combat troops. A total of 23,000 rose to 181,000 by year's end. There were over 1,600 deaths from hostile action.

America began to realize that a major effort was underway. Some began to choose sides. The terms "hawk" and "dove" slowly emerged, given national prominence for the first time, perhaps, in an hour-long television debate on March 8, 1965: "Vietnam: the Hawks and the Doves."

CBS Newsman Charles Collingwood quickly traced the developments from the French defeat in Indo China to the current growing escalation, spurred by events of the previous month. He called it the point of "crossroads" and turned to his hawks and doves, the first hawk being Senator Gale McGee (Dem., Wyoming) who said bluntly "planned escalation of the war in Vietnam is a necessary forerunner to any meaningful negotiations." This obviously was the Administration posture. Senator George McGovern (Dem., South Dakota) firmly replied, "there are problems all around the world that do not lend themselves to a military solution, and particularly a military solution imposed by foreign troops." In essence, the two Democrats had set the tone for the hawk-dove debate of the next four years.

The audience for that broadcast, as for similar debates, was small. The impact, however, may have been most meaningful. Television was beginning to spell out the importance of the issues by virtue of the special programming. Television was beginning to characterize the legitimacy of dissent by according the "other side" such prominence. The tactile promptings of the daily reporting from Vietnam and Washington were being supplemented by special broadcasts indicating the special nature of the subject.

Coverage of College Teach-Ins.

The news media generally, at about that same time, were beginning to report a growing phenomenon on college campuses: the teach-in. Like the sit-ins of the Black revolution, these were intellectual sit-ins to "debate" (i.e. criticize) U.S. policy in Vietnam. As the popularity of these teach-ins grew, sponsors of some of them got together and planned the first national teach-in, to be held in Washington on May 15, 1965.

At first the only interest in coverage beyond normal news broadcasts came from educational television. However when it was revealed that Administration spokesmen—primarily McGeorge Bundy, Special Presidential Assistant for Security Affairs—would participate, the networks became interested. CBS News was "pooler" for the networks as the dissenters gathered at the Sheraton Park Hotel. The educational broadcasters were a bit miffed as the networks took over but were mollified when told they could have the output free.

It was a strange mixture of people, as were other peace demonstrations to come. There were the bearded ones, the long-haired "hippy" types; there were middle class, suburban matrons and conservatively dressed (but liberally motivated) academics. The "hippy" element at one point stared at a CBS News technician, cameraman Bob Johnson, who had a beard. "One of ours has captured a camera," they joyfully whispered.

One of theirs had not captured the camera but many of theirs had captured the public eye on that Saturday. Educational television carried it live, and it lasted almost sixteen hours. Commercial television carried sections live and summaries in prime-time that night.

The great surprise, however, came just before the day of the massive teach-in. The star Administration spokesman, McGeorge Bundy, would not appear. At the last moment he was dispatched by President Johnson to the Dominican Republic on a "special mission." Angry dissenters said Johnson had done it to get Bundy out of the light of television exposure.

Fred Friendly called Washington and asked what might be done in the way of a "television teach-in." On the hunch that Bundy might have gone reluctantly and felt he owed a debt to his fellow academicians, I suggested a cable to Bundy in Santo Domingo, inviting him to such an event upon his return. We were right. Bundy did feel some obligation, no matter what his boss felt.

The next several weeks were spent in delicate negotiation to arrange the electronic confrontation. Friendly and Small visited Bundy in his office in the basement of the White House. There was agreement on his part but reluctance to be alone against one or several professors. We suggested two opposing teams. He agreed. Agreement with the anti-Vietnam professors was more difficult to bring about. They were not of a single mind, had no one leader, squabbled over minor details. At last they agreed to the general format but they balked at the suggestion that Eric Sevareid be the moderator. His reporting from the Dominican

Republic had struck them as pro-Administration.

I refused to offer any other moderator. If this debate were to be produced by CBS News, we would not give participants the right to choose the moderator. In addition, Sevareid was the finest moderator of discussion programs in all of television. The steering committee of the "professors" came to my office in Washington, still reluctant to agree to Sevareid though eager to have the debate with Bundy. I suggested a visit with Sevareid who never knew of their opposition. Ten minutes of conversation with Sevareid and they came away somewhat awed, considerably charmed and thoroughly agreed that he would be an excellent moderator.

The site for the debate was the Hall of Nations, an auditorium at Georgetown University. The broadcast was scheduled for 10 p.m. on Monday, June 21, 1965. The "hawks" included Bundy, Professor Zbygniew K. Brezinski of Columbia and Dr. Guy Pauker of the Rand Corporation, an expert of many years in Vietnam. On the "dove" side were Professor Hans Morganthau of the University of Chicago, the nation's leading spokesman for the "dove" cause at that time, Professor Edmund O. Clubb, Columbia's Asian expert, and John Donoghue, a Michigan State anthropologist who had just finished two years in Vietnam.

"Vietnam Dialogue: Mr. Bundy and the Professors" was conducted before an invited audience, half dove and half hawk in that auditorium and an audience of millions at home. If teach-ins took ten, twelve or twenty hours in campus settings, this one took only sixty minutes to go over all the major points of difference and end with Morganthau and Bundy barking unpleasantries at each other—Bundy noting Morganthau had been very wrong about Laos, and Morganthau replying that "I may have been dead wrong on Laos, but it doesn't prove I am dead wrong on Vietnam."

Morganthau later wrote me that television was beginning, even here, to give respectability to dissent. "For it demonstrated for all to see and hear that the opponents to the war were not wide-eyed idealists, irresponsible radicals, or eccentrics in general but well-informed, serious and responsible people who presented rational arguments. For instance, many people who were favorable to the Administration position have told me that they became dubious when they witnessed Bundy's attempts to discredit me personally rather than to meet my arguments."

The panel, the CBS News people and much of the audience repaired to a student tavern across the street to continue the dialogue over drinks. The television audience settled back to wonder about the policies of this country.

Those policies were defended, on April 7, in a televised speech by the President at Johns Hopkins in Baltimore. He said, "We are there because we have a promise to keep" and called for negotiations, but negotiations that would mark an end to aggression because "the appetite of aggression is never satisfied."

At about that time, President Ayub of Pakistan and later, President Shastri of India were scheduled to visit Washington. In large part because of American participation in an Asian war, these countries were becoming increasingly anti-American. The visits were "postponed"—perhaps, suggest Rowland Evans and Robert Novack in their book *Lyndon B. Johnson: the Exercise of Power*, because "Johnson did not relish the thought of them sniping at his policy on 'Meet the Press' and 'Face the Nation'."

After the television teach-in, Friendly, Herbert Mitgang and I went to Bill Moyers, the Presidential Press Secretary and suggested a series of prime time broadcasts, the first three of them to permit top level Administration figures to explain government policy in Vietnam. There would be no holds barred on the questioning, but the broadcasts would allow the Administration ample time for an orderly explanation of Vietnam.

Moyers was enthusiastic. The President agreed and permitted full cooperation from Cabinet members.

A series of four broadcasts were mounted under the "Vietnam Perspective" umbrella. The first, on August 9 featured Secretary of State Rusk and Secretary of Defense McNamara on "Vietnam Perspective: the Decisions"—an examination of how the U.S. got to its present position. The second, on August 16 was "Vietnam Perspective: How We Can Win" with ex-Ambassador to Saigon, General Maxwell Taylor and General Earle G. Wheeler, Chairman of the Joint Chiefs of Staff. The third broadcast, on August 23, was "Vietnam Perspective: Winning the Peace" with Secretary Rusk, Presidential Assistant McGeorge Bundy and U.N. Ambassador Arthur Goldberg.

On the three broadcasts there was penetrating questioning by CBS Correspondents Walter Cronkite, Harry Reasoner, Alexander Kendrick, Marvin Kalb, Peter Kalischer, and Richard C. Hottelet. A fourth broadcast was "Vietnam Perspective: A Day of War" and was carried at 10 p.m. on September 6. This broadcast, produced by Leslie Midgley and anchored by Charles Collingwood, saw five correspondents and fifteen cameramen deployed in different areas simultaneously to describe a single day in the war in Vietnam.

Three broadcasts had given the "big picture" from the State Department and the Pentagon. Now there was the soldier's war. Peter Kalischer, who had gone out with the Marines, summed up his day this way:

It's the end of the day for most of Bravo Company—thirteen Vietcong suspects rounded up and no casualties. Bravo has suffered

three killed and eight wounded since coming to Vietnam in June—
a five per cent casualty rate. It hasn't yet had a stand-up fight with
the Vietcong, and it may never have one. This was about an average
day. The men went looking for the enemy, but the enemy didn't
oblige. Frustration is now as much a part of their diet as C-rations,
in a war in which they're bullies for browbeating women and crip-
ples, and maybe dead fools if they don't. This is a political commis-
sar's war, and they don't have that rank in the U.S. Marine Corps.

Optimistic comments by General Westmoreland (properly modest in
respect for the enemy's ability) somehow had less impact than the film
and the words of the men in the mud. War is not pretty. This war was not
even clearly righteous. The impression of the American giant and the
little Asians haunted the report as it did so many others. No matter how
right the reasons, this war would never be successfully defended.

At home, debate grew.

Liberal groups like the Americans for Democratic Action and the
Friends Committee on National Legislation called for a cease-fire. Martin
Luther King was outspoken in criticism of the war. Defenders of the faith
did not always help. Senator Russell Long in a speech attacking "modern-
day appeasers" said, "We will do whatever is necessary, including fighting
a nuclear war, before we will surrender to anybody anywhere."

In October there were three days of anti-war demonstrations across
the country. Some 70,000 people participated in marches and rallies in
sixty cities. A young pacifist, Norman Morrison, set fire to himself at the
entrance of the Pentagon. In late November, 20,000 protesters held a
"March on Washington." Late in the year, a Senate group headed by
Majority Leader Mike Mansfield made a 35-day world tour which included France, Russia, Poland, Thailand, Vietnam, and a number of
other Asian countries—all with an interest in the war. On December 19,
Mansfield reported to the President. It was an extremely pessimistic
report.

One week later, President Johnson ordered a Christmas truce and
then a moratorium on the bombing of North Vietnam. The bombing halt
extended well into January, 1966. The Mansfield group had its report
published January 7, 1966 by the Senate Foreign Relations Committee.
It said that escalation blunted but has not turned back the drive of the
Viet Cong, the divisions inside South Vietnam remain unchanged, and
all of mainland Southeast Asia is "a potential battlefield."

TV Debates on Vietnam.

At CBS, Friendly planned for a series of debates to continue the
"Vietnam Perspective" broadcasts. One was scheduled for Sunday, Janu-

ary 30. Called "Congress and the War," we arranged for participation by Senators Stennis, Mundt, Morse, Clark and Representatives Boggs and Ford. Sevareid was to moderate; I was to produce.

On Saturday night, it started to snow. Early Sunday morning, I awoke to discover a record snowfall. My automobile was completely covered with drifting snow. I called Friendly and told him that it looked impossible, we could never get the crew and the guests into our studio for the broadcast. We would have to turn the time back to the program we had pre-empted: "Sunday Sports Spectacular." Minutes later Friendly called back. The sports people had planned on a live broadcast, cancelling it when they were pre-empted for "Vietnam Perspective." We would have to somehow get the broadcast on the air.

I called a nearby garage and asked if a tow truck could make it to my home in Bethesda. "Mister," said the garage man, "Impossible. A thousand guys are calling. You'd have to say some magic words to get me to your place."

"How about fifty dollars?"

"That's magic. I'll be there."

He came and we plowed through drifts to Sevareid's home, two miles away. Sevareid came out through hip-high snow and downtown we went.

The television crew came straggling in, car pools working their way through drifts of snow until the genius that was their boss, Charles Chester, had enough men to get us on the air. One of them battled his way up to Capitol Hill where Senator Mundt lived and brought him in.

The tow truck driver, his job in jeopardy, stayed with us long enough to get Senator Morse from the northwest end of town. We never did get Representative Gerald Ford who walked half a mile through heavy snow to a point where our second tow truck picked him up but he lived in Virginia and the bridges were all blocked with stalled autos. Local police picked up Senator John Stennis and brought him in. The only taxi driver we could find (and we quickly hired him for the next few days) went to Georgetown and brought in Senator Joseph Clark. Somehow, Congressman Hale Boggs managed to not only drive in from Bethesda without difficulty, but even managed to stop at church on the way in.

Our Washington staff struggled in. Sylvia Westerman and other girls in ski outfits, men in boots and heavy coats. When it was time to take air, we were ready with the single exception of Gerry Ford who was still valiantly trying to make it across clogged bridges, calling in periodically with progress reports.

The weather was cold but the debate was hot. For ninety minutes under the strong hand of Eric Sevareid, they covered the issues, concentrating on whether or not to resume the bombing.

Fred Friendly, in his memoirs, described the broadcast thusly:

Morse and Stennis were evenly matched, and for ninety minutes the two of them turned our Washington studio into the floor of the United States Senate. Toward the end of the program Stennis interrupted an attack on Morse and the doves to say: "This has been a real Congressional debate, (with) nationwide television coverage," and afterward Stanton called to say that it had been one of the best produced, most useful programs of its kind we had ever done.

There was an exciting response in Washington, in the press and in the mail. If it had made an impression on the White House that is not known. The next day, President Johnson ordered the bombing resumed. He also asked Ambassador Goldberg to take the Vietnam peace issue to the United Nations.

On Tuesday, CBS News presented a thirty-minute discussion with Senator J. William Fulbright, Chairman of the Senate Foreign Relations Committee and now the leading dove in high office. Fulbright was critical of the resumption of bombing, praised the action in the U.N. and asserted that "we were misled by this preoccupation with what has been called so often the international conspiracy of communism."

It was during this broadcast that Senator Fulbright confessed that he had erred in sponsoring the Tonkin resolution. Friendly later called it "a portrait of a tortured man." It certainly was a rare bit of television. An excerpt of Fulbright's comment:

President Johnson, in all honesty, inherited this situation. It had become quite substantial when he came onto the scene and he was presented with a very difficult situation. There was as many, as I recall it about 20,000 people, of our people there at the time of the Tonkin incident. That is substantial but nothing like now.

I regret that the President ever started the bombing and that much greater effort, this offensive for peace which has just been held —I regret that it wasn't engaged in before we ever became involved. But that is hindsight.

I don't wish to be too critical. Goodness knows, that is a difficult job and he did inherit a very difficult situation. And I don't think it is profitable or helpful to be too critical of that period now. And I have to say myself that I have played a part in that that I am not at all proud of, that at the time of the Bay of Tonkin I should have had greater foresight in the consideration of that resolution.

That would have been a good time to have precipitated a debate and a re-examination, re-evaluation of our involvement. And under the influences that existed then, it was during just the beginning of the Presidential campaign. I was very much a partisan in that campaign for Johnson, for the Administration. I disapproved of the statements of Mr. Goldwater and I went along with the urging, I may say, of the Administration.

I think it is a terrible situation we are in. I am hoping we can find an honorable way out of it. I do not wish to see it escalated into a war.

I do not believe in the Secretary's theory that this should be the proper place for a confrontation to destroy forever the idea that the wars of national liberation can succeed. This seems to me not an appropriate place for that. I think that if you are ever going to have it—I hope we don't ever have it.

I am not for any confrontation of that sort, by violence. But even if you should have it, this is a very bad place and very bad circumstances.

That is why I think this history is significant. We should never have a confrontation where there is any doubt about the justification for our particular part at that time in that particular incident.

Fulbright's "confession" of error in the Tonkin matter and his views generally made front page news the next day. On that day, I called Friendly to ask about hearings on foreign aid before Fulbright's committee. A few days earlier, Dean Rusk had testified and there had been an absorbing series of exchanges between the Secretary and dovish members of the Committee, including Chairman Fulbright. The witness that next day was David Bell, head of the Agency for International Development. The chief of AID is hardly the best known figure in the Administration but Friendly had been so disappointed in the comparatively brief treatment given Rusk, I felt he ought to know that the Foreign Relations doves had another Administration spokesman coming before them.

"Can it be covered live?" asked Friendly.

"Yes."

"I'll let you know."

He let us know—the answer was "yes." The other networks, as is customary, were told that there would be live cameras at the hearing. They asked that it be pooled. Early the next morning, CBS and NBC carried the hearing live. Probably no one was more surprised at this sudden notoriety than the witness himself, David Bell.

Bell could only speak to the AID program but the questioning, the extended remarks, and the exchanges between members of the committee turned it into a lively, unstaged Senatorial debate on Vietnam. CBS carried the morning session as did NBC. After a luncheon break, CBS returned to the hearing. NBC at first did not, then opted to join in continuous coverage. Friendly estimated that it cost CBS alone $175,000 in lost revenues.

Not everyone in the CBS family was pleased. Executives outside of the News Division were troubled by the costs and the precedent. Some affiliates complained bitterly because they, too, were losing considerable revenue (and had no voice in the decision).

It was announced that the next witness before Fulbright's committee would be General James Gavin, whose enclave theory was then popular among doves as a means to cut back on the military effort. CBS announced that it would carry Gavin. So did NBC.

In a sudden move that *Congressional Quarterly* described as "taking the spotlight from the Senate hearings," the President announced that he was flying to Hawaii to meet the leaders of South Vietnam. Gavin's day on the Hill was exciting television but only a prelude to an evening full of special reports on the Hawaii war conference. Around midnight, Johnson's plane had arrived in Los Angeles. Vice President Humphrey had flown there to meet him and was to continue on to tour Southeast Asia.

Friendly Resigns over Coverage.

The next witness before Foreign Relations was ex-Ambassador George Kennan who was outspokenly critical of the war. Friendly wanted to carry that live, too.

At this point, Friendly's fortunes and those of CBS News reached a climactic point. Jack Schneider had just been appointed to the newly created post of Group Vice President, supervising all broadcast activities of CBS. He found Friendly's arguments not persuasive enough and decided not to carry Kennan live.

Friendly called the situation "untenable," went to battle with Schneider's superiors, Stanton and Paley, and ended up quitting CBS News in a wild flurry of publicity. He felt he no longer had ready access to top management. They felt he did: Schneider *was* top management.

One could argue the merits and demerits of Friendly's crisis. The press did not. Almost without exception, they took his side, he always had been a popular figure with the critics anyway, and CBS was portrayed as the villain, keeping the people from the hearings. Kennan was carried live—on NBC. In one of the little ironies involved, it was CBS' turn to do "pool" and CBS cameras provided the pick-up.

There was never an official answer to Friendly's surprise resignation. There was an explanation of policy—it came in a letter from CBS President Frank Stanton to T. Thacher Robinson of Urbana, Illinois who wrote to complain:

Dear Mr. Robinson:

I fully understand the concern which led you to write me about the events involving CBS News last week. Having consistently taken a serious view of the responsibility of broadcast journalism to the American people during the twenty years I have been President of CBS, I must respond at some length to your comments.

The CBS Group Vice-President, Broadcasting, John A. Schneider, made an administrative decision not to broadcast live, on the CBS Television Network, the full testimony of another witness, Professor George Kennan (6 hours), a former ambassador to the Soviet Union. CBS News did keep its crews and equipment at the hearings and, in accordance with a prior agreement with the other network news organizations, originated the coverage which was carried by NBC. Mr. Friendly disagreed with the decision not to broadcast the Kennan testimony in its entirety on CBS and insisted upon our accepting his resignation.

The decision not to broadcast Professor Kennan's testimony in full may seem to you the wrong one. But it was neither a cynical nor an impulsive one. Decisions of this kind in broadcasting often have to be made before the full impact of the event is known. They must also be made in a contest that cannot always be wholly clear to the public. Factors governing such decisions include the television viewing habits of the public, the newsworthiness of the event concerned, and of the participants in it, the likelihood of time having to be made available for more significant future phases of the same event, the possibility of the specific matter of the broadcast's being handled with more meaning to more people in a later news broadcast or special summary, the announced intention of other broadcasting organizations to cover the event in its entirety, and other considerations.

Among the latter—but of no more weight than any other factor—is the necessity to maintain a sound and viable economy within the company. The cost of maintaining television and radio news organizations is enormous, and the major part of it must be borne by income from entertainment programming. The specific cost incurred by the CBS Television Network in covering the four days of the Vietnam hearings, for example, amounted to just under $1 million, and the loss in income for the stations which make up the Network is estimated to be over $1 million, in addition. Obviously, since CBS News cannot be self-supporting, we must pay some attention to the economics of broadcasting in making decisions involving such costs.

First of all, I want to assure you that CBS has believed—and continues to believe—that it has an obligation to report the Vietnam war and the issues surrounding it as fully, as revealingly, and as ably as it can. We believe that we have been conscientious and effective in trying to meet this obligation. In addition to daily reports from the battlefronts and the Vietnam countryside, CBS has also broadcast in peak viewing time many hours of special reports presenting the views of the Administration and of its critics both at home and abroad. Among those appearing on such reports have been Cabinet members, college professors and students, foreign statesmen, United Nations officials, and authors and journalists.

Seven weeks before they commenced, CBS urged the Chairman of the Senate Committee on Foreign Relations to permit live television coverage of the hearings on Vietnam that were the subject of the controversy that prompted your letter. We were aware that the hearings would constitute, on the whole, a valuable forum for enlightening the American people on our involvement in Vietnam, the forces that brought it about, and the implications to which it gives rise. On January 30, five days before the hearings opened, the CBS Television Network pre-empted an hour and a half for a special report, "Vietnam Perspective: The Congress and the War," presented live from Washington and marking the first major use of coast-to-coast television by congressional leaders to deliberate publicly America's conduct of the war. The CBS Television Network, thereafter, broadcast, in their entirety, the testimony of David Bell, Director of the Agency for International Development (7 hours, 12 minutes), General Gavin (5 hours, 11 minutes), who had gained widespread attention for his views on our military policy in Vietnam, General Taylor (6 hours, 33 minutes), military advisor to the President, who defended it, and of the Secretary of State, Mr. Rusk (6 hours, 3 minutes). In addition, the CBS Television Network pre-empted two hours of prime time for special reports summarizing and analyzing the hearings and their background, 10–11 p.m., February 8 and 18.

With regard to the Vietnam hearings, it was CBS's conclusion, rightly or wrongly, that the testimony of Professor Kennan, who had not been recently and prominently associated, as General Gavin had been, with criticism of U.S. policy and who holds no official position, as do Director Bell, General Taylor and Secretary Rusk, would not be of sufficiently general public interest or of sufficiently determining significance to justify pre-empting the some six hours of television time necessary to broadcast it in its entirety, but that the testimony could be best handled in the form of a succinct summary and important excerpts in later news and special broadcasts.

Decisions of this kind all too frequently involve borderline cases. The CBS Television Network broadcasts events that the other networks do not carry and sometimes omits those that another network may carry. We have been condemned as often and as severely by audiences for interrupting regular programming for such broadcasts as we have been for deciding not to do so.

I hope that, while you may fault us on a decision with which you may not agree, you will consider our overall coverage of the Vietnam war and our overall record in electronic journalism. I hope, too, that you will reserve judgment until you have seen our future contributions to public knowledge and understanding of the war and of all other significant news developments. I can, in return, assure you that CBS News has no intention of relinquishing its position of leadership in its field and the Columbia Broadcasting System, Inc. has every intention of continuing to give the News Division its full support, and encouraging it to do an even better job in the future than it has in the past.

> With all good wishes.
> Sincerely,
> Frank Stanton

February 25, 1966

The letter was released to the press. It was not warmly received. The critics were firmly lined up on Friendly's side. Friendly himself took issue with it suggesting that coverage of Rusk and Taylor were face-saving moves. The matter had ended his career at CBS News after sixteen years. "I left some of my youth and too much of my heart." A leader and a pioneer, Friendly left broadcast news to teach at Columbia University and serve on the executive staff of the Ford Foundation.

His leaving still did not resolve a network's dilemma as to when hearings or other prolonged events should be carried live and when they should be summarized. Newspapers are quick to side with the Friendly position but how many newspapers would give up many pages, most of an edition, to carry full text of a hearing? Few? Maybe none.

Some columnists dramatically summed up Friendly as a victim of the Vietnam War. Others hinted that CBS really dropped him because the network was becoming too critical of the war effort. The record before and since does not substantiate that.

The war, regardless of one broadcaster's fortunes, continued to escalate. By the end of 1966, there were 389,000 American troops there—an increase that more than doubled U.S. commitments. American dead numbered in excess of 5,000, almost quadrupling the 1965 toll and another 30,000 Americans were wounded—almost five times as many as the previous year.

Escalation of the War and the Coverage.

In October, President Johnson went to a war parley in Manila, meeting with the leaders of six Asian nations involved in the war. He toured Australia, South Korea, New Zealand, the Philippines and even paid a surprise visit to the troops in Vietnam itself ("Come home with that coonskin on the wall"). CBS, which had not engaged in as much "live" coverage of hearings as did NBC (72½ hours of Senate hearings in 1966), did a great deal in the way of special broadcasts, particularly during the President's Asian swing. The series of "instant" specials on that trip were more colorful than substantive but each was a reminder again of the war still in progress.

It was an election year, 1966, and most politicians were skittish about Vietnam as an issue. There were a number of "peace" candidates. With few exceptions they did badly. As the President flew home, it was widely reported that he would campaign for candidates in the closing days of the election. He denied this on arrival but the networks showed film of the preparations for Johnson in numerous cities. His credibility was again damaged.

It was to be damaged even more during 1967 when the Senate debated the Tonkin Gulf resolution of three years earlier, the go-ahead Lyndon Johnson had received from Congress. It was obvious that many who supported it then, opposed it now. CBS News Diplomatic Correspondent Marvin Kalb revealed that "contingent drafts" of the Tonkin Resolution had been prepared for some time prior to the incident, in effect were in the pockets of top Administration officials. He noted that a number of Senators now believed the Tonkin attacks were merely pretexts to get such a resolution approved "on a wave of emotion about American ships being attacked on the high seas."

Early in 1968, Fulbright was to hold more hearings on Tonkin and despite a carefully documented defense by Defense Secretary McNamara, there were serious questions about the entire incident which "legalized the war." Committee member Frank Lausche (Dem., Ohio) said of an unpublished committee staff report on the matter, "Every statement in this secret report tends to prove that we should not have done what we did . . ." Senator Albert Gore (Dem., Tenn.) said, "The Administration was hasty, acted precipitately, inadvisably, unwisely, out of proportion to the provocation." He said the "Congress and the nation were misled about the . . . operation."

The Vietnam commitment had risen to half a million American soldiers. The Vietnam opposition similarly escalated—at one rally alone, in New York on April 15, 1967 some 100,000 protesters took part in spelling out displeasure with the war. All three networks carried special documentaries on the war. They were frequently critical.

In October, over 55,000 persons took part in a March on the Pentagon. It ended with a nighttime "siege" of the Pentagon parking lot, hundreds of arrests, and one brief clash between demonstrators and troops at the Pentagon door.

Harris and Gallup polls showed diminishing support for the war.

On November 30, Senator Eugene McCarthy (Dem., Minnesota) announced that he would enter four Presidential primaries to demonstrate opposition to the Johnson policy in Vietnam. Though New Hampshire was not one that he named, it became the first and most significant of his primary races.

And then, in early 1968, came Tet.

Tet is the Vietnamese Lunar New Year and there was to be the usual pause in the fighting. Instead, the Communist force launched the heaviest and most coordinated offensive of the war, attacking thirty provincial capitals, airfields, U.S. bases and particularly bloody assaults on Saigon and Hue.

It came at a time when Americans thought that the enemy was in pretty bad shape and there might be some hope that they would enter negotiations, accepting the President's offer to halt the bombing in the North. Something like 50,000 Viet Cong and North Vietnamese troops attacked. Boldly they seized and held the U.S. Embassy in Saigon for six hours. The fighting raged on for weeks. Before it ended, there were 2,000 U.S. dead and twice that number of South Vietnamese killed (estimated on March 6) and our military estimated 50,000 enemy soldiers killed. Almost 10,000 civilians were killed, 40,000 homes were destroyed and over 800,000 new refugees created.

Walter Cronkite returned from a personal tour of the fighting and gave a strongly critical report on a CBS News special report.

Presidential Press Secretary George Christian privately informed me later, "Believe me, the shock waves rolled through government." Why? "When Walter returned from Vietnam, I think his reports disturbed a lot of people about the conduct of the war; pessimism breeds pessimism. I do think he gave an honest reporter's view. But he is a household name far more than other newsmen; he is the man millions rely on for their summary of the news every day; he is not identified as an editorialist, but as a reporter of great objectivity."

Similar reports were heard on other networks. The major news figures like Cronkite were having quite an effect. Howard K. Smith of ABC News was openly hawkish and Chet Huntley of NBC was considered an Administration supporter but the vast majority of broadcast newsmen seemed to be reporting anti-Administration views. Most felt they showed objective balance but to those within the Administration it seemed to be largely anti-Johnson, anti-Vietnam.

George Christian: "I don't think it's proper for Brinkley to say, 'It appears the Administration isn't as interested in peace as it says it is' . . . I recall one of Frank McGee's Saturday reports in which he editorialized for a full two minutes against the war."

How much impact do television newscasters have? Far more than any journalist in the other media, with few exceptions, because they are more personalized, more intimate, more a part of the home. I asked Senator George McGovern about this once. His reply: "We have perhaps reached an era in the electronic media where the reporters of the news— are newsmakers themselves. Where the news is not so much reported as it is made by television. I have had some South Dakotans tell me that they put more faith in what a well-known newscaster reports than what a politician says."

Again the Question of Patriotism.

Cynicism about the war was common. High officials began getting touchy. Secretary of State Rusk in an off-the-record "background" session with reporters was indignant as they pursued him with questions about Tet. The *Wall Street Journal* revealed the substance of his remarks which it termed an "extraordinary tirade."

Said the Secretary, "None of your papers or your broadcasting apparatuses are worth a damn unless the United States succeeds. They are trivial compared to that question. So I don't know why, to win a Pulitzer Prize, people have to go on probing for things one can bitch about when there are 2,000 stories on the same day about things that are more constructive in character."

On that February day, Rusk asserted, "There gets to be a point when the question is, whose side are you on. I'm the Secretary of State, and I'm on our side."

It is easy to turn to Ambrose Bierce's observation that, "In Dr. Johnson's famous dictionary, patriotism is defined as the last resort of a scoundrel. With all due respect to an enlightened but inferior lexicographer I beg to submit that it is the first."

But Dean Rusk was no scoundrel. Dean Rusk *is* a patriot but one who has been wearied and worried by press treatment of the war, frustrated, obstructed, baffled and for a man with almost Oriental patience, somewhat exasperated. The Secretary feeling a deep sense of purpose, of doing what needed to be done, finds the war going badly at that moment, the press at his heels, and the public swinging away from the Administration. Rusk was also angry at the press, particularly television, for its treatment of one particular facet of dissent—the crowds who would picket, heckle, and disrupt public appearances by himself and other top Administration officials.

When I once queried George Christian about television coverage of dissenters after the 1968 campaign, he replied, "Hubert Humphrey was distressed all through the campaign by TV's preoccupation with protesters at his speeches. Yet there's no question that heckling is part of the story, so it's difficult to criticize any of the media for this. The main problem is with overemphasis of the protesters—and I speak of all the media—is the impression it creates that a public official does not have public support. Like Oriental water torture, the drip-drip-drip finally leaves such an impression."

I recall Secretary Rusk giving me a finger-wagging lecture on "television's preoccupation" with these pickets while it pretty much ignored the substance of the speech given. "A few pickets," he said, "seem to be more important than the Vice President or the Secretary of State. How do you defend that?"

Such outbursts by the Secretary were rare. Rare in private, unheard of in public. Their importance is less the frailty of the man than the immense frustrations of the office.

As the Tet attack was finally contained, Rusk was persuaded to appear in open session before Foreign Relations for the first time in two years. For two days, Rusk gave a superb defense of the Administration position—testimony carried live during the day on NBC and in prime-time condensations by ABC and CBS at night. The dexterity of Rusk's performance was matched by the eloquence of his detractors on the committee. All participants had come to the hearings well prepared, well briefed.

Jack Gould, in the *New York Times*, noted the observation of a committee member sympathetic to Rusk, Senator Karl Mundt (Rep., South Dakota), that somehow the Administration has not been successful in getting its point of view across to a country now seriously divided. Added Gould, "It might be argued that a spontaneous television program, embracing conflicting points of view, might be even more effective in reaching the general public. Television has the ability to personalize staggering problems, something the print media cannot hope to duplicate."

Rusk's testimony ended when Chairman Fulbright noted that though the hearings were on foreign aid, he "believed" the Secretary had reason to suspect that the Vietnamese war would come up. Rusk allowed himself an easy smile and responded that he, too, had an inkling that the topic would arise.

Washington buzzed with instant critiques of Rusk's performance. Most agreed he had done well. Even his critics called it a brilliant defense of the indefensible. At the White House, the "reviews" were ecstatic. From the President on down, all were overjoyed with Rusk.

There was less reason for joy at the White House before the day ended for that day was March 12, 1968, the day of the New Hampshire Presidential Primary.

It was hardly known nor little remembered but Eugene McCarthy didn't get the most votes in New Hampshire. Lyndon Johnson did. But McCarthy won New Hampshire. He won with only 42.2% of the vote, some 7% less than Lyndon Johnson (49.2%) despite the fact that McCarthy alone was on the Democratic ballot; Johnson's votes were all write-ins.

McCarthy *did* win the majority of the New Hampshire delegates (Johnson supporters had put up too many candidates and they split his vote) but most Americans in a very short time were under the impression that McCarthy had swamped LBJ. Why? Because it *was* a remarkable victory and the first glaring sign of how much political strength there was in the anti-war feeling.

Robert Kennedy saw it. The very next day, he said he was reconsidering whether or not to run for President and three days later formally became a candidate.

Lyndon Johnson saw it. Within three weeks he stunned the nation and withdrew from politics.

It happened on the night of March 31, 1968. It was in Lyndon Johnson's nature that he allegedly never asked for time from the television networks. Though there was ample precedent going back to Truman, President Johnson never asked. He would simply indicate that an appearance "was available for live" through his Press Secretary. With few exceptions, this was the pattern of his years in office.

On March 31, it was different. The White House asked. It wanted to be sure that his address was carried.

CBS was the "pooler" and Don Richardson produced. He knew it was very important when he was handed an advance text but he did not fully realize how important—because the closing paragraphs were *not* in that text.

Richardson was extremely nervous because there were delays in the President's oval office and it was barely moments before air as the President turned to the cameras, ready. "Tonight," he began, "I want to speak to you of peace in Vietnam and Southeast Asia . . ."

After a brief reference to the current situation and to the Communist attack during Tet which had "failed to achieve its principal objectives," the President came quickly to the point of his prepared text.

> I am taking the first step to de-escalate the conflict. We are reducing—substantially reducing—the present level of hostilities.
> And we are doing so unilaterally, and at once.
> Tonight, I have ordered our aircraft and our naval vessels to make no attacks on North Vietnam, except in the area north of the Demilitarized Zone where the continuing enemy buildup directly threatens allied forward positions . . .
> I call upon President Ho Chi Minh to respond . . ."

The President then went on to note that our resolve continues, that the military position was strong, our South Vietnamese allies recovering from the Tet offensive and stronger than ever, etc. He called for the talks to start soon, announced that Averell Harriman would represent him, even repeated the offer made three years earlier at Johns Hopkins to help create a TVA-type project in the Mekong Delta. Experienced President-watchers grew uneasy. Lyndon Johnson had more to say. The text didn't indicate it—the text was wending its way to a close, to a sentence that read, "Our reward will come in the life of freedom, peace and hope that our children will enjoy through ages ahead."

At this point, had he followed text, he would normally just say good night. But there was more:

> What we won when all of our people united just must not now be lost in suspicion, distrust, selfishness, and politics among any of our people.
> Believing this as I do, I have concluded that I should not permit the Presidency to become involved in the partisan divisions that are developing in this political year.
> With America's sons in the fields far away, with America's future under challenge right here at home, with our hopes and the world's hopes for peace in the balance every day, I do not believe that I should devote an hour or a day of my time to any personal partisan causes or to any duties other than the awesome duties of this office—the Presidency of your country.
> Accordingly, I shall not seek, and I will not accept, the nomination of my Party for another term as your President.
> But let men everywhere know, however, that a strong, a confident, and a vigilant America stands ready tonight to seek an honor-

able peace—and stands ready tonight to defend an honored cause—whatever the price, whatever the burden, whatever the sacrifices that duty may require.

Thank you for listening.

Good night and God bless all of you.

The effect was stunning. America was shocked. On CBS, White House Correspondent Dan Rather and Congressional Correspondent Roger Mudd, assigned to comment after the address, were flabbergasted. Asked for comment, Mudd suggested, "I'd like to go home and think about it and come back tomorrow."

The President was later to insist that the decision had nothing to do with Vietnam or McCarthy in New Hampshire; it had long been planned. Few believed that. Most of America was convinced that you could add one more to the Vietnam casualty list.

Three days later, Hanoi said it was willing to talk.

TV'S Role in the Peace Movement.

The war, by Election day, 1968, had seen almost 29,000 American boys killed (about 45% of them in 1968), over 80,000 wounded that year alone and according to the Budget Bureau was to cost $26.3 billion in fiscal 1969.

As talks began in Paris, well over half a million Americans were serving in Vietnam. The talks, most predicted, would follow the pattern of the Korean settlement: long delays, continued fighting and more deaths until agreement was finally reached (it took over twenty-four months of negotiating before the final cease-fire in Korea). Nixon, on taking office, replaced chief negotiator Averell Harriman with Nixon's 1960 running mate, Henry Cabot Lodge. Lodge left, frustrated by the lack of progress at the end of 1969. At that point, American casualties had exceeded 300,000 with some 40,000 deaths. Though President Nixon had started troop withdrawals (the number of troops dropped to around 475,000 by year's end) and a plan to beef up the South Vietnamese to take over the war, public protest continued. In Washington on November 15, 1969 an immense crowd (variously estimated from 250,000 to 500,000) gathered at the Washington Monument in an afternoon of protest, the largest such protest in American history. Though public opinion polls showed most people in support of the President and opposed to such protest movements, they were showing the majority in favor of getting out. This was quite different from the support Lyndon Johnson could rally in his earliest years in office.

How did it happen? How did the tide of public support turn to put a President out, to force conclusion of a war in terms less than heroic? Just how important *was* the role of television? James Hagerty, former Presidential Press Secretary to Eisenhower and later a top executive at ABC, said simply, "By showing war in its stinking reality, we have taken away the glory and have shown that negotiation is the only way to solve international problems." Psychiatrist Frederick Wertham, by the way, took Hagerty to task for this, saying TV was "hardening us to war rather than educating us against it."

The Hagerty view is the "war-in-the-living room" theory so widely held. Among those sharing respect for the impact of television is the distinguished Swedish sociologist Gunnar Myrdal who explains the vast participation of the young in the protest movements by noting, "Every child knows about the physical horrors of the Vietnam War. This is not fiction. Real people are killed. We see them lying dead. The effect is that youth discovers the credibility gap. It sees the horrible reality of the war. It feels that it is being talked to by liars. To young people this is serious. This is what roused the generation. This is what has given us the present period of protests and demonstrations."

Myrdal even suggests that the course of history would have been changed had television been around fifty years earlier: "If we had had television in 1918, we would have seen Woodrow Wilson, Lloyd George and Clemenceau making peace. We would have seen the poor refugees coming out of Turkey. Later we would have seen the bombing of Ethiopia. We did not see these things. We were protected from the horrors of the world."

Senator Fulbright once wrote me, "The impact of 'bringing the war into the living room' has indeed revealed to the people the savage character of this war and, I believe, caused them to consider its justification more closely than they would have otherwise." Another prominent leader of the anti-war intellectuals, Professor Hans Morganthau put it this way: "The impact is bound to be a revulsion against war . . . a war may be justified on political and military grounds, but the public at large will refuse to support it after witnessing on television the human suffering all wars inevitably cause."

One of the most perceptive viewers of television's impact, because his job was to do so for the President of the United States, is former Presidential Press Secretary George Christian. When I asked him about this, he noted that one of television's weaknesses is that cameras have access to the American side, warts and all, but not to the other. The result: "It's difficult for anyone to be militant when he watches stacks of American bodies being loaded into helicopters. The viewer also gets the very definite impression from TV that this is an American war: Yankee *vs.* Vietnamese. Aside from the atrocities during the Tet offensive and the burning of the Montagnard villagers, enemy brutality to Vietnamese civilians is not a regular commodity on television news."

It is a common aphorism that wars take on a life of their own beyond the control of the men who start them, the men who fight them. Television coverage of war may have some of this same characteristic. The impact is beyond any one group to control—the men who start the wars, the men who report them, the men who try to stop them.

Early in 1969, columnist Stewart Alsop offered a fascinating look into the minds of the men who ran the Vietnamese war under President Johnson. In the February 17, 1969 edition of *Newsweek*, Alsop did a column entitled "The Lessons of Vietnam" based on his conversations with Johnson advisors, men like Rusk, McNamara, Taylor, William and McGeorge Bundy, Nitze and others—with the assurance that no one would be quoted by name.

Several of these "anonymous" quotes are especially interesting. First, "the basic cause of dissent . . . was a kind of national guilt feeling, the feeling that we were acting like a big bully beating up a little guy." This is what Christian called "Yankee vs. Vietnamese." Television pictures of the tall, straight Americans and the tiny, Asian prisoners were imbedded in the public mind. Alsop's unnamed sources also noted the failure of the Administration to tell its story successfully. "This has been the most over-explained war in history. The trouble was, any explanation would do— for that particular week. LBJ kept Congress in hand for a long time with those amazing briefing circuses. But the time came when nobody would listen to him but the American Legion and the Amvets."

Credibility: It wasn't just gapping, it was dragging; it was so badly bruised at the end that hardly anything could be believed. Why? Several instances have been cited—Tonkin, the aborted campaign swing in '66, etc.—and books have been written on the subject. Sometimes there was candor and events overtook fact, the Administration spokesmen appeared to be untruthful. Other times there was premature exuberance. Other times, they just plain lied.

For a long time before the end, the press just would not trust officialdom. The reverse quickly became fact as well. Christian complained, when I asked about this, "Several highly-respected newspapermen have told me it is difficult for reporters of some publications to cover the war objectively. If they file a story unfavorable to the general editorial position of the paper, it winds up inside. If they play to the editor's opinions they make page one every time."

Christian and his colleagues apparently wondered if they could not use television better. "We sometimes talked of arranging special programs —perhaps regular interviews with Ambassador Bunker and the military leaders—in hopes of counteracting unfavorable impressions of the war and our objectives. We usually abandoned these as unworkable over the long haul. We pored over thousands of feet of good film photographed by AID representatives and others, depicting the very real progress in the villages and the contributions of non-military American men and women working to improve the lot of the people. But we never did much in this direction, because it smacked of propaganda and I guess we were gun-shy."

One of Alsop's sources echoes this last thought: "We decided to win this war without any beating of drums or war propaganda. I wonder now if we can win a war that way. In fact, I wonder now if you can fight a war without censorship of the news, television especially."

One wonders how common was this view—"censorship of the news, television especially." The temptation must have been great.

After he left office, Lyndon Johnson wrote an article on his relationships with the press and made this observation:

> I believe I was the only President in this century who presided over a war in which there was no censorship whatever of news dispatches. The effect of bringing Vietnam and all its travail onto the evening news screen will not be known, I believe, for a long time. It made the reality of that war more vivid, certainly. It may also have intensified the public's frustration over not being able to finish it off quickly, or at least to see battle lines on a chart changing as our troops moved forward from town to town. Showing the suffering and the savage combat with an elusive enemy was the price we paid for a free press. It was a price worth paying, all things considered, but it was still a heavy price for the nation.

I once asked Senator Eugene McCarthy when the tide turned, when the opposition became respectable, when it could be joined without fear of being damned as a radical. He said he was sure that the time was in the winter of 1966–67 when the long bombing halt ended and attacks on North Vietnam were resumed. He didn't think television had much to contribute to the change in public opinion but he confessed that he watched it very little.

Others would not agree. Senator McGovern: "It lends credence to the dissent." Hans Morganthau: "Television gave dissent a 'respectability' it could not have received in any other way." Senator Fulbright once wrote me that he felt it was the common sense and wisdom of the dissenters, not television, that gave them respectability but he added, "Perhaps I am arguing only whether the medium is the message . . ."

A defender of the Administration would look at it differently. Senator Gale McGee of Wyoming, when I asked him about it, noted that "the individual citizen became more vulnerable to the harangues of those who would exploit the heart rather than appeal to the head . . . I agree in the main with those who contend that television in its coverage of what we call dissent . . . has been too easily distracted by the relatively few dissenters who have captured attention from the medium and thus robbed TV coverage of the balance it should have."

It is not a hawk alone that takes television to task for its preoccupation with the more colorful, more flamboyant events. Professor Morganthau, when I asked about weaknesses in the medium, noted, "The weakness of television . . . is inherent in the nature of the medium; for what is newsworthy is the extraordinary incident which the viewer is inclined to take as the whole story. It requires a particular skill and judgment for television coverage to put the extraordinary incident into the context of the whole story. I have no doubt that this can be done. I have no doubt either that it has not been done in the past."

Senator Fulbright feels, too, that reporters don't always grasp what is important: "I suppose we all have different views as to what is trivial and what is important in the life of our country, and especially in our Government." Fulbright, in comments to me, was philosophical about this: "Personally, I believe that on the whole the TV companies have been responsible in their coverage of these events. No doubt the flamboyant and extreme cases attract more attention than more normal activities, but the same is true throughout all our lives, and applies to newspapers and common gossip, as well as other things."

The protesters learned that outrageous action could capture the attention of the media. In many ways they became more adept at winning television coverage than the so-called experts, the high-paid advisors on Madison Avenue who are so fervently wooed by aspiring political candidates. The success of protesters in getting television exposure has been the bane of conservatives. In a speech heavily critical of television, Vice President Spiro Agnew, late in 1969, asked, "How many marches and demonstrations would we have if the marchers did not know that the ever-faithful TV cameras would be there to record their antics for the next news show?" Yet, as time went on, television reporters as others made careful measure of these efforts and bent over backwards at times to have balance.

Still, when thousands protest, is it not proper that there be coverage? For that matter, one man with a view worth considering should be able to get that view known.

Television is a medium of impressions. If balance is a goal, whether it parades under the guise of fairness doctrine or equal time or "giving both sides" as if there are just two sides to everything, balance must be tempered by the nature of television. The same amount of time will not balance a bland defense of an Administration posture against a dramatic picketing of the Administration spokesman making that defense. They remember less of what he said than that moment when the protesters walked out or walked in or shouted or whatever.

No matter how carefully television copy explains that these protesters are few in number or atypical of the audience, the impression is there, the impression of strong opposition.

So, too, is the treatment of the war itself. No matter how much attention is paid to the "good" things happening in Vietnam, it is the bloody, bloody that people remember. George Christian put it this way once, in a letter to me: "All of the networks have done excellent jobs of reporting on refugees, pacification, elections, etc., in occasional Vietnam specials. Unfortunately, the daily diet is killing, killing, killing, which I guess is what war is all about."

There is much that one can criticize in television's coverage of the Vietnam war and much that can be praised. In the end, it was the war itself—not television—that brought it to Paris for talks after bringing it to American homes for disapproval.

That is how it should be. It is in those homes that the final judgment on our Government and how it is run should always be made.

CHAPTER 8

A TIME TO KILL
AND A TIME TO HEAL

AMERICAN PRESIDENTS have been fatalistic about assassination.

Abraham Lincoln, the year before Booth's bullet killed him, said, "If I am killed, I can die but once; but to live in constant dread of it, is to die over and over again."

James Garfield once said, "America is the place where you cannot kill your government by killing the men who conduct it."

William McKinley, reportedly his last words as he died of an assassin's bullet, said, "It is God's way. His will, not ours, be done."

And John F. Kennedy in a campaign plane, turned to the late Charles Von Fremd, a CBS News correspondent, and mused that any madman with a rifle and a telescopic sight had a chance to kill a President. There wasn't much you could do to prevent it.

When a madman fired from the Texas Book Depository in Dallas on November 22, 1963 a President was killed—John F. Kennedy. On the morning of his death, President Kennedy glanced at a full page ad in the *Dallas News* accusing him of pro-Communist activity and he said, shaking his head, "We're really in 'nut country' now."

His closest confidant, other than his brothers, was Theodore Sorensen. In a biography of the President, Sorensen wrote:

> "The only two dates that most people remember where they were," Kennedy once said, "were Pearl Harbor and the death of President Franklin Roosevelt." No one will forget where he was when he first learned, disbelieved and learned again of the death of President John Kennedy. No one will forget how his widow, eyewitness to the lowest level of human brutality, maintained the highest level of human nobility. No one will forget how low the flags seemed at

half-mast on the crisp New England kind of day when they buried him at Arlington Cemetery.

The intellectual who had written in 1960 that Kennedy, like his election opponent, was not "a man at whose funeral strangers would cry" was proven wrong.

November 22 will indeed be burned into the memory of those who lived that day. In no small part, it will be remembered because from mid-day on that Friday until the President was buried four days later, American television played a role that no form of communication known to man had ever played: it made all of a nation, witness to and participant in a national catharsis.

Theodore White in *The Making of the President, 1964* wrote that, "Nothing like this had happened in the history of the human race—so large a participation of mankind in the mortal tragedy of a single individual." *Newsweek* said it another way, "The greatest escapist medium ever devised made escape impossible."

First word came at 12:34 p.m. Dallas time, 1:34 in New York. It was a UPI line—one sentence long—which read, "Three shots were fired at President Kennedy's motorcade today in Downtown Dallas." It wasn't even preceded by the usual warning "BULLETIN." There was momentary "hash" on the wire as the UPI New York bureau squelched all other bureaus from filing material and moved the line: "DA IT YRS NY"— "Dallas, it's yours. New York."

The next line read "no casualties reported" but within moments came "FLASH. KENNEDY SERIOUSLY WOUNDED PERHAPS SERI-OUSLY PERHAPS FATALLY BY ASSASSINS BULLET."

The network newscasters were on the air with the bulletin—grim-faced and careful not to say more than the bulletin material indicated. Facts began dribbling in from their own reporters and both UPI and the Associated Press were now filing.

At CBS News, word came from the News Director of the Dallas affiliate, Eddie Barker of KRLD-TV, that the President was dead; he had it from a doctor at Parkland Hospital. Walter Cronkite, in New York, continually referred to this report but emphasized that it was not official. At 1:33 p.m. in Dallas—59 minutes after the first UPI bulletin, Malcolm Kilduff, as Assistant Presidential Press Secretary confirmed it—the President was dead.

The networks stayed on the air, under instructions from the top leadership of each. They were told to keep on the air, not to return to normal programming. For how long? "We'll decide that later," was the reply. Ultimately the answer came: for four full days.

During that period, this one story—this "only" story—was to be carried on CBS-TV for over 55 hours, on ABC-TV for 60 hours and on NBC-TV for 71 hours and 36 minutes. NBC on Sunday night, as crowds filed past the President's casket, lying in state in the Rotunda of the Capitol, decided to stay on all night without narration, only appropriate music: it was on the air continuously for over 41 hours from Sunday morning until well past midnight on Monday. Between them, the networks employed 2,100 men to handle the coverage and the cost in lost advertising, according to *Variety* was $40 million.

The audience was the largest in history. In New York City alone, it was estimated that the average family watched 34 hours of television during the four-day span. On Monday, the day of the burial some 95% of all television sets in New York were operating. Streets were deserted, businesses closed, stores empty.

A moving review of television's role by George Rosen in *Variety* began, "One of the worst hours in the nation's history has produced television's finest." He went on to say that, "A murderer's hand that squeezed a $12.78 rifle in Dallas, within minutes, flipped 50,000,000 TV dials to a new kind of communication between the TV screen and almost 200,000,-000 viewers . . . For TV was the catalyst, the ever present force, which forged a unity of national grief. With it, and largely because of it, the nation moved—as one—from incomprehension to shock to anger to grief to mourning to apprehension to resolution. Television, as one participant —there were no mere 'observers' in this tragedy—put it, became a 'cathedral' for all people everywhere."

"Everywhere" exaggerates not too much. Portions of the live coverage were carried by satellite to twenty-three countries and another 600 million people (the combined population) had an opportunity to watch some of the coverage. NBC fed the programming via the Relay satellite to the networks linked by Eurovision and Intervision (the Iron Curtain countries). Most carried it live, some carried it delayed.

Though the coverage included network pick-ups in most major cities (many for interviews and man-on-the-street reaction), it came primarily from Dallas, Washington and New York. Equipment and manpower were rushed to these cities from all over the nation. On Friday, television followed the story in Dallas until the plane carrying his body and the new President arrived in Washington at dinnertime. The big Dallas story in the late afternoon and evening was the search for the killer and the arrest of the suspect, Lee Harvey Oswald.

In Washington, there was the bright television spotlight piercing the darkness of Andrews Air Force Base. A yellow lift truck edged up to an open door in Air Force One and the casket was lowered to the ground. Jacqueline Kennedy—proud and straight—followed at its side, Robert Kennedy now at her side. The first words to the nation from the new

President followed. Lyndon Johnson saying, "I know the world shares the sorrow that Mrs. Kennedy and her family bear. I will do my best. That is all I can do. I ask for your help—and God's."

The long day drew to a close. In Dallas, Lee Harvey Oswald was arraigned for the murder of policeman J. D. Tippit. In Washington, the President's body was at Bethesda Naval Hospital. During the night, it would be brought to the White House, Jacqueline Kennedy still at the side of the casket, still wearing the dress she wore then, the blood-stained dress. Much of the Cabinet and Press Secretary Pierre Salinger had been over the Pacific in a jet heading for Japan when it happened. They were back now. The networks worked through the night to prepare for the next day's coverage, consulted with Salinger and his staff on what was ahead.

Saturday was a rainy day in the Capitol city. Dignitaries filed into the White House to pay their respects. On a catafalque in the East Room of the White House, John F. Kennedy lay in state. The networks kept switching from the somber dignity of Washington in mourning and the messages of grief from around the world to the chaotic scene in Dallas, particularly the wild atmosphere at police headquarters. Local law enforcement men came down the corridor crowded with reporters to hold aloft the assassin's 6.5mm rifle. The prisoner himself was seen. Information poured forth.

Between scenes of actuality, the networks ran eulogies, on film, in panel discussions, even in concerts to commemorate the nation's mourning.

Then came Sunday. The rain was gone in Washington, a chilly sunshine in its place. The morning moved on slowing in anticipation of the procession that would take the President's body to Capitol Hill. Networks were filling with religious commemorations.

Then it happened.

Lee Harvey Oswald was being taken from the Dallas city jail to the County jail. NBC switched live as the accused man, flanked by detectives, stepped onto a garage ramp in the jail basement. Suddenly, out of the lower right hand corner of the TV screen, came Jack Ruby and a shot rang out.

Tom Pettit, NBC's man at the scene shouted in disbelief, "He's been shot! He's been shot! Lee Oswald has been shot!"

At CBS, which had been taping, there was an immediate live switch to Dallas and subsequently, a replay of the shooting. ABC-TV was caught without live cameras on the scene (their cameras were at the County jail waiting his arrival there) but there was an immediate bulletin. For the first time in history, a homicide had been carried "live." An eerie television first in a weekend that already hd its full share of real life shock.

The networks could not dwell on the new blood spilled in Dallas for, back in Washington, the procession to the Capitol was beginning. Out of the White House came Mrs. Kennedy, dressed in black, her two small children at her side. Slowly the caisson which had carried Franklin D. Roosevelt in 1945, carried John Kennedy along the route he had travelled a thousand days earlier to his inauguration. With an honor guard from all the Armed Forces and muted drums setting the slow pace, the caisson moved toward the Capitol. At the plaza before the east front, it stopped and pallbearers unlashed the flag-draped casket and took it up the long steps into the center Rotunda. There it was silently lowered onto Lincoln's catafalque.

Three speakers eulogized the dead President in brief ceremony. There was Chief Justice Earl Warren, Speaker of the House John W. McCormack and Senate Majority Leader Mike Mansfield. "A piece of each of us died at that moment," said Mansfield, "Yet in death he gave of himself to us. He gave us of a good heart from which the laughter came. He gave us of a profound wit, from which a great leadership emerged. He gave us of a kindless and a strength fused into a human courage to seek peace without fear." And then, in silence, television cameras showed Mrs. Kennedy and her daughter go to the bier. The young widow kissed the flag that covered the casket. The child reached under it and touched the coffin.

As the ceremonies took place, in Dallas Oswald died in the emergency room at Parkland Hospital, a few feet from where John Kennedy had been declared dead just 48 hours earlier.

Through the afternoon and evening and then the long, cold night the people came, came to the Capitol Rotunda. Before morning, an astounding number had filed by. Some estimates say 250,000 had filed by—some waiting six to eight hours in a line that was as much as two miles long.

Now and then, among these figures of average Americans, came some of the famous: astronaut John Glenn, President de Valera of Ireland. And shortly after nine o'clock, Mrs. Kennedy suddenly appeared unannounced. With Robert Kennedy next to her, she knelt beside the coffin and then departed again. What television didn't show, what television didn't know, was that she and the dead President's brother walked for some blocks, apparently unnoticed by the thousands of waiting mourners, before getting back into a limousine and leaving.

On Monday morning, the pilgrimage past the bier ended. The big bronze doors were closed. Shortly before 11 a.m., the pallbearers from the Armed Services carried the President back down the long steps for his last journey. Six gray-white horses, three of them riderless, pulled the caisson. Behind it came a riderless horse, Black Jack by name, with empty boots reversed in its stirrups to mark the death of the rider. Slowly the processional came down Pennsylvania Avenue and then before the White House. The Kennedy family came out and walked behind the casket, his brothers at each side of his widow.

The Supreme Court, the Cabinet, members of the Congress followed. Then came the honored guests from overseas. Through the Northwest Gate of the White House, normally an entrance gate, came President deGaulle of France, Chancellor Erhard of West Germany, Queen Frederika of Greece, King Baudouin of Belgium, Haile Selassie of Ethiopia, President Macapagal of the Philippines. A startled television cameraman stuttered to his director, "I've got a whole bunch of kings!"

They walked to St. Matthew's Cathedral where Richard Cardinal Cushing celebrated the Pontifical Requiem Mass. The Most Reverend Philip M. Hannan, Auxiliary Bishop of Washington gave the eulogy and included words from the speech that John Kennedy never gave, the luncheon speech scheduled for Dallas on November 22:

> Finally, in his last hours, President Kennedy had prepared these words for Dallas and for the nation:
>
> "The righteousness of our cause must always underlie our strength, for as was written long ago, except the Lord guard the city, the guard watches in vain."
>
> The following is one of his favorite passages from Scripture, from the Book of Ecclesiastes, the third chapter:
>
> "There is an appointed time for everything, and a time for every affair under the heavens.
>
> "A time to be born, and a time to die. A time to plant, and a time to uproot the plant.
>
> "A time to kill, and a time to heal. A time to tear down, and a time to build.
>
> "A time to weep, and a time to laugh. A time to mourn, and a time to dance."

The services ended, Cardinal Cushing blessed the casket outside the Cathedral, and the march resumed—south to the Lincoln Memorial, around that shrine to another martyred President, across the bridge over the Potomac and into Arlington National Cemetery. There the dignitaries gathered at graveside for the final moments. Overhead fifty jets, one for each state, flew by. Then Air Force One flew over alone.

Cardinal Cushing spoke the last words, "O God, through whose mercy the souls of the faithful find rest, be pleased to bless this grave and Thy holy angels to keep it . . . the body we bury herein, that of our beloved Jack Kennedy, the 35th President of the United States . . ." The flag that had covered the casket was folded and presented to the President's widow. Holding Robert Kennedy's hand, she quietly left Arlington.

Those were the scenes that television showed between November 22 and November 26, 1963. They were scenes that seared into the American mind.

"The Kennedy funeral," wrote Marshall McLuhan, "manifested the power of TV to involve an entire population in a ritual process."

To bring about this ritual process on television, the networks accepted and succeeded at a challenge that none ever expected. Elmer Lower of ABC called it "the toughest job I have ever had in thirty years in journalism."

There are a host of stories that could be told at all three networks, in Dallas, in New York and in Washington, stories about that remarkable four-day period. Perhaps a feel for them can be had in the telling of just one story, as one network handled the story in one city, Washington.

Shortly after the funeral, the CBS director of public relations in Washington—the late Dudley Harmon—interviewed this author to capture the essence of what had happened during that period. The interview gives some feel for what all networks went through in Washington and in other cities.

Q. How did it begin for you?

A. It began on the 22nd—I was in my office with Frank Fitz-Patrick and Don Richardson. We were simply going over the list of news contacts. When the first bulletin hit, Don Bowers came running in from the desk and said, "Kennedy has been shot." I guess like everyone else we just didn't know what that meant.

Q. Did you think it was a joke?

A. No, no, no. You took one look at his face and you know he was serious. And then someone said, "Is he dead?" And the answer was, "We don't know, we just know he's been shot." We came running out shouting, "We need remotes at the White House, Lyndon Johnson's house, and the Hill."

Q. As you came out of the office you were—saying—how did you decide so quickly?

A. Those were the logical places to go, and it was kind of silly to come out barking orders because we were all going right to the machines first to see what was on the wires. After checking the wire, I went to see Don Cooper of WTOP, and ordered remotes. We ordered lines—we didn't even have that many remote units.

We sent one hurrying to the White House—the big truck—we sent one towards the Hill. We didn't have a third, really, so we improvised—we took a Greenbriar station wagon and put the guts of a remote unit into this little wagon and headed it towards Lyndon Johnson's house.

I checked the wire again; by this time CBS was on the air. For TV we needed someone in the studio, Neil Strawser, with Herman at the White House. Our other White House correspondent, Bob Pierpoint, was in Dallas with the President. We started giving New York material from here to fill. At this time, the President's fate was still in doubt. Then I called Baltimore—the CBS affiliate there, WMAR—and we asked for their remote unit and they said they would send a remote unit down. They asked—where does it go? I told them just to call me from the edge of town when they arrived, and then I called New York and asked for more people and more equipment.

Q.   How many people did you want?

A.   They were going to send down Art Kane to help with general stuff, Norm Gorin, the director, and Don McGraw, who is a technical expert for us, and Sid Kaufman came with him. At this point, they were all going to come, and a remote unit they said— and at least one more remote truck would come down during the night.

Meanwhile by this time we were on the air steadily with material for both radio and TV. We started working on getting a remote at Andrews Air Force Base, because the body was going to be back at 6:30 p.m. By this time, it was about 5:15. We had very little time to work.

We didn't have a remote unit—we improvised one. Then we found that Congress had closed down and we started that Hill remote unit towards Andrews. We actually had two going at one time. The telephone company said that they could not provide more than one line at a time. It had to be a pool line—NBC—I think NBC—had that line. All three networks had units on the way, but it became a pool with NBC. Charles von Fremd went out to do radio from there and ended up being on both radio and TV, describing the arrival.

Meanwhile we had a White House remote working and we were able to feed material from the White House. As I said, on the Hill it was film. We were just calling everyone—you know—trying to find more people, and bring in everyone in sight.

Well, you know that first night—I don't know how long—I don't remember how long we stayed on the air. Until he arrived at 6:30, the story was still largely in Dallas. We were filling, even before 6:30 we were getting the films of all the people. . .

Q.   I remember Mansfield was being interviewed . . .

A.   The leaders of Congress—the man in the Senate who heard the news and went and told Teddy Kennedy—you know Teddy was presiding over the Senate. All of these people—you know, I think we were the only ones to get McCormack.

The film kept flooding in, we kept throwing it on the air, and Neil Strawser wouldn't know sometimes what film we had next.

Friday night was a night of reaction and for finding out as much as we could. At the end of the day on Friday we had a pool meeting. It is my vague memory we had scheduled it to start at 12:30 or 1:00 in the morning. We decided to go to ABC (it was nearest the White House), and we were to go on from there to the White House to meet with Salinger. Salinger had not arrived back from the Pacific, so we went to ABC and had a pool meeting and a draw to see who would coordinate.

ABC immediately removed itself, said it did not have the facilities to coordinate anything this elaborate. In this case, we went on and flipped the coin. CBS was chosen and I immediately put Art Kane in charge of producing for the pool. It is really pool coordinating because much of the production is a three-way decision—still, he had a tougher job, really; he was kind of a federal arbitrator and producer at the same time.

Norman Gorin was put in charge for direction of the pool. This meant that Bob Vitarelli of our staff would direct for us, Bob Camfiord would direct from somewhere else. He ended up directing for CBS and its contribution to the pool, which was all coverage of the Hill itself.

I immediately assigned WTOP directors at our spots at the Capitol Plaza and at the White House and at our spot at Lyndon Johnson's home, and around 2:30 or 3:00 a.m. we finished the initial meeting with the pool to set up the general rules on who would cover what.

From there we went to the White House and met with Salinger. I will never forget seeing Salinger, because you know Salinger, you know him to be a jovial, genial character, and in his face you could see the entire tragedy written out at that moment. Later that morning he was pretty much restored, not to his jovial self, but to a cool, hardworking, self-contained self. But at 3:00 a.m., his face seemed drained of emotion. Leonard Reinsch from Atlanta was there also, and I really don't know where he came from. He is the man in charge of televising conventions, inaugurals and all the rest for the Democrats.

I remember Mac Kilduff, the other aide to Salinger (with Andy Hatcher), walking in. Kilduff we had on film late in the evening and he looked awful, tears streaming down his face. It was his job to announce that the President was indeed dead. By this time he had had a chance to shave and freshen up and really looked better than most of us.

When we had finished that meeting we had live cameras ready, though none of us were on the air. We were coming back on the air at eight in the morning. We knew that Mrs. Kennedy was coming back from the Bethesda (Naval) Hospital where the body was to be prepared, and they were to come back to the White House. We walked out with Reinsch and with Hatcher to decide where to place our live cameras. Our live units were at the White House to record bringing the body to the White House.

That having been done, we decided—Don Richardson was with me—that here was a chance to witness a bit of history, and I knew we wouldn't get out of that control room much for several days. We decided that we wanted to see John Kennedy brought back to the White House. I remember they looked like little smudge pots, little flames lining the driveway, and they had a small company of military marching ahead. The cars came with the family. Mrs. Kennedy got out—I will never forget—she was still wearing the same dress with blood on it. You know, it stunned you. Well, from there—neither Don nor I had eaten since that Friday . . .

Q. What time was that?

A. It was now about 5:00 in the morning, Saturday morning. We went to Georgetown, had breakfast with the camera crew; Don, Bruce Hoertel, Milton Bittenbender and myself.

Q. At the diner there?

A. I don't know the name of the place—it is across from our lab at Prospect Street. Then we came back here and then Don went to one room where there's a couch, in Pierpoint's office. I stretched out on a couch in my office, but kept picking up the noise from the newsroom, so I went into Crawford's office, and I slept there. Less than an hour. Then there was a call—there had been a problem about the White House remote. Well, that was all right—we had that straightened out before we went on the air that morning. By 9:00 in the morning, we had to be down to the Hill for a pool meeting . . .

Q. Did you feel horrible, Bill?

A. No.

Q. Or were you too excited then?

A. I didn't feel a thing. I guess I slept about six or seven hours over the four days. I didn't feel a thing until maybe Thanksgiving Day or later, and then it caught up with me.

We went down to the pool meeting at the Rotunda, and the first thing we found out was that—as usual—the non-experts were setting up the stands backwards so that our cameras would get the backs of people. We insisted that they be turned so we could see people's faces as they came past the casket, and that was arranged. We went upstairs to the gallery and continued meetings involving pool coverage.

At that time the word was that he would be buried back in Boston. To handle things until then, we had committed most all of our equipment between the group of us. Later we learned he was to be buried here, at Arlington.

We had also made arrangements to carry church services. NBC was setting up at the National Cathedral—that would be a pool. We were setting up at Saint Matthew's where his final services were to be.

By now it was driving rain, and Don McGraw, Frank FitzPatrick and Don Richardson drove back to Broadcast House in the rain.

We went past the White House and then—I don't remember why we went past, for some reason or other we decided we would go past the White House—and this was a mistake, because we got jammed in traffic. Even in the heavy rain people were going by, people were standing. People kept coming all the time.

We got back to the office and discovered among other problems that some mikes had washed out in the rain, and correspondents were working from inside the remote truck at the White House. We started rotating equipment to get more mikes down and to continue the coverage on into the night on Saturday.

Let's see—Saturday night we met, I think, at NBC—one in the morning or so—and this is when we discovered that they were going to bury him in Arlington. We needed more equipment, we kept calling New York for more equipment. We weren't getting much equipment, but we learned they would send down another handful of technicians. Because suddenly we had the pool problem, as well as our own piled on CBS, we had technicians who had worked around the clock, just staggering around 36 hours or so without sleeping. We had to get some of these men in some kind of shape because we knew we now had more days to go, and more remote spots.

The pool meeting in the wee hours of Sunday morning was designed to plot out what we would do at Arlington, and whose responsibility it was. ABC was to take part of the parade route to the church and back. We had the church and we had to take up the parade route at 17th and Constitution Avenue all the way over to Arlington, and then back if needed.

And now we had our additional commitments—we had to find new ways to get more men and cameras down. And I remember getting back to the office and finding that Dave Dugan and—I had asked for him—and Dave Dugan was coming down and so was Bill Leonard to help us on Sunday and Monday, and they were both very fine, and a great deal of help; Dugan on radio and Leonard on television.

But I needed more people—I needed a couple more radio voices —we had put all our leg men on radio—everyone was performing superbly—something about the event brought out the very best in just everyone. They covered themselves with glory and of many of them—I have heard this of George Herman many times since but it could have been said about almost any of them—that their taste was impeccable. And this was true.

But we plotted out what we did—I remember coming back and there was a question to ask Hatcher, and I called the White House, and I remember the girls at the other end said, "You wouldn't have me wake him up at this hour," and I said, "We'll, it's not so late," I said, "It's only 12:30." And she said, "Look at your watch again." I did. My watch had stopped and it was now 3:30 or 4:00 in the morning.

Sunday started and Sunday was a big day—this was the day for the eulogies in the Rotunda and the bringing of the body up, and we were ready all down the Avenue, except that we had a remote camera set up at 4th and Constitution. The police called and said they had torn down our platform and carried it off because an assistant police chief who gave permission had forgotten to pass it on. No one could find him now, and they said it was—as far as they were concerned we didn't have a permit. But this didn't matter, it turned out, because the Chesapeake and Potomac had forgotten to put in a line, or didn't have the line to put in there, so we lost that remote position. We converted into an audio remote and Bill Leonard did voice over the pool picture from that spot. And did it very well.

We carried the ceremony to the Rotunda. The moment the eulogies began we discovered that the pool—and this was the only serious technical flaw in the pool—that it had garbled audio. We don't know—I believe a later check indicated that the Signal Corps, which had been involved in the "mults" at the Rotunda, had loused it up. But in any case it was not good TV audio, we found after they got through about one sentence. We checked radio. It was right, so we switched to radio and we carried radio audio throughout the Rotunda ceremony. ABC—I don't know what they did—I don't think they ever got decent audio.

NBC called our people in New York and begged for our audio, saying they were getting this garbled audio, and we gave it to them, and they ended up with CBS radio, and it was Ted Church, who was assigned to radio, not television, whose voice you heard between the eulogies, and heard on both networks—on both CBS and NBC.

Q.   He sounded as though he were crying.

A.   Well, I don't think—I think all of our people were genuinely moved, and you could get that in their voices, but I don't think any of them really broke down, although there was great emotion.

Our problem that day was that they would not permit a flash unit in the cortege, so you had permanently stationed cameras, and they were so far apart—four blocks apart, perhaps each one— that the correspondents—couldn't see enough. And beyond that, we didn't have monitors, because you just couldn't have enough for the needs of that short period—and correspondents not having any other way to know what the picture was, we talked them through on the program interrupt, and we—well, to begin with, we told them it wasn't necessary, they all know—we told them to say as little as possible. But some things had to be said, and so when they would make the turn on Pennsylvania Avenue, and the rear camera showed the Capitol looming up behind the cortege, I would get on program interrupt and just softly say, "Now you see the Capitol," and then the correspondent would come in and gently say, "Now you see the Capitol."

Once in a while we would simply close our mikes and we'd tell them, "We are killing your mike, we will go with natural sound for a little bit." That way they knew they could relax a moment. But none of our correspondents talked too much or needed to be reminded. They were great.

The one fluff along that line which was rather amusing—this was a new experience for some of our newer people, legmen, and Stanley Levey, the man who covers labor and business for us.

And Stan was—as I say, we were all quite carried away by what was being done, and I said to him, "Now Stan, it's moving a little closer to you now—you don't see it yet, you don't have to talk yet, just wait a few moments, then when you see the head of the cortege, then you can mention it. Don't answer me, because your mike is open, but that's what you are to do."

And a voice over the air said softly, "Okay, Bill." And you can bet that there was quite a reaction in the control room to that. But this was not a serious error.

And so the story was carried to the Capitol—Marvin Kalb was there for TV, Ted Church for radio, Roger Mudd was outside, and the thing that happened, of course, just before it all began, was the killing of Oswald. This presented us with an interesting dilemma— what do you do in terms of good taste, and I consulted with Ernie

Leiser and I didn't have to because we both agreed that the thing to do was, once the cortege started, no references to Oswald, or minimal references to Oswald.

And I think in the whole several hours the only reference—once or twice a correspondent said, "The crowd here does not know yet about Oswald," or something like that. The news had spread pretty quickly through the crowd.

Mudd did magnificent work over simply the picture of people filing past during that night. And again this night went—this Sunday night we went off the air I think before midnight—11:30 or so, as I recall. NBC stayed on. And we had another pool meeting. This one I was late to because again I had to juggle manpower—the problem the next day was, how do you cover a procession that now is twice as long as the one that used up all your manpower today—and then you have a grave-side commentary to worry about.

The answer was, as the cortege left, one by one we would relieve the correspondents and skip them over to another spot. Bill Leonard was the first to be relieved—well, actually, it was Tony Sargent, he went to 17th and Constitution. Bill Leonard went to Arlington, so-and-so went so-and-so and by the time the people had reached the White House, and the procession went to the church, we had deployed all our correspondents to new positions. Mudd left the Hill, went on top of the Lincoln Memorial, so that he could walk around physically and follow the cortege as it wound around and headed up towards Arlington. And so this is how we went into the day of the funeral.

There was one other problem Sunday night. The pool called Frank and they said, "We need morning clothes for all the technicians." And, bless FitzPatrick, you know he's my kind of guy, the thing he said was not, "Oh my God, it's Sunday night in Washington. How am I going to rent morning clothes?" But he said, "What sizes?" And he got them, got them that night. I guess we both left here about the same time, in the wee hours.

Also Sunday we produced an hour talk show with four Senators here. And we had the job of continually cutting in and out of programming showing the arrival of the Mikoyans, the Erhards, the Prince Philips and all the rest and it was my duty to tell four U.S. Senators that de Gaulle was due any moment—we may have to leave them in the middle of their program, and they said they understood full well but actually they went on for 52 minutes, and then we cut away for de Gaulle and they felt they had done it so well they didn't want to finish and they had ended on a good note. Since then Hugh

Scott and "Scoop" Jackson who were on the program—Pastore, also, I believe—told us that they have had quite a bit of response from that program.

But anyway, Monday was the day, the unforgettable day of that funeral and when it ended, our camera at the White House began picking up the dignitaries coming from Arlington and going to see Mrs. Kennedy, and George Herman had the very tough job of describing them. We knew very few of them, mostly the very famous.

At the graveside we had one technical trouble that—we had far fewer than we should have had—but we had one that was interesting.

We had a line from Bill Leonard to us—a broadcast line—but our program interrupt line with which we communicate with him went out. And I don't know how it was done, but somehow his technicians rigged up a radio phone set-up of some kind from Leonard to a phone booth 150 yards away. The engineer called from the phone booth and we relayed all cues through this man and it went flawlessly —you know, in a million years you couldn't do that again.

And then the Attorney General of Texas—cuss his name—called up and in the middle of this said he is holding a vital news conference right after the funeral, and this could mean only one thing— that he really had something significant to say about Oswald. We had to be there. It was at the Statler Hilton.

We called the Hilton and we rushed people over—we moved units over—NBC did, and the man got up and gave a little Chamber of Commerce speech about Texas won't let this crime go unsolved, etc. etc. And that was it—there was no news conference—there were no questions, that was all. It just was tremendous added strain to something that was already rupturing our ability to cover.

And then the State Department was going to open up its reception. Well, NBC had a camera loose which had been relieved earlier that day from a position on the parade route. We moved it over there—it became pool camera.

We drew for pool voice position. Marvin Kalb was to do narration, and for an hour and fifteen minutes or so he described and identified this fantastic collection of foreign dignitaries, and did a beautiful job.

And we again just stayed on the air. CBS went to Herman and Pierpoint now—both at the White House for some more fill until the network was ready to gear up later that evening for the big two-hour twenty-minute wrap-up on the entire four days. And . . .

Q. How many cameras did you actually have down here?

A. I don't know—you know, when you pool produce, it merges into the pool, and I don't know—I guess the pool had twenty-five cameras, maybe more—we had six, ten, twelve, about fourteen remote cameras. There were so many, you know, heroes of the day—Bill Crawford did production with me, Paul Liebler did the Mass at the church, and did it magnificently. At one pool meeting NBC wanted to offer Frank Blair for commentary and the other networks allowed they would just as soon have Father Hurley and not an NBC voice doing commentary.

Q. Well, he did a marvelous job . . . It was funny—it seemed to me you were operating with practically the same staff you always have in Washington, because I remember for the March on Washington there seemed to have been forty people down here from New York.

A. Yes . . .

Q. Perhaps this time they were all out and never had time to come to the office.

A. We probably tripled the number of technical people—this from New York, Baltimore, Philadelphia. On-the-air personalities, we had less than we had on August 28—we had just two additional people.

Q. Dave and Bill?

A. Right. And we used almost everyone at WTOP—one of the blessings was the WTOP had very little to do on the air so their people were relieved—their technical people were available to us. So much of what happened—I really don't know—having people like Clucas in radio—you can just turn loose and they won't even bother you unless they have a serious problem—tremendous help—and Don McGraw at TV in New York who did the same on the television side. McGraw did the pool—he got away once and got back to his motel room and I got him out of the shower and had to put him to work on something else.

Q. He was down at the Capitol the whole time or was he here in the control room?

A. Well, he was at the Capitol and at the pool meetings, and when you are not on the air you are setting up the next day's coverage. The nicest thing said, I have told other people this but there were lots of nice things said, all of us know that, and one of the pleasant things for me was Monday night about nine or so when we had just about wrapped up everything—we had, I think, one last commitment to the final show, I called my lady and told her I was coming home and she was going to make a steak. I looked at my desk which was now like three inches deep with paper. There was a telegram from my former boss, you know, and this kind of thing . . .

Q. Barry Bingham?

A.   No, this was Vic Sholis, and this kind of thing made you feel pretty good but the nicest thing said was said not then, but afterwards. A British TV producer named Jeremy Isaacs, who produces for Associated Rediffusion—he does a program called "This Week" and he was in my office. Isaacs said, "You know, we have been preparing seven years to cover Churchill's death. And the television people meet often, sometimes monthly, and we'll never match there what you have done here." It was just the nicest compliment in the world.

Q.   Just one question, Bill. Did you yourself, were you able, actually, to see any of this on television?

A.   Oh, I saw a great deal from the control room. To begin with, I guess I was on the intercom four or five hours a day—when there was a funeral cortege to the Capitol on Sunday, and then on Monday to the Capitol to get the body to the White House—to the church—to the cemetery. I was never fully conscious of all of it really, except that I know that whenever I watched it, it was in good taste. And this pleased me. I saw very little—we had an NBC monitor in the control room—we didn't have enough monitors so that the control room could also see ABC—I never did know what they had—and we didn't hear NBC—but it just—whatever I saw was going right. But we always had to look two steps ahead. And it all goes very, very quickly.

Q.   I was just thinking what a pity you couldn't be like somebody who could really sit and watch it from beginning to end, because it was so terrific, as everybody has said. It's a shame that you couldn't enjoy—enjoy is the wrong word to use—but appreciate what a viewer, you know, without worrying about the next . . .

A.   Four days of coverage, three networks—in the abstract you would say, gee, it would be great if you could sit down with three monitors or just look at all the kines for one and then the other.

Q.   Will they ever be shown?

A.   There is just too much. You couldn't do that. CBS is, well, they are not just preserving all of it but they are, the last program—two-hour- twenty-minute sum-up, and condensing it, I think, to a one-hour program, maybe for internal distribution—may never see air, may just be to give to people who are involved.

Q.   Were you able to see the two-and-a-half hour one?

A.   No.

Q.   That's too bad.

A.   I used to say there were only a handful of television programs that affected history, and this was right. One was when Nixon gave his "Checkers" speech, and another was the "See It Now" on Mc-

Carthy and there are only a few like that. But you got to this, this was not . . . this was the people, and the average American watched a lot of television during those four days, people lived that story as no other people in history will ever live it. People feel a closer identification with those four days because of television than any other people ever felt over any other event. And it was vicariously being with Mrs. Kennedy every step of the way.

Looking back over those remarks almost half a dozen years later, one is puzzled. Instead of awe for the impact of those four days, there is a sense of exuberance, a heady feeling of accomplishment, wonder that it could come off successfully at all. The mood seems incongruous. Those four days were historic, in television's history and the nation's. Why not reverence for history instead of a sense of "We did it!"?

The explanation is that while those producing the coverage knew what they had done, they had little grasp at the time of what television had done. The television crews and editorial people felt the emotion of the moment, some worked with tears in their eyes at times. They didn't know how much of this emotion carried through to all America.

It was a feat of great technical accomplishment—to fill all that time and to fill it meaningfully. That was the reason for exuberance when it all had ended, for the feeling of "We did it."

It is only afterwards that television learns how much it did. In the case of matters which shake up the public, reaction comes quickly. In the case of the Four Days, it came differently. Many of the television people who worked through those long, long days did not learn until it was all over that their own families watched in stunned silence, that the streets were empty, the stores with few customers. America was stilled.

A glowing tribute came in November of 1963 from Senator William Proxmire of Wisconsin, often a critic of television. "Not only was the coverage dignified and in immaculate taste," he said in a Senate speech, "it was remarkably competent and frequently it soared with imaginative, if tragic beauty. The intelligence and sensitivity of commentary and continuously expressed dedication to this country's strength and solidity in its hour of terrible grief was superb. This marvel of the 20th century—television—displayed what an amazing contribution it can make to instilling in Americans a sense of this great country and what it stands for."

Senator Proxmire had summed it up well in that single paragraph. Television had accelerated the healing process of a nation rent with a tragic wound. It came at a moment where senseless brutality seemed to shake up a nation's psyche and it reminded all of the strengths of a great country.

It was the conduit of continuity.

In the years that followed, during the rest of the decade, American television handled many events of prolonged duration—space shots, political conventions, the long election night in 1968, international crisis. The lessons of the Four Days, when television was compelled to take the air continuously without warning, served as reassurance that it could be done and as a guide telling how to do it.

It is a tragic footnote in television history that these lessons were used in comparable situations twice in one year. In April of 1968, Martin Luther King was assassinated and television was a force in calming the Negro population, ten per cent of a nation, ten per cent convinced that the White Man had stooped to this, stooped to killing the most charismatic leader of the Black Revolution.

[Riots broke out across the nation's big cities. But the rioting was contained within a matter of days. The prime reason was the vastly improved treatment of the outbursts by local officials, including rapid introduction of heavy local and military law enforcement units. A secondary contributor to restoring the peace was the unprecedented television coverage devoted to the death of a private citizen. In some countries there is tradition for this. In America, national mourning has traditionally been limited to the death of Presidents and war heroes. France, for example, was moved to national mourning by the death of Camus. No American author or other private person has ever had something similar until the April 4, 1968 killing of Martin Luther King.]

For Blacks, angry and frustrated, there was a less than subtle suggestion that someone cared, that "The Man" cared, the Establishment cared. The expressions of shock included the full spectrum of America from the President to the man in the street, the white man as well as the Black. Networks ran prime-time specials. On CBS a round-table of prominent Negro leaders including Roy Wilkins and Whitney Young ran well beyond midnight. ABC's "Joey Bishop Show" was devoted entirely to Dr. King's memory. The television concern with the story extended to Tuesday, April 9 when all three networks carried full, live coverage of the funeral in Atlanta. For over seven hours, three American networks carried the story. It had to have a calming effect.

The words spoken by the leading television news figures were eloquent witness to the sense of loss America felt. The comments of NBC's Chet Huntley were an example: "Again we are made to look like a nation of killers at a time when our detractors and unbridled critics and adversaries had already advanced that damaging assertion. The perpetrator of this deed brings down upon all of us the painful charge that we Americans are prisoners of violence and destruction and death. What others think we are, however, is less important than what we are; and we are poorer as a consequence of this . . ."

Television had again served as a palliative, for the second time in less than five years.

Tragically, it was compelled to assume that healing role still again in just two months. Senator Robert Kennedy was assassinated in a Los Angeles hotel on the night of his victory in the California Presidential primary.

NBC's Edwin Newman grimly observed, "There's something unreal about this. All the wheels go around; we handle it as we did before. Nothing changes—only the names."

Again programs were pre-empted and replaced by special tributes to the fallen Kennedy. Panel discussions by friends of the late New York Senator replaced entertainment programs. On the Saturday of his burial, services at St. Patrick's began a full day of telecasting—lengthened by the failure of the funeral train to meet its schedule and thus carried on into the night.

The networks were prepared to carry it through burial at Arlington at dusk. Instead the much delayed train extended the day. Lights were available in some areas in Washington but not in others. There were eerie but dramatically effective moments where only automobile lights could be seen as the cortege wound its way from Union Station to Pennsylvania Avenue, down around the Lincoln Memorial passing Resurrection City— the Southern Christian Leadership Conference "tent-in" of Negro poor— and across the river to Arlington.

Mourners held candles in the darkness as Robert F. Kennedy was lowered into the ground at the edge of his brother's burial plot.

Quite late that night, television's latest homage to tragedy ended.

CHAPTER 9

THE POLITICIAN
AND THE TUBE

In February of 1963, not long after the off-year elections in the United States, that sometime observer of American mores, Mr. Nikita Khrushchev, addressed his own countrymen in Moscow and explained the American election scene: "A sort of show takes place. During such shows, demonstrations are demanded for votes for the elephant while the other party asks to vote for the donkey. Political advertising in the United States has much the quality of theater advertising . . . Television in America can drive you crazy from morning to night. You get snowed under by speeches from the elephant and the donkey."

The history of broadcasting, back to the very first days of radio, is entwined with the reporting of politics. The history of politics, from the first days of broadcasting, is entwined with attempts to use the airwaves to woo votes.

In the beginning there was the word—and in broadcasting the beginning word was election returns. Lee DeForest used his experimental radio station at High Bridge, New York to carry the 1916 election returns of the Wilson-Hughes contest. In 1920 the Inaugural broadcast of the first licensed commercial station, KDKA in Pittsburgh, carried the Harding-Cox election returns.

Four years later, radio was used for campaigning in a Presidential election. William G. McAdoo made a series of broadcasts seeking the Democratic nomination as did Calvin Coolidge five months before the Republican convention. That 1924 Democratic convention was carried on radio for all 103 successive ballots, a seventeen-day affair. For the first time a Democratic convention was "witnessed" by thousands outside of the hall and it was being witnessed at its worst, something that would be echoed forty-four years later in television treatment of the 1968 Democratic convention.

The 1924 campaign saw both John W. Davis and Calvin Coolidge use broadcasting extensively, primarily Coolidge who rarely left the White House. The Democrats spent $40,000 on radio and the GOP three times that amount. It would cost that much today for just a minute or two on prime-time TV. One full hour coast-to-coast cost only $4,000 in 1924. There were three million radio sets that year but when Al Smith challenged Herbert Hoover in 1928, you could reach forty million Americans by radio. The political "commercial" was born that year—the Republicans putting on 6,000 "Minute Men" to make short radio talks using canned scripts provided by the National Committee.

The *New York Times* saw great possibilities for radio. In an editorial the ecstatic *Times* called the political effect of radio "the greatest debunking influence that has come into American public life since the Declaration of Independence."

And in August of that year, unnoticed by most people, was the use of the first television remote: a pickup of Governor Smith accepting his party's nomination from the steps of the New York Capitol in Albany. The signal was telecast by General Electric over its station in Schenectady, fifteen miles away.

Four years later, in 1932, the political parties were spending $5 million on radio as Roosevelt ran against Hoover. And a few weeks before the election, the Democratic National Committee experimented with a television program over W2XAB. Featuring entertainers for FDR, the broadcast was produced at CBS studios in New York. The audience consisted of invited news reporters. There were eighteen million radio homes that year and thirty-three million when Franklin Roosevelt ran again in 1936. James Farley, who managed his campaign, said radio's role could "hardly be overestimated" in combatting the one-party (Republican) press.

Political chicanery in the use of broadcasting was getting common. One questionable technique emerged that year. Senator Arthur Vandenberg went on CBS to "debate" the voice of FDR on recordings. Twenty-one of the sixty-six CBS stations cut it off immediately. Another twenty-two reportedly cut it off, returned, cut it off again and returned again. Broadcasting's tenderness about the treatment of politicians was evident even then.

In 1940, television covered political conventions for the first time. The audience consisted of 40,000 to 100,000 persons in two cities, Philadelphia and New York.

Television was fairly dormant in the war years but radio was very much a part of the 1944 campaign. Madison Avenue, worried critics reported, had taken over the political campaigns. Hollywood production talent and Hollywood stars were used in profusion. The one-minute "spot" and the station break were used continually. News coverage of the campaign was extensive. One poll, by the National Opinion Research Center, said that 56% of some 2,000 people polled, felt they got the most accurate news about the campaign from radio. Only 27% mentioned newspapers, less than 6% cited magazines.

The War ended, 1948 became television's tentative beginning as a political force. Not that the audience was big (there were only 350,000 homes with sets and only three dozen stations on the air) but it was an audience of enough substance to attract the political eye. It was also the year of the first "great debate" (on radio) involving Presidential hopefuls.

Ex-Governor Harold Stassen of Minnesota faced New York Governor Thomas E. Dewey in debate during the Oregon primary. They met May 17, 1948 in the radio studios of KEX, Portland and the debate was fed to three networks. Dewey was the favorite in the primary and, as front runner, took a tough posture on the rules of the debate. Despite Stassen protests, Dewey ruled out audience. They each spoke for twenty minutes and then had half that time for rebuttal. Stassen was first, Dewey followed and, on his insistance, had final rebuttal.

The debate was dull, the ground they covered was old, a local paper called it "Tweedledum and Tweedledee." Dewey won the primary and no one thought the debates made much contribution. Well, almost no one. The *Washington Star* said of such debates: "They are educational in character, they put the speakers on their mettle, they reveal weaknesses which are obscured in ordinary campaign speech-making. If there were more of them, we would have better campaigns, candidates better prepared to discuss the real issues of the day and an electorate composed of the American radio public, better able to judge both issues and candidates."

Great debates were still a dozen years away but the next four years did see the development of television as a political campaign device without precedent. And why not? The potential audience had grown from under half a million in 1948 to over eighteen million television sets in 1952, most of them with multiple viewers.

It is questionable whether Adlai Stevenson could have won that election, with or without television. It is not even questionable, however, that Governor Stevenson, one of the most accomplished orators of the 20th century, had no talent for television. He was forever polishing his eloquent, witty speeches to the very last moment. They were never timed right, never on teleprompter. He was always rushing toward the end, always spilling over and being cut off the air.

On the other hand, Madison Avenue worked out a careful campaign for Dwight Eisenhower. It is said that Batten, Barton, Durstine and Osborne orchestrated Ike's half-hour appearances in a three act play. Act One was a heroic arrival, Ike coming through the back of the auditorium, working his way through the wildly cheering throng, mounting the platform, waving, smiling, looking at Mamie, holding up arms to stop applause while grinning at its continuance. Act Two was the speech. Act Three was the departure, a reverse of Act One. The speech was never more than twenty minutes long. The appearance was a blend of carefully planned pageantry. Stevenson was a little known Governor of Illinois against an extremely popular war hero. The Republican campaign managers were happy to continue that theme on television.

The Republicans also made heavy use of "spot" television, the quick impression, twenty seconds, one minute, even station breaks. Not every station would carry these political "commercials." The Westinghouse chain said it wouldn't take spots, that the issues could not be discussed in one minute. They were the exception; most stations took the business gladly.

Thomas Dewey had rejected heavy use of short spots but those running the Eisenhower campaign were glad to have them. There were a series of twenty-second and sixty-second announcements that began with an announcer triumphantly noting "Eisenhower answers the Nation!" This was followed by an "average citizen" asking a question and a brief reply by General Eisenhower. All of this was scripted by Rosser Reeves, a famous advertising agency executive, best known for "hard sell" commercials. The "citizens" were filmed in many different locations. The Eisenhower replies were done in a single day, fifty of them, in a studio in Manhattan. The replies were then spliced to the questions.

The GOP planned a saturation campaign with these spots. They were to spend $1,500,000 during the last two weeks of the campaign for the television scheduling of these spots. Stevenson's people learned about the campaign and informed the candidate. He joined them in rejecting a similar campaign. He said he didn't want to be merchandised "like a breakfast food."

Still the Democrats did use some spots and both parties made heavy use of short, five-minute broadcasts. These were placed in the last five minutes of popular programs, designed to ride piggy-back on their audiences. The audience for a half-hour, purely political broadcast is usually very small.

There was a singular exception to this general rule, a spectacularly successful television half-hour, perhaps the most important network "paid political" of all time. It was the so-called "Checkers" speech of Richard M. Nixon.

Nixon and the Checkers Speech.

On September 18, 1952 the *New York Post* ran a front page headline: *SECRET NIXON FUND.* The story, by Leo Katcher, began, "The existence of a 'millionaire's club' devoted exclusively to the financial comfort of Senator Nixon, GOP Vice Presidential candidate, was revealed today." It told of seventy-six Californians who had contributed $18,235 to a fund subsidizing Nixon's political activities as a U. S. Senator from their state.

The first hint that Nixon had regarding interest in the fund came the previous Sunday after he had appeared on NBC's "Meet the Press." Following the telecast, one of the panelists, columnist Peter Edson, privately asked him about rumors of a supplementary salary of $20,000 a year contributed by a hundred California businessmen. Nixon said the fund was to pay for travel, printing, extra clerical expenses and other matters strictly political which could not be billed to the government. It had been set up after his 1950 election by Dana Smith, his Finance Chairman and he referred Edson to Smith. Smith confirmed the existence of the fund, said it was limited to individuals not corporations and to $500 contributions so that no one could be accused of buying favors.

After the *Post* article, prominent Democrats attacked the fund. Democratic Chairman Stephen A. Mitchell demanded Nixon's resignation, called the fund "a subsidy from persons with an interest in federal legislation." Mitchell said Ike must "cast away either his principles or his running mate." Newspapers across the nation carried the story. Many editorialized about the morality of such a fund. Even some Republicans were critical. Then-Republican Senator Wayne Morse called the fund "unwise policy." The chairman of the Wisconsin Eisenhower-Nixon committee, Wilbur Renk, said Nixon was "honest" but "dumb," was morally wrong and should resign. A poll of 100 newspapers, most of them pro-Republican, showed two-thirds of them opposed to Nixon after the disclosure.

The people around Eisenhower began to panic, many talked of losing the election. The Republican National Chairman, Arthur Summerfield, openly argued that Nixon should be kept on the ticket but reportedly every other major Republican on the Eisenhower train was ready to drop Nixon. Sherman Adams and Herbert Brownell telephoned California Senator William Knowland, in Hawaii, to fly back immediately and join the Eisenhower train. Knowland, it was said, would be the substitute for Nixon if needed. Ironically on arrival, Knowland argued for Nixon's retention.

Nixon issued an explanation, a statement of "basic facts" but it was lost in the wave of speculation over whether General Eisenhower was dumping his running-mate. Ike didn't help matters when he talked to reporters informally and said he believed Nixon innocent of any wrong-doing but he would have to prove it. "Of what avail is it for us to carry on this crusade against this business of what has been going on in Washington if we, ourselves, aren't clean as a hound's tooth?"

The press on the Eisenhower train was now openly predicting Nixon's removal and 90% of them were said to be convinced that he was a campaign liability. They seized on the "clean as a hound's tooth" remark as symbolic of Eisenhower's assumption of Nixon guilt. They were saying Nixon would have to quit or be dropped.

Nixon's advisors, primarily William Rogers (named Secretary of State by President Nixon sixteen years later) and Murray Chotiner, urged him to fight it out. Chotiner came up with the idea of a television explanation saying, "Every time you get before an audience, you win them. What we have to do is to get you before the biggest possible audience so that you can talk over the heads of the press to the people. The people, I am convinced, are for you but the press is killing you." They rejected the suggestion that they go on network panel shows ("Meet The Press" had extended an invitation); Chotiner wanted the case stated without interruption by unfriendly press questioners.

The pressures mounted. On Sunday, Harold Stassen sent a 300-word telegram advising resignation, even offering a suggested text for the withdrawal message. That afternoon, Thomas E. Dewey called, urged Nixon to go on television and end with an appeal to the viewers to send in their verdict. Nixon liked the idea.

That night, General Eisenhower called. He, too, urged a television appearance. Nixon asked if Ike would make his position clear after that. Eisenhower said he hoped that wouldn't be necessary. Nixon pushed for an Eisenhower declaration and the Presidential candidate replied, "We will have to wait three or four days after the television show to see what the effect of the program is." Arthur Summerfield said the Republican National Committee would pay the $75,000 cost of the broadcast.

Two days later the broadcast was to originate from NBC studios in Los Angeles. Those days were spent in preparation. The problem of a Nixon counterattack was solved on Monday when the *Chicago Tribune* reported a Stevenson fund solicited from businessmen in Illinois. There was no question of Stevenson receiving money, this was a fund to induce young men "not blessed with independent income" to go into government service, their state salaries supplemented by bonuses from this fund.

Stevenson was virtually alone among Democrats in not attacking Nixon when the *Post* story broke, saying, "Condemnation without all the evidence, a practice all too familiar to us, would be wrong." Nixon supporters were less charitable than Stevenson, Murray Chotiner saying, "He was hiding something—otherwise he would have been at your throat like the rest of them." Whether the Illinois fund was something the Demo-crat was hiding or not (he said it had never been secret) it *did* provide ground for counterattack.

Nixon continued to work on his television script through Tuesday, the day of broadcast. An hour before he was to leave for the television studio, Tom Dewey called. "There has been a meeting of all of Eisen-hower's top advisors. They have asked me to tell you that at the conclu-sion of the broadcast tonight you should submit your resignation to Eisenhower. As you know, I have not shared this point of view, but it is my responsibility to pass this recommendation on to you."

Nixon was stunned.

"Hello," said Dewey, "Can you hear me?"

Slowly Nixon asked, "What does Eisenhower want me to do?"

Dewey hedged, he had not spoken directly to Eisenhower.

Angrily, Nixon refused to tell him what he would do: "Just tell them that I haven't the slightest idea as to what I am going to do and if they want to find out they'd better listen to the broadcast. And tell them I know something about politics too!"

With that, he slammed down the receiver.

Nixon drove to the El Capitan Theatre in Hollywood that night, Tuesday, September 23. The theatre was empty except for television technicians, the press corps was parked in another room with a battery of television sets.

What followed from 9:30 to 10 p.m. that night was one of the most remarkable single performances in the history of politics. It mixed simple and direct response with cutting counterattack with homey touches, so corny that they could be viewed as a satire on political addresses on tele-vision, including wife and (reference to) dog.

He began, "My fellow Americans, I come before you tonight as a candidate for the Vice Presidency and as a man whose honesty and in-tegrity has been questioned." He explained the fund, defended it on legal and moral grounds. He read opinions from auditing and legal firms.

Nixon was sitting at a desk, Mrs. Nixon at his side watching him. When he turned to her, so did the cameras. About half way through the broadcast, he moved out from behind the desk and stood talking directly to the audience. He spelled out his personal finances: a 1950 Oldsmobile, a small equity in a home in California in which his parents lived, $20,000 equity in his house in Washington, no stocks or bonds, a little life insur-ance. He then listed a few debts.

Then came the "hearts and flowers":

> Well, that's about it. That's what we have. And that's what we owe. It isn't very much. But Pat and I have the satisfaction that every

dime that we have got is honestly ours.

I should say this, that Pat doesn't have a mink coat. But she does have a respectable Republican cloth coat, and I always tell her that she would look good in anything.

One other thing I probably should tell you, because if I don't they will probably be saying this about me, too. We did get something, a gift, after the nomination. A man down in Texas heard Pat on the radio mention the fact that our two youngsters would like to have a dog and, believe it or not, the day before we left on this campaign trip we got a message from Union Station in Baltimore, saying they had a package for us. We went down to get it. You know what it was?

It was a little cocker spaniel dog, in a crate that he had sent all the way from Texas—black and white, spotted, and our little girl Tricia, the six-year-old, named it Checkers. And you know, the kids, like all kids, loved the dog, and I just want to say this, right now, that regardless of what they say about it, we are going to keep it.

Nixon then slipped into the political counterattack. First, with subtlety, he called Governor Stevenson a fine man "who inherited a fortune from his father" and added, "But I also feel that it is essential in this country of ours that a man of modest means can also run for President, because, you know—remember, Abraham Lincoln, remember what he said —'God must have loved the common people, he made so many of them'." Then the strokes of counterattack came stronger—the Stevenson fund and the fact that Stevenson's running-mate, Senator John Sparkman of Alabama, had his wife on the payroll. "I would suggest that under the circumstances both Mr. Sparkman and Mr. Stevenson should come before the American people, as I have, and make a complete financial statement as to their financial history. And if they don't it will be an admission that they have something to hide."

It was at this point that Nixon moved to the front of his desk, praised Eisenhower, condemned the "Truman-Acheson Administration," accused the State Department of mistakes that caused the war in Korea, and damned corruption in Washington. Then came the clincher, the plea for public support:

And now, finally, I know that you wonder whether or not I am going to stay on the Republican ticket or resign. Let me say this: I don't believe that I ought to quit, because I am not a quitter. And, incidentally, Pat is not a quitter. After all her name was Patricia Ryan and she was born on Saint Patrick's Day, and you know the Irish never quit.

But the decision, my friends, is not mine. I would do nothing that would harm the possibilities of Dwight Eisenhower to become President of the United States. And for that reason I am submitting to the Republican National Committee tonight through this television broadcast the decision which is theirs to make. Let them decide whether my position on the ticket will help or hurt. And I am going to ask you to help them decide. Wire and write the Republican National Committee whether you think I should stay on or whether I should get off. And whatever their decision is, I will abide by it.

But just let me say this last word. Regardless of what happens, I am going to continue this fight. I am going to campaign up and down America until we drive the crooks and the communists and those that defend them out of Washington. And remember, folks, Eisenhower is a great man. Folks, he is a great man, and a vote for Eisenhower is a vote for what is good for America.

Time had run off, the last few words cut off. He had meant to tell where the telegrams and letters should be sent, where the National Committee was located, but he didn't have time. He didn't need it. Before he left the buildings, the network switchboards lit up and the response poured in. Nixon was not without humor about the "Checkers" speech. As they reached the street, a big Irish setter came bounding up to the Nixons, his tail wagging. Turning to Mrs. Nixon, he said, "Well, at least we got the dog vote tonight."

Sixty million Americans saw or heard the speech. Between one and two million telegrams and letters with three million signatures came in, overwhelmingly pro-Nixon.

Eisenhower asked Nixon to fly to Wheeling, West Virginia where he would be the next day. Ike met the plane, went up the steps and down the aisle and grinned, "You're my boy." They went to Wheeling Stadium for a joint appearance and as they came out, Bill Knowland went up to congratulate Nixon who, emotionally spent, looked up with tears in his eyes. Knowland placed an arm around him, Nixon wept in his shoulder, and news photographers captured the final moment in the "Checkers" crisis.

Republicans were jubilant. The mail ran 350 to 1 in Nixon's favor. Enough letters enclosed campaign contributions to more than pay the $75,000 broadcast charge that Arthur Summerfield had approved. Summerfield was with Eisenhower during the Checkers broadcast and the General turned to him and said, "Well, Arthur, you sure got your money's worth."

Summerfield polled his national committee. He reached 107 members and they were all pro-Nixon. Summerfield said it was "the turning point of the campaign." Democrats were dismayed by the powerful reaction. For many, it demonstrated the brute impact of television in politics. Liberals were appalled by the immodest use of emotional appeal—the dog Checkers, the Republican cloth coat, the poor boy who wants to be President. They scorned the appearance, made jokes. Most of America did not.

Variety shared the liberal dismay. They "reviewed" the broadcast as a soap opera: "Just Plain Dick." Said the review:

> GOP Vice-Presidential candidate Richard M. Nixon, facing an $18,000 gift fund rap, went before the TV cameras last Tuesday (23) in the best tradition of the American soap opera. It was as slick a "production" as anything off the Anne Hummert belt line, parlaying all the schmaltz and human interest of the "Just Plain Bill"—"Our Gal Sunday" genre of weepers.
>
> The only thing missing was the organ background music as Nixon, appealing for a commutation of sentence with a faithful wife as the major prop, turned in a performance that would have gladdened the hearts of the Dancer-Fitzgerald-Sample soaper fraternity. Translated into a commercial suds saga, it would have been a cinch to garner a renewal for at least another 52-week cycle.

Variety, having had its fun over the mawkish emotionalism in the Checkers presentation, offered a "straight" comment: "Regardless of what party or cause the viewer championed, it was a brilliant feat in political journalism. It was, too, a major test for TV, demonstrating once and for all (and something the commercial boys can learn from) that, with a good script, good casting and topflight production, you can't miss."

There have been few telecasts that changed the course of history, perhaps only two that changed political history, the Nixon-Kennedy debates being the other. This was the one in which the medium was the carrier, the message was that of the candidate. It was a virtuoso performance. One can argue that it matched the mood of that moment; at another moment it might seem too corny to be effective. That matters not. The right moment is the only moment in a political race. This single performance by Richard Nixon carried him on to the Vice Presidency and, though future defeats seemed to doom him, was one moment necessary to fulfill his destiny—winning the Presidency in 1968. Without Checkers, Nixon might well have been dropped from the ticket. American history would have been different.

How powerful television was and how few believed it could perform such a miracle. A critique after the fact might show that the issue was quickly dispensed with and the bulk of the performance dealt with other matters, most of them highly personal and seemingly irrelevant to the matter at hand. Perhaps. But the electorate acts with instinct in its measure of a man, issues rarely command the hand that marks the ballot.

It was Nixon's unhappy fate that eight years later, television with similar instancy should serve to deprive him of the Presidency. In that case, television debate did as much for young Senator Kennedy as television did for Richard Nixon in 1952: it caught America's fancy, not as conclusively perhaps, but enough to elect an opponent of Richard Nixon's.

We shall examine the great debates of 1960 later but perhaps we should start with Kennedy's own use of television in other aspects of that campaign. He, too, found it tremendously effective, particularly in overcoming a major handicap, that of being the first Roman Catholic to run for President of the United States.

Kennedy Uses TV to Fight the Catholic Issue.

The Kennedy personality was perfect for television. Marshall McLuhan is one of many to call him "the first TV President." He was handsome, suave, witty, yet serious, obviously bright and exuding sincerity. McLuhan attributes one other element, an apparent indifference to the goal that makes him attractive to the viewer. McLuhan describes him as "a somnambulist, a highly motivated dreamer who prefers to remain insulated from a frightening world." This aloofness is political dynamite on television, says McLuhan who feels Kennedy "had that indifference to power without which the TV candidate merely electrocutes himself."

But that was the style of the man ("style" in connection with Kennedy was ultimately to become a cliche) and not the substance. Substance and issues can be hidden in campaigns. American history is full of campaigns in which the candidates said little of consequence, exposed nothing of their inner beliefs, offered just a passing gesture towards matters of great moment. John Kennedy, even if he chose this route, could not duck one issue. His Catholicism was so well publicized, he could no more ignore it than could Malcolm X pass as a white man.

How to deal with the issue? The opportunity presented itself in Bible Belt country, where Protestant fundamentalism was as strong as the winds that swept across the Texas prairies. The Greater Houston Ministerial Association invited him to discuss religion. He decided to accept, to make an opening statement and then submit to any question the ministers might offer. On September 12, 1960, some 300 ministers and 300 spectators gathered in the ballroom of the Rice Hotel. John Kennedy came in, just before 9 p.m. after a full day of barnstorming across Texas.

His remarks were fairly brief and worthy of note. Some excerpts:

> . . . because I am a Catholic, and no Catholic has ever been elected President, the real issues in this campaign have been obscured—perhaps deliberately in some quarters less responsible than this. So it is apparently necessary for me to state once again—not what kind of church I believed in, for that should be important only to me, but what kind of America I believed in.
>
> I believe in an America where the separation of church and state is absolute—where no Catholic prelate would tell the President (should he be a Catholic) how to act and no Protestant minister would tell his parishioners for whom to vote—where no church or church school is granted any public funds or political preference—and where no man is denied public office merely because his religion differs from the President who might appoint him or the people who might elect him. . . .
>
> I do not speak for my church on public matters—and the church does not speak for me.
>
> Whatever issue may come before me as President, if I should be elected—on birth control, divorce, censorship, gambling, or any other subject—I will make my decision in accordance with these views, in accordance with what my conscience tells me to be in the national interest, and without regard to outside religious pressure or dictate. And no power or threat of punishment could cause me to decide otherwise.
>
> But if the time should ever come—and I do not concede any conflict to be remotely possible—when my office would require me to either violate my conscience, or violate the national interest, then I would resign the office, and I hope any other conscientious public servant would do likewise.
>
> But I do not intend to apologize for these views to my critics of either Catholic or Protestant faith, nor do I intend to disavow either my views or my church in order to win this election. If I should lose on the real issues, I shall return to my seat in the Senate, satisfied that I tried my best and was fairly judged.
>
> But if this election is decided on the basis that 40,000,000 Americans lost their chance of being President on the day they were baptized, then it is the whole nation that will be loser in the eyes of Catholics and non-Catholics around the world, in the eyes of history, and in the eyes of our own people.

When the questions came, he handled them deftly in the spirit of his opening remarks. There were questions about Vatican influence, about Church direction in public life, about an interfaith dedication he failed to attend years ago. Typical of Kennedy's treatment of the Ministerial questions was his reply to a question about South American persecution of Protestant missionaries in Roman Catholic countries. Said Kennedy, "One of the rights I consider to be important is the right of free religious practice, and I would hope that the President would stand for these rights all around the globe without regard to geography, religion, or . . ." He never finished; audience applause drowned out his final words.

That chronicler of candidates, Theodore White, wrote of that remarkable evening in Houston, "He had for the first time more fully and explicitly than any other thinker of his faith defined the personal doctrine of a modern Catholic in a democratic society. How much effect he had that evening no one can tell. He had addressed a sullen, almost hostile audience when he began. He had won the applause of many and the personal sympathies of more; the meeting had closed in respect and friendship. But how far the victory in this hall would extend its glow no one could measure."

Television cameras filmed the appearance and excerpts were on newscasts across the country. Kennedy supporters, however, found a better use for the film. They edited the Houston appearance and carefully placed it on local television stations across the country. It was not shown on network television; that could be a problem since the volatile issue was hard to judge and might backfire in any given community. But used in specific areas where local Kennedy leaders felt the sting of anti-Catholicism, it was a remarkably effective document. As White put it, "Kennedy Volunteers were to use the filmed record over and over again in both Catholic and Protestant areas of the country for the next seven weeks; it was to be their basic document; no measure is available of how many millions saw the film played and replayed."

The Paid Political Telecast.

Paid political broadcasts such as "Checkers" in 1952 and the Kennedy "Catholic" film in 1960 are the exception rather than the rule. They were dramatically effective and capable of attracting large audiences. Most political telecasts of half-hour or one-hour lengths are not, except in the closing days of an exciting campaign.

The more common experience is that political broadcasts of length command a much smaller audience than the regularly scheduled entertainment they replace and that this audience is largely of the faithful, the already devoted followers of the candidate. Political managers much prefer shorter broadcasts including the twenty-second, thirty-second, and one-minute "commercial." These short takes oversimplify, often mislead, and certainly are pure propaganda but, in the words of one astute national political expert, "Your audience can't get away from you." Further, the audience is not likely to be offended—it interrupts their evening for just a passing moment, just as ordinary commercials do. Longer broadcasts, and even those five-minute television postcripts to entertainment, can irritate. Pre-empting a favorite program can infuriate. In 1952, Adlai Stevenson replaced "I Love Lucy" and received a telegram reading "I like Ike and I love Lucy. Drop dead."

The short takes are largely the product of Madison Avenue experts who care less for nicety than for impact, result. At times their search for impact can strike for the belly, little caring if it is above or below the belt. Some classic examples were rolled out by the Democrats in the 1964 Presidential campaign. One showed a little girl licking an ice cream cone as a soothing woman's voice explains that people used to explode nuclear bombs in the air and the radioactive fallout made children die. A treaty would ban that but a man who wants to be President voted against it, "His name is Barry Goldwater." And if he's elected they might start testing again. As she continues, a ticking Geiger counter wipes out her sound and then an announcer urges the audience to vote for Johnson, "the stakes are too high for you to stay at home."

Even more devastating was the "Daisy" commercial for Lyndon Johnson. This brief epic showed a little girl in a meadow, picking petals off a daisy. She counts: "One, two, three . . ." and then a male voice overrides her and growing louder says, "Ten, nine, eight . . ." counting down to "three, two, one, zero." The screen goes black and suddenly there is the mushroom cloud of an atomic blast. As the shock waves begin to fade, the voice of Lyndon Johnson intones, "These are the stakes. To make a world in which all of God's children can live, or go into the dark . . ." And over the dark screen, the announcer's voice again, "The stakes are too high for you to stay home."

Republicans howled in protest at this use of television, this obvious attempt to portray Barry Goldwater as a trigger-happy candidate who would recklessly sanction the use of atomic weapons. Even Johnson's running mate, Hubert Humphrey, called the spot "unfortunate." The issue was particularly sensitive to Republicans. Senator Goldwater had discussed, on ABC's "Issues and Answers," the possibility of using low-yield atomic weapons in Vietnam to "defoliate" the jungle and expose enemy supply lines. There was quite a controversy over this suggestion, one which ignored the Senator's additional comment that he did not think this was a course to follow.

NBC, which ran the commercial for the first time during "Monday Night at the Movies" on September 7, 1964 received thousands of telephoned protests. Republican National Chairman Dean Burch called the "Daisy" spot "a new low in American politics."

Burch, by the way, met with Democratic National Chairman John Bailey for a biennial ritual, the signing of a "Code of Fair Campaign Practices" under the sponsorship of the Fair Campaign Practices Committee. He took the occasion to rip into Bailey for the offending use of television. Bailey said the image of Goldwater was one he himself had created and you could hardly blame Democrats for exploiting it. The spots, however, were subsequently dropped.

Other Democratic television spots, less controversial, also punched away at Goldwater. One simply showed a telephone ringing and ringing until a hand reaches for it. The hand stops. A voice asks, "Who do *you* want answering the phone when Khrushchev calls?" A particularly effective spot shows a pair of hands slowly tearing a Social Security card in two. It was to encourage the thought that Goldwater opposed Social Security. Among older Americans, it had considerable impact.

On the Republican side of the TV picture was a film that became famous, yet never saw air. It was called "Choice" and was scheduled to be shown to a daytime audience on NBC.

Democrats got their hands on a copy of "Choice" and it became an underground-film sensation in Washington. It was hard for a news reporter to avoid invitations to private showings by the Democrats. They hoped, correctly as it turned out, for a great turning of the press stomach and resulting stories attacking the Republican film as scurrilous. The film, sponsored by "Mothers for a Moral America," a front created by the Citizens for Goldwater-Miller, was to depict the low state of America under Lyndon Johnson. It offered lurid scenes of Negroes rioting in the streets, strip teasers, teenagers in exotic and erotic dances, looting, drugs, a Mardi Gras scene with a man in a fig leaf, etc. There was even a man, suggestive of Lyndon Johnson, racing in an auto and throwing a beer can out the window to remind one of reports that LBJ had been drinking a can of beer while racing his Lincoln Continental around the LBJ ranch. And there was a long, lingering shot of a rack of pornographic books, the one in the middle bearing the title *Jazz Me Baby.*

With the showing of the film, gleeful Democrats also provided an alleged transcript of the planning meeting of the film makers who created "Choice." They talked of "appeal to raw, naked emotions." They spoke of appealing to the rural audience which considers city life evil: "This film will obviously and frankly just play on their prejudice." They talked of finding "powerful film, gut film" and repeatedly called for appealing to "fear and anxiety."

Even as these private showings were being "sponsored" by Democrats, the President of NBC, Robert Kintner had demanded deletions, including a scene showing a topless bathing suit. He termed it an "appallingly tasteless production" and called it to the attention of Candidate Goldwater and the Republican National Committee. Goldwater who had not seen the film, checked on it, told reporters that it was "nothing but a racist film" and immediately ordered that it never be shown. On television, it never was.

Four years later, each party was compelled to withdraw commercials considered "too rough."

The Republicans had a spot silently showing battle scenes in Vietnam, rioting in the streets, starving children. Between each of these grim sequences was inserted a passing close-up of Hubert Humphrey. He grins in one of these. It ended with the Nixon campaign slogan "This time vote like your whole world depended on it." The Democratic National Committee called it "the epitome of gutter practices." It was withdrawn from the Nixon television campaign though not before Nixon's campaign manager, John Mitchell said, "It ill behooves the Democratic National Committee to complain about this spot when compared with its media attempts to relate Richard Nixon to the atomic bomb and the vilification the Humphrey campaign had heaped on Governor Agnew."

He referred to commercials which the *Washington Post* called "the old mushroom cloud bit, employed to emphasize Barry Goldwater's supposed weakness for nuclear weapons . . . exhumed to dramatize the same insinuations about Mr. Nixon" and a series of commercials hitting at Spiro Agnew. The Maryland Governor, Nixon's running mate, had made some unfortunate slips of the tongue during the campaign and the Democrats were capitalizing on them. One spot showed a man laughing over a screen with the message "Spiro T. Agnew for Vice President" and ends with the thought "If it weren't so serious, it would be funny." Another emphasizes a beating heart to remind the audience that Agnew would be just a heart-beat away from the Presidency.

The *Washington Post* during the 1968 campaign took issue with some of the tasteless commercials, particularly the one intercutting a grinning Humphrey with scenes of violence: "Concededly, the political commercial can be a blunt instrument and as the campaign has warmed up, some of them, on both sides of the battle, have gotten increasingly blunt . . . If, as NBC argues, a provision of law which forbids censorship of political broadcasts is really so sweeping that it forces networks to air anything, however tasteless—which we somehow doubt—then that law ought to be changed. In the meantime, the Nixon-Agnew ad men need to strike a somewhat finer line between what is fair comment, whether funny or unfunny, and what is sick."

Before the campaign was over, the Nixon forces spent an estimated $12 million on political advertising. Humphrey who had money troubles early in the campaign, spent perhaps $9 million. Most of this money went to television though Nixon made superb use of radio, a medium most politicians were forgetting. His ad agency representative said, "It's a terrific medium because it's flexible—no production costs—and it's a bargain."

The Costs of TV in Campaigns.

Overall, politicians were estimated to have spent $36 to $40 million on television during 1968. Senator Robert Kennedy, before his death, was said to have spent $7 million just in the primaries. Some place the television costs at $50 million or more. It was the most expensive campaign in history. One FCC report said it was double the cost of 1964.

In Presidential years, campaign costs for everything including television have escalated from $140 million in 1952, to $155 million in 1956, to $175 million in 1960, $200 million in 1964 and $250 to $300 million in 1968.

Interviewed by Walter Cronkite on the night of the Indiana primary in 1968, Robert Kennedy said, "Where the expenditures go is for television. We could cut down 80% of our expenditures if television wasn't so expensive."

On the other hand, there is a great deal of television exposure, perhaps the most valuable kind, that does not cost a penny. It is in the day-to-day newscasts and the special documentaries during political years.

Before he left for the New Hampshire primary in the winter of 1968, I had lunch with Senator Eugene McCarthy. He laughed and said he planned to use television a lot, and not spend very much. He said that a serious candidate can always get a lot of exposure and also had the opportunity to demand equal time. He planned to do both. When I suggested that equal time did not always come easily, the Senator archly replied, "The networks don't act from principle, they react from fear."

McCarthy was to get a great deal of television exposure in the year that followed. He took to the medium easily, was one of the most comfortable and convincing of all candidates using television. He was so good that a rumor persisted that somewhere in the McCarthy entourage was a disciple of McLuhan, a television expert that molded the candidate in the epitome of McLuhan's "cool" man. The Senator denies this. After the election, he told me that he, too, had heard such reports. "If they saw the last minute changes we made because of budgets and other problems, they would hardly consider that an expert was preparing the broadcasts. I didn't do a thing in 1968 different than I had been doing on television when I first ran for office in Minnesota."

McCarthy was a favorite of the Sunday panel programs. He even participated in one, before the California primary, in which he used his biting wit mercilessly to "abuse" the three-man panel on "Face the Nation." His supporters enjoyed it so and felt him effective enough to warrant purchasing the videotape and showing it again on "paid" time. One of the panelists, David Broder, later said that he, Martin Agronsky and David Schoumacher were called "the three stooges."

1968, as the Presidential election before it, did not have as much "free" time as in 1960 after Congress suspended the equal time rules to permit the Kennedy-Nixon debates (we'll examine this fully in the next chapter) but the 1959 Congressional action permanently freed the Sunday panel programs. Richard Nixon seemed to be ducking these until very late in the 1968 campaign when he finally agreed to go on "Face the Nation" and then "Meet the Press." He did so after the Democrats made campaign issue out of the fact that he had not been on such broadcasts for several years and certainly not during the campaign.

There had been debates over whether candidates should duck interrogation and stick to a controlled television environment, one they control. Nixon had done a series of question-and-answer broadcasts with "typical" citizens but the atmosphere for those was carefully created. Both Nixon and Humphrey, on election eve, held two-hour-long telethons taking questions from voters which their aides carefully screened.

F. Clifton White, the perceptive manager of Barry Goldwater's campaign for the Presidential nomination, looked back at Nixon's 1968 campaign and said, "I think the fact that Mr. Nixon did accept (Sunday panel appearances) even though toward the end of the campaign, indicated the opportunity we have here both through our own television medium, press and the public, to say that a candidate for public office is going to have to expose himself to the public through a medium that large numbers of people are going to observe . . . beyond the controlled medium, where they do it themselves. They will use the control and I think they have a legitimate right there, because I think the candidate had the right to present himself in what he feels is the best posture in making the points he thinks are most important and significant, and then in addition to that, I think the public should demand that he also be exposed to the television medium in an uncontrolled situation."

Nixon did very well at the two such appearances and, as his subsequent handling of Presidential news conferences proved, is most able at the give-and-take of such encounters. There are added values in handling antagonistic questions in terms of TV image.

Outside of extraordinary presentations or moments of high public interest and involvement, the most persuasive television influence in a campaign comes in the coverage given a candidate in regularly scheduled newscasts. The audience for Sunday panel programs, even in election years, is fairly small—though this is swollen by the widespread coverage given these broadcasts in all media, including broadcasting. On the other hand, the evening newscast on CBS or NBC has an audience of fifteen to twenty million and ABC half that.

More and more, political campaigns try to tailor the candidate to television exposure. Timetables of major appearances are rearranged to compensate for TV deadlines. Exclusive interviews are granted. Newspaper reporters are kept waiting until TV commitments are met.

It is not as easy for a candidate to grasp the impact of short film clips on television. His publicity people can't give him a scrapbook of clippings as they can with newspaper coverage. It soon is evident, however, from the comments of the people he meets and the mail he gets, that the public reacts strongly to television news.

The Effect of Vote Projections.

In this regard there is concern over one impact of television reporting, its last impact in any campaign. There are those who feel that network "projections" of election returns can hurt the turn-out in areas where the polls are still open.

Networks are sensitive to this, also. Dr. Frank Stanton of CBS has long advocated a 24-hour voting day, with all polls closing at the same moment. NBC and ABC have advocated a variation of this—a single closing time across the nation, all polls closing simultaneously.

One who is convinced that projecting the vote can effect the turn-out is Pierre Salinger who left the White House Press Secretaryship to run for the Senate in California in 1964. He believes that network projections of Johnson's landslide victory caused 300,000 voters to stay home in California.

That year, Art Buchwald turned his considerable satirical talent on the topic and envisioned a voter who refused to be discouraged by news reports and planned to vote anyway, the polls in California still being open. A friend tries to stop him and asks, "Do you want Walter Cronkite to be mad at you?"

Salinger take the matter soberly, however, and says, "I seriously question that the right to cover an election also includes the right to discourage voting by declaring that your vote or mine can't influence the outcome." He concedes that it would not have made a difference in his own defeat (he lost by over 100,000 votes at a time when the head of his ticket was overwhelmingly the winner in California) but calls the process "a grave threat to the democratic process." Sociologists examined California, under a CBS grant, and found no evidence that the early projections inhibited the vote, either in the numbers that turned out nor in the man they voted for. Other studies reached similar conclusions. Voters expressed concern that a bandwagon effect could result but gave no evidence that it really had.

Some of the 1964 studies implied that the possibility existed that television could affect voter turnout in Western states if the election were close, 1964 being a landslide. NBC conducted a study in 1968 to find out. Using a sample of 2,000 voters (one-third of them in the East for contrast), NBC concluded that television had minimal effect in changing voting patterns in states where the polls were still open.

Voters who changed either their turnout plans or switched candidates in the West were not significantly different from voters in the East who did not look at television returns before voting. Voters in Western states were statistically the same as fellow Westerners whether or not they were exposed to television election returns before the polls closed. NBC said, "We can conclude with a high degree of confidence that television election broadcasts have no detectable influence on voting behavior—in *close* elections, as well as in *landslide* contests."

A Congressional examination of the question before the 1968 election concluded that no restrictions on the broadcasting of election returns were warranted. One study showed that voters didn't fully trust the projections (the networks have been wrong on a number of occasions) and tended to rely more heavily on raw vote totals and electoral vote totals.

Salinger recommends, as a means of avoiding "electronic disenfranchisement," the 24-hour poll closing at the same time. It should be noted, however, that in 1968 CBS News experimented with the polling of voters as they left the voting booth. It was found that many voters were willing to reveal how they cast their ballot and, with proper samples, these revelations could be projected with a remarkable degree of accuracy to give a final result. This practice could negate the values of the 24-hour plan should the nation elect to go that way and the networks decide to stay in the projection business.

It should be clear that these electronic projections are *not*, as Salinger and other critics (including many in Congress) seem to think, a "prediction." The systems used were brought to a high polish by CBS News President Richard Salant using Lou Harris and his organization to set up the first VPA, Vote Profile Analysis. They are simple sampling techniques, exactly like those used by pollsters in creating statistical samples. They do not speculate on what people say they are going to do but are samples based on actual votes cast in the past.

States and Congressional districts are broken down into model precincts. These are chosen to reflect the electoral ecology of that area accurately. Part-time employees phone in the results from these precincts which number just a few thousand. As representative of the whole, the model is translated by computer quickly to show how each state was voting.

This is not a use of prediction. It is a scientific sampling, small enough to gather quickly and project onto the bigger scene, hopefully reflective of the total and thus giving the state-by-state result.

Pre-election pollsters, who faced a very tough time in 1968 when they showed Nixon far ahead until the closing days of the campaign, have similarly been criticized for "predicting." They stress that they simply tell what is happening at any given time, not what will happen in the future, George Gallup defended his craft in 1968 by saying, "The fact still remains that a President is elected when the people go to the polls. Not when the polls go to the people."

Television reports only the voting trends it can identify by magnifying sample precincts to represent the whole, precincts chosen because they would do just that. Some confusion results from the tense employed by broadcasters as they describe the returns. They often report returns as if the story changes: "Nixon is pulling ahead" or "Humphrey is starting to rally in Missouri" or "Wallace is slipping in Arkansas." The fact remains, saying so does not make it so. The only votes that count in the end are those already sealed in ballot boxes and voting machines. The official count makes them official; television does not.

CHAPTER 10

IN TV DEBATE GATHERED

WHEN ABRAHAM LINCOLN debated Stephen Douglas in Illinois, it attracted a large audience for its time. Estimates range from a low of 1,500 people to a high of over 15,000 attending one of those seven debates. When Richard Nixon debated John F. Kennedy on television, 102 years later, the audience for the first broadcast was estimated at 75 million.

The ratio in audience between the first Lincoln-Douglas encounter and the first Nixon-Kennedy debate has been placed at 6,250 to 1!

NBC estimated that 120 million persons in the United States saw one or more of the debates. Individual broadcasts recorded 65 to 75 million persons each, the average was about 71,000,000 viewers. In *The Making of the President, 1960,* Theodore H. White called the television debates "a revolution in American politics. This revolution had not been made by one of the three men on the screen—John F. Kennedy, Richard M. Nixon or Howard K. Smith, the moderator. It was a revolution born of the ceaseless American genius in technology; its sole agent and organizer had been the common American television set . . . it was to permit the simultaneous gathering of all the tribes of America to ponder their choice between two chieftains in the largest political convocation in the history of man."

The idea for the television debates was first put forward on a radio broadcast in 1952. Senator Blair Moody (Dem., Mich.), appearing on CBS Radio's "The People's Platform" on July 27 of that year said, "I think it might be very good for CBS or NBC or someone else to put on a series of debates between General Eisenhower and Governor Stevenson . . . because I would like to hear the relative views of these two men contrasted with each other."

Dr. Frank Stanton of CBS wrote Senator Moody and pointed out that the Congress would have to change Section 315 of the Communications Act of 1934 to permit such debates. Stanton sought reaction from the candidates themselves. Eisenhower's advertising agency consultant, Ben Duffy, President of Batten, Barton, Durstine and Osborn, felt the debates would be great for television but not for Ike who, Duffy felt sure, could win without them. Governor Stevenson was said to be "terribly eager" to participate.

NBC wired both candidates offering time for a debate on both NBC radio and television. The offer was declined. NBC then offered side-by-side interviews of each candidate, each of them sitting in a separate studio. This, too, was declined.

What was Section 315 that inhibited Frank Stanton? The key line in the brief three paragraph statute reads, "If any licensee shall permit any person who is a legally qualified candidate for any public office to use a broadcasting station, he shall afford equal opportunity to all other such candidates for that office in the use of such broadcasting station."

That means that General Eisenhower and Governor Stevenson on television would compel the networks to give "equal time" to all other candidates for President. Enough to give Frank Stanton pause? Well, the next time Ike and Adlai ran, in 1956, there were at least seventeen candidates for President. The other fifteen candidates received less than 1% of the vote but would have had to get equal time. The candidate for the Christian Nationalist Party in 1956 is said to have received a total of eight votes. There were 62,000,000 votes cast in 1956.

In that year, Section 315 arose in a silly matter. The President was scheduled to deliver a talk on behalf of the United Community Fund. CBS would not carry it after the FCC advised that it would then be obliged to give equal time to all Presidential candidates. Adlai Stevenson wrote CBS assuring it that he would not ask for time. CBS sent for and received similar assurances from the candidates of thirteen other parties before it agreed to schedule President Eisenhower.

Later in the campaign there was a crisis in the Middle East. Britain, France and Israel invaded Egypt. The President addressed the nation on all networks. Governor Stevenson this time demanded equal time to express his views on the crisis. The FCC was asked for advice. The FCC said it could not grant an immediate ruling, the issue was too complex. With the election very close, the networks decided to grant Stevenson the time. Afterwards the FCC ruled that they didn't have to, that the President had addressed the nation in his role as President, not as a candidate.

Such incidents have haunted broadcasters from the earliest days of election coverage. Early in 1952, William F. Schneider declared himself a Republican candidate for President and demanded equal time of CBS.

The network refused, said he was not a serious candidate, was just seeking personal publicity. The FCC ruled otherwise under Section 315 of the Communications Act. CBS gave Schneider two half-hours on the network. That was more than the Republican party gave him—William F. Schneider could not even get a ticket to the 1952 Republican convention.

Section 315 is Amended.

One perennial candidate for high office, including the Presidency, was a Chicago carpenter named Lar Daly, who insisted on being called Lar "American First" Daly, who campaigned in a red, white and blue "Uncle Sam" suit with high hat, satin-lapeled jacket and striped trousers. Daly, no man to fuss over protocol or party, filed for Mayor of Chicago in 1959 on both the Democratic and Republican tickets. It was his thirteenth try for public office.

Mr. Daly was a careful television viewer and kept records of his opponents' appearances on local television. He compiled a list of five such appearances and then fired off a 2,000-word telegram to the Federal Communications Commission asking for equal time.

Two years earlier, the FCC had turned down a similar request. Never had the Commission granted equal time for appearances on newscasts. This time it did. In a four to three vote, on February 19, 1959 the FCC ruled that the Chicago stations must give free and equal time to the man in the "Uncle Sam" suit.

The industry was shocked. Among the five instances cited by Daly were brief film clips of the major candidates filing their nominating petitions, the incumbent Mayor opening the annual March of Dimes drive, and the Mayor greeting the President of Argentina as he arrived on a formal visit to Chicago. Three of the four Chicago stations, following the FCC directive, agreed to give Lar Daly sixty-six minutes of time. He used it to express his position in the Mayor's race including, incidentally, his suggestions that public schools be abolished and that gambling be made legal.

The fourth station, WBBM-TV (owned and operated by CBS) protested the FCC ruling and appealed for reconsideration. Dramatically, as the FCC started hearings, CBS cancelled a "Face the Nation" appearance of Senator Hubert Humphrey because he might be a candidate for President in 1960. Humphrey, denying this at that moment, sharply responded that the networks were engaged in a little high-powered lobbying.

Indeed, on July 26, CBS offered that rare network phenomenon, an editorial, on the topic. Dr. Stanton personally spoke to the issue, then before the Congress, and said that without remedial legislation "we will have no choice but to turn our microphones and television cameras away from all candidates during the campaign periods."

Congress amended Section 315 to solve the Lar Daly "problem." It exempted *bona fide* newscasts, news-interviews, news-documentaries (providing the appearance of the candidate on same was incidental to the subjects covered), and live coverage of *bona fide* news events including political conventions.

Early in 1960, legislation was proposed to provide "free" time to candidates. The cost of a political campaign was going up rapidly, primarily the increased cost for broadcast time. NBC offered a series of eight hour-long editions of "Meet The Press" to the Presidential nominees for joint appearances. "Meet The Press" was now exempt from the restrictions of Section 315.

Earlier, on the day of Nixon's nomination in Chicago, NBC proposed a series of Great Debates and on that July 27th reached John F. Kennedy first (the other networks had similar offers in hand). He accepted immediately, eagerly and without qualification. Nixon issued an acceptance that night with certain provisions attached to the acceptance. The other network proposals were also accepted.

Congress went into a post-convention session and, with both candidates now willing to debate on television, earlier proposed legislation for free time was dropped. Instead, on August 24, the House approved Senate Joint Resolution 207 which suspended Section 315 for the 1960 campaign.

Television debates were now possible.

To Debate or Not to Debate.

A number of Nixon supporters urged him not to debate. In subsequent years similar advice has been given the "in's" suggesting that debates did not favor the well-exposed, much publicized incumbent but rather his lesser known opponent.

President Eisenhower joined the chorus of opponents. He was described as "very much opposed" to television debates, feeling the man in office would be second-guessed by the man on the sidelines. Warned Eisenhower, "Don't build him up by appearing with him on television."

Nixon, however, was perfectly willing to take on Kennedy. It is said that he was confident he would win a debate after watching Kennedy's acceptance speech in Los Angeles. Nixon felt Kennedy spoke too fast and that his normal use of words was too complex to appeal to the average voter. Nixon, of course, had scored remarkably well on television in two previous campaigns, particularly during the "Checkers" appearance. He had been a college debating champ. Furthermore, Nixon did not want to appear to be ducking a fight.

There was one more, major reason. In the debates, he could face an audience of millions of Democrats, Independents and the all-important "undecided" vote. Regular political broadcasts had little appeal to anybody other than the party faithful. In 1960, Democrats outnumbered Republicans three to one in registration. This was a chance to get to them.

CBS and NBC had offered eight hours of time, ABC three hours. The value of this time, if purchased, was about $2,000,000. The networks made it clear that this was not "free" time, that they meant to exercise editorial control. NBC saw no objection to "appropriate" sponsorship of the debates but CBS publicly opposed sponsorship and the question was closed.

On August 9, the first meeting was held at the Waldorf-Astoria in New York to discuss the debates. The network committee consisted of the news chiefs, John Daly for ABC, Sig Mickelson for CBS, William McAndrew for NBC, and Joseph Keeting of Mutual. Kennedy was represented by J. Leonard Reinsch and William Wilson; Nixon by Fred Scribner, Herbert Klein, Carroll P. Newton and Edward "Ted" Rogers. They agreed on having debates. The Nixon people wanted a single, "sudden-death" debate; the Kennedy advisors wanted five. They agreed on four, all to be completed by October 21 (the Democrats wanted it later), all to be worked into the candidates' travel schedules by mutual agreement.

Kennedy's TV expert, Leonard Reinsch, was terribly confident. "Every time we get those two fellows on the screen side by side, we're going to gain and he's going to lose."

On August 31, they met again to discuss format. In his telegram of acceptance, Nixon had stipulated that the debates be held without prepared text or notes, without interruptions, and with time for questioning by panels of newsmen. The negotiators agreed that the first and fourth debates consist of opening statements (Kennedy getting first position in the first debate, Nixon going on first in the fourth debate), questions from the newsmen, and closing statements by the candidates. This format was set by the Nixon-Kennedy representatives who rejected Mickelson's proposal of an "Oregon" style debate in which the candidates questioned each other.

It was agreed by all sides that a pure debate should be rejected, it would not hold an audience. The Lincoln-Douglas debates were "pure" and lasted three hours each, with an hour for the opening debater, ninety minutes for the other man and the remaining half-hour for the first speaker. No panel questioned them.

They also agreed on dates and places. The first debate would be produced by CBS News for the "pool" in Chicago on September 26. The second would be by NBC on October 7, the third to be produced by ABC on October 13 with one candidate in New York and the other in Los

Angeles, and ABC would produce the last debate in New York on October 21.

There was disagreement on the format of the second and third debates, the networks still wanting "Oregon" format, the candidates' representatives insisting (and prevailing later) on a format that called for a question to the first candidate, a comment by the second candidate, a question for the second, a comment by the first and so on. There was disagreement over the make-up of the newsman panel and here the networks prevailed. They insisted that the panels for debates one and four consist of network newsmen only, the panels for debates two and three be split with two network reporters and two newsmen from the print media. The Kennedy representatives were particularly adamant about more newspaper men on the panels but the networks stuck to their suggested arrangement.

The First Debate.

The first broadcast was produced by Don Hewitt and moderated by Howard K. Smith, both of CBS. The panel of newsmen included Bob Fleming (ABC), Stuart Novins (CBS), Sander Vanocur (NBC), and Charles Warren of Mutual. The first debate was to be limited to domestic issues with opening statements of eight minutes each, questions and closing statements of three minutes each.

Kennedy crammed for the night carefully. His staff had a Sears Roebuck foot locker full of research material, their portable campaign research library. For twenty-four hours at the Knickerbocker Hotel in Chicago, they worked to condense the material to fifteen typewritten pages covering a dozen subject areas.

The morning of the debate, September 26, they met with the candidate for a session of questions and answers. Kennedy rejected their suggested eight-minute opening and dictated another of his own. The rest of the morning, the advisors grilled John F. Kennedy on the issues. It ended with Kennedy dispatching them to research some questions he had raised on his own.

The Democratic candidate then had lunch with his brother Robert, Theodore Sorensen and pollister Lou Harris. After lunch, Kennedy spoke to the United Brotherhood of Carpenters and Joiners. They had heard Nixon early that morning and proved to be an extremely hostile audience. It is said they hoped to psychologically disturb the Republican candidate. To Kennedy they were friendly. After his talk, the Senator returned to his room at the Ambassador East Hotel and napped until 5 p.m. Arising, he lay on the bed in a white T-shirt and army pants, answering questions from brother Bob, Sorensen, Harris and the researchers Richard Goodwin and Meyer Feldman. The researchers had reduced the essential material to fact cards which the candidate gaily sent spinning to the floor after each topic was covered.

Richard Nixon, in contrast, was bone tired. After addressing the union audience, he returned to his room at the Pick-Congress and went into seclusion, only Mrs. Nixon present. His frantic television advisors were unable to reach him with details of the setting of the debate and related matters. He did take a long phone call from running mate Henry Cabot Lodge who, it is said, urged him to be careful to avoid the "assassin image."

When he left the hotel for the CBS studio, a television advisor was allowed to share his auto with him and hastily brief him. The ride took ten minutes.

Kennedy, meanwhile, had dinner in his room and dressed. He pocketed a stop watch and headed for the studio. He arrived at 7:30, about an hour before air time.

Richard Nixon got there a few minutes earlier and had the bad luck to strike an already injured knee against the car door. The knee, badly hurt in a similar accident at Greensboro, North Carolina, suffered a painful crack.

Executives of all three networks met the candidates as they arrived. Nixon was taken before the cameras that he might be seen "on set." His advisors asked for minor changes in the lighting which were done. Kennedy then went before the lights for a similar three-minute "look-see." No changes were asked for nor made.

The top CBS make-up expert was flown in from New York but neither candidate availed himself of her services. Frances Arvold, later teased about Nixon's make-up, was limited to making up the network newsmen. Nixon had vetoed the suggestion of Ted Rogers that he wear make-up. Instead he asked Ev Hart of his own staff to apply some "beard stick" powder (Max Factor's "Lazy Shave"). Kennedy had a dark tan from open-car campaigning in California and decided to go without make-up of any kind.

Don Hewitt, who was director as well as producer, had wanted an audience. Failing that, he extended the audience concept to the panel of newsmen, seating them with their backs to the camera. He described them as "sort of the front row. The (television) audience was sitting back behind the cameras and the reporters were sort of asking questions that the audience would have asked had they been there." Hewitt planned to use reaction shots, the showing of one candidate listening while the other talked. Ted Rogers objected to this (the Kennedy people wanted it) because Rogers felt Nixon's appearance was critical and that this would distract the audience from what was said. Hewitt's superiors told him to shoot the broadcast as he saw it. He did.

Rogers also requested that Hewitt avoid left profile shots of Nixon. As it happened, no profile shots were used. Nixon personally asked Hewitt to avoid taking reaction shots of him while he was wiping perspiration off his brow. Hewitt agreed but inadvertently included one such wiping during a wide shot.

At 8:30 p.m. (9:30 in the East), the first debate took air. Howard K. Smith said, "Good evening. The television and radio networks of the United States and their affiliated stations are proud to provide facilities for a discussion of issues in the current political campaign by the two major candidates for the Presidency."

After the ground rules were explained, Kennedy spoke first and came out attacking. He talked about unemployment, the Puerto Rican and Negro victims of discrimination, the plight of the farmers, the medical costs for the aged, underpaid teachers, and the failure of the Eisenhower Administration. He said for eight years America was stuck on dead-center and he wanted to move ahead. Nixon was later to call it a "very shrewd, carefully calculated appeal, with subtle overtones, that would have great impact on a television audience." Nixon also observed "he spoke as effectively as I have ever heard him"—so much for that earlier evaluation by Nixon of Kennedy's shortcomings as a television speaker.

Nixon went on to defend the eight years of Eisenhower, calling it the greatest period of progress in American history. He said that the Republicans "cared" about the downtrodden every bit as much as the Democrats, the only difference was how to solve the problems. Kennedy wanted costly Federal programs; Nixon wanted emphasis on individual iniative and private enterprise. The difference, he implied, was between a bureaucratic society and a free society.

Then came the questions. One, Nixon conceded, was especially damning. In an August 24 newscast, President Eisenhower had been asked, "What major decisions of your Administration has the Vice President participated in?" Ike replied, "If you give me a week, I might think of one."

The President was chagrined to find that remark given wide publicity and called Nixon to explain it. He was being facetious and never expected the press to take it seriously. The press, by the way, at the next Eisenhower news conference, failed to ask the same question again.

As Nixon feared, the question came up during the first debate. Sander Vanocur of NBC asked it and Nixon fielded a reply but, he later observed, "I am sure that to millions of unsophisticated televiewers, this question had been most effective in raising a doubt in their minds with regard to one of my strongest campaign themes and assets—my experience as Vice President."

Nixon's weakness appeared to be his reliance on normal techniques of debate, rebutting and refuting, correcting his opponent's inconsistencies or errors. Nixon addressed himself to his opponent. Kennedy addressed himself to the television audience.

The debate ended at the appointed time. The candidates shook hands. Newsmen asked them who had won and Nixon said that would be known on Election Day.

He returned to his hotel suite and got the first inkling of bad news about his appearance. His longtime personal secretary, Rose Mary Woods, said her parents had called from Ohio asking if Nixon were ill. They said he looked pale and tired. His own mother then called and also asked if he was feeling all right. His doctor arrived in the suite and told him, "You looked weak and pale and tired tonight on TV because, in fact, you *are* weak and pale and tired—even though you don't feel that way at all, in your own mind." Nixon weighed himself, discovered that he weighed 160 pounds, ten pounds below his normal weight and the lightest he had been in the last thirty years.

During the next few days, private and public polls showed that the general public thought Kennedy was the winner. Newspapers hedged, perhaps because of the sensitiveness of declaring a winner. Many called it a "dead heat." Mr. Nixon felt that newspapers called it close because they listened for content. He noted that those who listened to the debate on radio instead of television felt he had won. Ralph McGill of the *Atlanta Constitution* agreed. Kennedy looked better, he wrote, but of persons listening on radio, "They unanimously thought Mr. Nixon had the better of it."

This was little comfort to Nixon—the big audience was watching television.

The *Chicago Daily News* added its own element of excitement to the post-debate period. It ran a story headlined "Was Nixon Sabotaged by TV Make-up Artists?" and quoted the business agent of the Make-up Artists and Hair Stylists of America, John Hall, as saying that it was an unprofessional job. The story was repeated widely, CBS was much criticized. A few days later, the *Daily News* ran a follow-up story quoting Herb Klein as saying Nixon was made up by his own man. Ted Rogers pointed out, "No TV camera, no make-up man can hide bone weariness, physical fatigue."

The association between Richard Nixon and theatrical make-up remained in the public mind for years to come. Reflecting on the 1968 campaign, Nixon's TV advisor Frank Shakespeare recalled, "The single greatest request that we had from international networks, from networks in Europe, and networks in the United States, from picture magazines, from newspapers had to do with a rather extraordinary subject. Everyone wanted a film, or photograph, or to write about Richard Nixon putting his make-up on." The impact of the first debate was a lasting one.

Nixon's "loss" was serious, not on any scale of debating points but in terms of Kennedy's new stature. It didn't matter that there were three more debates. It didn't even matter who won unless the winning was overwhelming (and none were). What mattered was that "young" John Kennedy was now at an equal plane, a serious candidate, able to hold his own and even beat the debating master. He had taken a quantum step up. Ike had warned, "Don't build him up." He was "up" now.

The Second Debate.

The second debate, on October 7, was to be held in Cleveland originally but facility problems prevented that. Washington was chosen. The air time was 7:30 p.m. EDT. The producer was NBC Vice President Julian Goodman (later President of the network) and the moderator was Frank McGee of NBC. The panel included ABC's Edward P. Morgan and CBS's Paul Niven as well as two non-network reporters, Alvin Spivack of UPI and Hal Levy of *Newsday.*

Subject matter was unlimited. There were no formal statements, only answers to questions and replies to answers of the opponent. The first was limited to two-and-a-half minutes per answer, the latter to one-and-a-half minutes per rebuttal or comment.

Tension from the campaign was being felt. The Kennedy people were unhappy over the lighting. Senator Kennedy wanted to know why there were more lights at his side of the set. Brother Bob Kennedy, standing in Nixon's spot before the broadcast, wanted to know why there were more lights on *that* side. After thirty minutes, they were satisfied. Nixon took only five minutes to be satisfied.

Nixon brought his own make-up man, Stan Lawrence, a professional who stayed with him for the remaining debates. Nixon looked better for another reason. Dr. Malcolm Todd had prescribed four rich milk shakes a day. The candidate had regained the lost weight.

The director, Frank Slingland of NBC, took a rather remarkable precaution during the broadcast. He counted each reaction shot, to make sure that each candidate had an equal number. He timed each one to grant stop-watch equality.

This debate dealt with foreign policy, primarily, including Castro, the U-2 spy plane incident, and the defense of Quemoy and Matsu. Nixon did very well and was flooded with congratulations. One newspaper chain reported "Nixon is back in the ball game." James Reston in the

New York Times wrote, "Nixon clearly made a comeback, came out ahead."

The Third Debate.

The third debate, in terms of content, was nothing spectacular. They went over the Quemoy and Matsu debate again and moved on to bigotry, labor unions, and gold outflow. Nixon criticized Harry Truman's use of questionable language.

The third debate, however, was the first truly electronic debate. ABC's Donald Coe produced with Nixon originating in Los Angeles and Kennedy in New York. The moderator was William Shadel of ABC and the panel included NBC's Frank McGee, the late Charles Von Fremd of CBS, Douglas Cater of *The Reporter*, and Roscoe Drummond, the columnist. The panel was in Los Angeles but in a separate studio from that of Nixon. The air time was 7:30 p.m. EDT on October 13.

ABC went to great pains as had the other networks earlier. Since the New York studio was distant from "suitable" office suites, they even built a cottage in the studio for Kennedy's use as dressing room, office and lavatory.

Coe spent hours arranging a "Lincoln-Cherney debate." Using actor Dan Lincoln who had Kennedy's coloring and physical characteristics and actor Richard Cherney who resembled Nixon, Coe had them stand in the set so that his technicians could match a perfect "split-screen" shot. It was used just once on the actual broadcast.

There was one internal dispute during this debate. Kennedy brought three documents with him—a copy of an Eisenhower letter on U.S. treaty agreements relating to the Taiwan Straits, a quote from John Foster Dulles and a page from a book by General Matthew Ridgeway. The Nixon side protested, noting that his original acceptance included the condition that no notes be used. The Kennedy side said they had never acknowledged this as a condition.

The Fourth Debate and the Non-Debate.

ABC also produced the last debate, at 10 p.m. on October 21. Quincy Howe was moderator and the panel was all broadcasters again: John Edwards of ABC, Walter Cronkite of CBS, Frank Singiser of Mutual and John Chancellor of NBC.

The format was exactly the same as the first debate but the subject matter here was foreign policy. Theodore White called it the "dreariest" of the debates. James Reston called it "highly repetitive." Curiously, the audience for the debates which had dropped during the second and third, rose for this last encounter, almost matching the immense audience for the first debate. Perhaps it was the lateness of the hour—election day was just two weeks away.

Oh—ABC remained painstakingly fair. They built a cottage for Nixon to match that Kennedy used in the third debate. They were identical even to the finished exterior. It was "modified colonial" in design.

And so the debates ended and a non-televised debate began. It was a debate over holding a fifth debate. Several leading Democratic Senators (Pastore, Monroney, and Magnuson) had suggested it one day after the second debate. The networks checked the candidates. Kennedy agreed; Nixon strategists decided to hold out until they saw how Nixon did in the fourth debate. Nixon suggested that the Vice Presidential candidates debate. He later urged that a fifth debate might put Lyndon Johnson and Henry Cabot Lodge on for part of the hour. This was in a 1,000-word telegram obviously designed for press consumption; most of it dealt with his differences with Kennedy over Castro.

Meetings were held. The networks even agreed on a producer, CBS; a place, Washington; and a date, October 31. Fred Scribner for Nixon and Leonard Reinsch for Kennedy compromised on a format—one giving ten minutes each to Vice Presidential candidates and then a panel quizzing the Presidential nominees. At one point, the Republicans even suggested a camera set up in Central Park to take questions from anyone who wandered by. The networks shuddered and said it could draw 100,000 people to the park making security and production impossible.

Debate No. 5 almost came to be but on October 28, Reinsch wired Scribner under Kennedy's name. Scribner felt the telegram implied bad faith on his part. Scribner showed network representatives a reply saying that there would be no more negotiations until Kennedy apologized. Debate No. 5 died right there.

Assessing the Debates.

The great debates were over. Kennedy would win the election by an extremely thin margin (112,000 votes) and the pollsters and social scientists would explore the meaning of the unusual face-to-face encounters on television.

The average family, they reported, saw quite a bit of it. Nine out of ten families saw at least part of one debate. Over half of TV families saw three debates, over a quarter saw all four and the average saw a total of 53-minutes. Elmo Roper said that 57% of the people felt the debates influenced their vote. Something like 3,400,000 credited the debates alone for their choice. Something like three out of four of these chose Kennedy over Nixon.

Who won? Dr. George Gallup's poll said 42% of Americans gave it to Kennedy when the debates had ended, 30% to Nixon, 23% called it a draw and 5% were undecided.

John Kennedy on November 12 said, "It was TV more than anything else that turned the tide."

Nixon was right about radio. Studies indicated that people who followed the debates on radio only believed Nixon had won all four.

The impact on voters that politicians rarely reach was tremendous. Paid political half-hour broadcasts during the campaign followed the usual pattern. They attracted 30% less audience than the program they replaced. The four debates, on the other hand, averaged 20% *more* audience than the entertainment programs they pre-empted. NBC President Robert Kintner noted that the total audience for all four debates was larger than the electorate itself; more people saw the debates in part or whole than actually voted. "If the candidates had met to debate daily in New York's Yankee Stadium before a capacity crowd," he said, "it would have taken them almost five years to be heard by that many people."

Richard Nixon gave his own impressions of the debates later in his book *Six Crises* and saw them as a permanent fixture. He also, ironically, called for the kind of debate that his advisors and Kennedy's had rejected.

Looking to the future, the incumbent—or whoever represents an incumbent Administration—will generally be at a disadvantage in debate because his opponent can attack while he must defend. But joint TV appearances of candidates at the presidential level are here to stay, mainly because people want them and the candidates have a responsibility to inform the public on their views before the widest possible audience.

In future campaigns, however, I would suggest that debates would be more interesting and would serve a more useful purpose if they were limited to specific subjects with only the candidates participating, and if the time allowed for discussion were two hours rather than one so that a subject could be discussed in adequate depth. This was the pattern of the Lincoln-Douglas debates of 1858, to which the 1960 series was often and quite erroneously compared. Every possible effort should be made from the standpoint of makeup, lighting, and other technical factors, to see that the candidates are on even terms. This last objective is easier said than accomplished. As my television adviser, Ted Rogers, commented after the campaign, "It is almost impossible to get a bad picture of Kennedy because of his coloring. On the other hand, it is difficult to get a good picture of Nixon."

I have no complaints and am doing no second-guessing on that score, incidentally, but one possible improvement would be to have debates in future campaigns conducted as was our third round, with the candidates in separate studios, allowing for the special kind of lighting that is needed and appropriate for each.

Columnist Max Lerner saw debates as a permanent part of American politics. "We may be pretty certain," he wrote, "that no Presidential candidate in future elections will dare turn down a request from his rival for a series of debates. Whether for good or ill, the political TV debate as a method in Presidential campaigns is here to stay."

He was wrong. There were no debates in 1964. There were none in 1968.

Not everyone was pleased with the 1960 debates. Columnist David Lawrence called them "a discouraging development in American politics. Showmanship has converted the duel between the candidates into a dramatic contest in facial make-up and theatrical tricks."

Max Ascoli in *The Reporter* said candidates in TV debates "are bound to behave like two talking Univac machines, each conditioned to recite a pre-taped message in answer to a foreseeable challenge from the other." He called the debates "four nightmarish hours" and said they could undermine representative institutions, that "these nation-wide town meetings were nothing but electronically contrived bad dreams."

Famed historian Henry Steele Commager saw the debates creating a Gresham's Law of politics—"the glib, the evasive, the dogmatic, the melodramatic, the meretricious will drive out the sincere, the serious, the judicious, the sober, the honest in political discussion." Commager, nine days after the last debate, wrote an article for the *New York Times* taking issue with Arthur Krock of that publication who had written, "The public will demand these joint appearances in all future Presidential campaigns." Said Commager, "Let us hope not."

His article was entitled "Washington Would Have Lost a TV Debate." He quotes Jefferson as authority that Washington was slow to react and though his judgment was as sound as any, it was "little aided by invention or imagination." Jefferson himself, said Commager, studiously avoided public confrontation, didn't even read his own messages to Congress but sent them instead. Aaron Burr, he continued, would have beaten Jefferson in debate. Henry Clay would have won over Andrew Jackson who would have lost his temper. Lincoln's stories were too long. Wilson needed time to think, also had a hot temper. "Instead, of our major Presidents probably only Franklin D. Roosevelt had the wit, the resourcefulness, the self-assurance, to do well in such televised press interviews."

Richard Salant of CBS News took issue with the Commager thesis:

More than 75,000,000 people watched the first debate—and almost as many the last. Their interest was sustained not only throughout each debate, but throughout all four debates. Certainly the candidates aimed their remarks at what they felt was the largest common denominator of the electorate, but they nevertheless sustained the interest of the many minority groups which made up the majority.

I also disagree with Mr. Commager who, I feel, does little to support his own argument about the major Presidents' ineptitude at debate by pointing out that Mr. Lincoln, in seven stirring debates with Douglas, succeeded in educating "not only the voters of Illinois, but posterity as well." My personal feeling is that Mr. Lincoln would have been magnificent in debates—on or off television—and in this feeling I join President Kennedy, who wrote before the election that "the quiet dignity of Lincoln . . . would have been tremendously effective on TV." I also like to think that Washington, despite his methodical manner and false teeth, would have had the appeal of an Eisenhower. To believe that the people would have rejected Washington is to damn not television, but the people.

The game of "what might have been" is fascinating for armchair history buffs. The game of "what might be" remains for broadcasters. The great debates had tremendous effect. One fallout was the frightening of politicians.

Why they were The Last Debates.

When the matter see-sawed in and out of the Congress in 1968, as it had for the previous eight years, the broadcast industry sought suspension or removal of the equal time provision. There was early encouragement. On May 29, the Senate passed Senate Resolution 175 suspending Section 315 as it applied to the 1968 Presidential campaign.

The proposed suspension came after hearings conducted by the Senate Commerce Committee. The Committee reported that it had the assurance of broadcasters that in addition to free time for the major party candidates, significant time would be provided the nominee of any important third party movement, an obvious reference to George Wallace. The committee report emphasized that the measure in no way diminished the statutory responsibility of broadcasters to provide fair coverage of a cross-section of political opinion. The committee vote was unanimous. The day after it was reported out, the Senate agreed to a voice vote. The bill was passed on to the House and was to take effect on August 31, after the major parties had chosen their nominees.

August 31 came and went without similar House action. The House Commerce Committee under Chairman Harley O. Staggers (Dem., W. Va.) held sporadic meetings, did nothing until the Congress recessed for the political conventions, and showed no great interest in quick action when the Congress returned. Both Vice President Humphrey and his Republican opponent, Richard Nixon, at that point said they favored televised debates similar to the Nixon-Kennedy debates.

Meanwhile, the FCC issued a statement to "clarify" Section 315 for individual stations on August 21. It began by saying it "encourages" stations to make their facilities available to candidates but reminds them that legally qualified candidates have the right to equal time, without any right of censorship by the broadcaster. Thus, the FCC warned, no broadcaster can dictate program format, participants, length of program, and times of taping and broadcasting. If a candidate declines such condition while his opponent or opponents accept it, he still has equal time rights under Section 315.

Rather than encourage broadcasters to expand their journalistic function to better serve in a campaign year, authorities in Washington seemed more concerned with such reminders of statutory limitations. Some members of Congress said if broadcasters really wanted to help candidates, they should simply cut their rates. One key figure was reportedly campaigning to expand the law and prohibit stations from editorials endorsing candidates, even if equal time is offered to the opposition candidate.

When Congress returned after the political conventions, the House Commerce Committee acted. It changed the Senate resolution to include George Wallace in debates and sent the matter on to the full House. By this time, candidate Humphrey was eager for debates, front-running Nixon was strongly opposed and vowed never to engage in a three-way debate with Wallace.

On October 8, the matter came before the House. Republicans engaged in a procedural filibuster, calling for roll-call after roll-call and forcing a round-the-clock session. The Republicans said they were doing it to dramatize the need for Congressional reform. Democrats accused them of trying to block any broadcast debate. The session ended after 32 hours and 17 minutes, second longest House session in history. Some 45 roll-calls had ensued, by far a record number. The final vote was curiously lopsided, 280 to 35 in favor of broadcast debates. Presumably, few were eager to be *on record* in opposition.

One day later, the House version of the measure went back to the Senate for action. A boycott openly led by Republican Leader Everett

Dirksen blocked any quorum in the Senate and the measure was "indefinitely postponed," killed for the Presidential year.

At no time in the period since 1960 have Congressional leaders shown any inclination to make debates possible on a permanent basis. One election at a time and be careful to see whose ox will be gored. At no time has Congress been eager to extend Section 315 suspensions to contests other than Presidential. Privately Congressmen confide their fears that some handsome young opponent may rise over the horizon and, thanks to a television debate, send Mr. Congressman into premature retirement.

The great debates were a great experiment. Congress was not ready to take it out of the laboratory and permit public consumption of Election Year television colloquy.

CHAPTER 11

IN POLITICAL CONVENTION GATHERED

TELEVISION AND POLITICS blended in 1952 as the national political conventions were televised for the first time. Over 100 stations were on the air and over 18 million television sets were in the hands of Americans.

The audience for convention coverage that year was immense. Estimates say over 55 million people saw some part of the network coverage. For the first time, they were able to see more than people in the convention hall. This might have been disturbing to some delegates and more so to newspapermen. It reminds one of Jackie Gleason's witty description of television critics as men describing an accident to eyewitnesses. Home viewers saw more than newspapers could give them.

Not everyone approved. One magazine of that day warned that, "Television, fixing its prying and disillusioning eye on the antics and asininities of our shirtsleeved statesmen in Convention assembled, is likely to so disgust the plain citizen that he may continue to withhold his vote until zero is reached."

ABC said from the start that it would carry "gavel to gavel" coverage in 1952 but the other networks seemed inclined to go easier. CBS promised a minimum of 20 hours of each convention, NBC a minimum of 30 hours each. As it turned out, all networks stayed all the way. With some sessions going into the wee hours of morning and one Democratic convention day lasting 14 hours non-stop, all three networks devoted long hours to the meetings, a total of 70 hours for the Republican gathering and 77 hours of Democratic conventioneering.

When it was over, the promised 20 or more hours stretching to 144 hours, the networks were proud of their work. The Radio Corporation of America took an ad in the *New York Times* to note: "With the aid of television, we had what amounted to the biggest town meeting ever held . . . 60 million people had front row seats."

Terribly conscious of all those front row seats, convention planners began tailoring the quadrennial meetings to match the eye of the camera rather than the presence of those on-the-scene. Leonard Hall, then Chairman of the Republican National Committee said, "We must choose able and personable candidates who can 'sell themselves' because TV has changed the course of campaigns."

His party made changes in 1952. The ultimate nomination of General Eisenhower rather than Senator Robert Taft was the result of the credentials fight in the '52 convention. The doors to credential committee hearings were closed to television but cameras set up outside the door (quickly dubbed "The Glass Curtain") and television interviewed participants to the meetings. Their comments were televised minutes after they emerged from the room, developments were reported across the country moments after they occurred. Sig Mickelson, then head of CBS News, said, "If the television eye had not been focused on the credentials committee at the 1952 Republican National Convention, Senator Taft might have been nominated rather than General Eisenhower."

J. Leonard Reinsch, who handled television for the Democrats that year said, "The nominating convention took on a new dimension—that of a giant political rally. The penetrating and merciless eye of the camera brought television in the forefront as a means to involve the American public in the political convention. It also exposed national leaders and party officials to the risks involved in subjecting their platforms and policies to the American electorate."

There were also risks in having the TV eye there all the time. After watching the Republican convention on television, Reinsch ordered the telltale red lights on the cameras concealed so delegates would not be aware of being on camera. He didn't like the reactions he saw among GOP delegates. Speeches were shortened. Prayers to open or close sessions were limited to two minutes.

More changes were made at the next convention. The Democrats moved the platform proceedings to the week before the convention. Daytime sessions were dropped, welcoming speeches limited, tedious parliamentary moves curtailed. Sessions were scheduled with prime time audiences in mind. Even demonstrations for candidates were limited and the traditional seconding speeches for Vice President eliminated.

The Republican President watched the Democratic convention and ordered his party to initiate even greater changes to accommodate television. He wrote the party Chairman Hall, "Len, I presume you are getting one thousand suggestions as to how to run a convention, and perhaps most of them get in the wastepaper basket, and maybe these will too, but here they are: 1. No long, dreary speeches." Mr. Eisenhower listed twelve more suggestions and when he got to number 14, he wrote, "I repeat the first. No long, dreary speeches."

Wrote Hall later, ". . . television has compelled parties to tighten up their conventions and keep something going on at all times. That's why I believe you will never see the time come again when you have thirty ballots to select a candidate. You just can't bore a nationwide television audience that much."

The Democrats that year introduced still another innovation to capitalize on television: a movie. It was called "The Pursuit of Happiness" and was produced by movie-maker Dore Schary, narrated by a young Senator from Massachusetts named John F. Kennedy. The only thing wrong with this filmed history of the Democratic party was that it was pure propaganda.

Two networks showed the film but CBS News cut away from it to devote its air time to other aspects of convention coverage. Democratic Party Chairman Paul Butler was furious. When the film ended Butler addressed the convention and accused CBS of breaking faith. The delegates were angry. Some even stormed the central camera stand and shook it violently, something that was hardly appreciated by cameramen from other networks and newspapers who were perched on the shaking stand.

Butler charged CBS with breaking a commitment. The network denied that. Frank Stanton said, "Those who make news cannot, in a free society dictate . . . to what extent, where and how" it is covered. Another CBS comment: "The right of CBS to be bored must be defended." Robert Kintner, then President of ABC, issued a statement supporting CBS and the right of "each network (to) exercise its own editorial judgment."

Politicians were discovering that the alluring lady, television, had a mind of her own. They didn't like it.

Even then there were grumblings that conventions should be changed, not to accommodate television but to keep it from dominating the proceedings. There were complaints about television reporters working freely about the floor; complaints that television cameras were finding delegates reading newspapers instead of listening to the business at the rostrum. Indeed, television always seemed to zero in on delegates who, from boredom or fatigue from the more festive aspects of a delegate's life, were sleeping in their chairs.

Yet, to this day, politicians realize how valuable is the exposure, how important the communication with America and they are reluctant to move against television. They are, however, always aware that it is there.

In 1964 at the Republican convention in San Francisco, the Goldwater people who controlled the convention proceedings (and ultimately nominated Chairman William Miller to be Goldwater's running mate) rearranged the schedule to minimize a platform fight initiated by liberal Republicans. President Eisenhower spoke before instead of after the reading of the platform. The platform reading itself was expanded from a 25-minute condensation to a droning, 90-minute recitation of every last word.

When these delays ended, the opponents were allowed to speak. Nelson Rockefeller was the key spokesman. By the time he got to the lectern it was well past prime time in the East. The session ended well after midnight in California, three hours later in the East. Television exposure of the internal battle was successfully minimized.

That convention saw one unique event: a television reporter arrested on camera. The reporter in question was John Chancellor, arrested ostensibly for obstructing the aisles. As the cameras followed the policeman escorting Chancellor out of the hall, the witty reporter ended his comments with "This is John Chancellor, somewhere in custody."

We noted earlier that after the first televised convention, a magazine said television would show the "antics and asininities of our shirt-sleeved statesmen." A dozen years later, following the 1964 Republican convention, television had offered a "picture of confusion, noise, impossible deportment and indifference to what is being discussed at the platform." So spoke an angry Dwight Eisenhower who said the American people were "horrified."

General Eisenhower was addressing the Republican National Committee and he wanted conventions cleaned up. It was said that a young lady related to Ike had been trampled on the convention floor and had narrowly missed serious injury. The former President called for a strong chairman with "dictatorial" powers, a limit of five minutes to all floor demonstrations, the barring of all reporters and cameramen from the convention floor and a curtailing of the number of delegates and alternates permitted to attend a convention.

The National Committee ordered a study of convention procedures. The committee conducting that study reported in January of 1967 at the New Orleans meeting of the GOP National Committee. It recommended that the convention try to eliminate the center camera stand. It called for fewer cameras elsewhere on the floor. It implied that reporters should be kept off the floor and interviews with delegates be conducted in a designated area elsewhere in the building. Though the number of floor passes was limited at the next convention (Miami in 1968), these suggestions were largely ignored. Perhaps the lure of full television coverage was too attractive.

On the other hand, the committee did make a number of suggestions obviously designed to trim the ship, to make the program more attractive on television. They called for a limitation on honorary speakers, drastic cuts in special presentations, restricting welcoming speeches to one, reducing paid entertainment, providing "the best professional assistance to speakers" so that they look and sound good, and strict enforcement of rules limiting nominating and seconding speeches (fifteen minutes to nominate; four seconding speeches of five minutes each).

They also asked that the rostrum be designed to eliminate a mass of people in the background which the committee found distracting. They said, "The background for a speaker as seen by a televiewer is a mass of people's faces, constant movement and distractions," Note the concern over how a speaker is "seen by a televiewer." This change was made in Miami in '68.

The committee noted that demonstrations after a nomination created "a dangerously overcrowded situation" and recommended that demonstrations be restricted exclusively to delegates and alternates with everyone else banned from the hall. Newsmen, however, were not banned; the restriction was modified in practice.

As to the reading of the platform, the committee noted that this results in "multitudinous complaints" and that observers feel "it tends to sound dull and uninteresting and that it is too time-consuming." It was recommended that the convention planners study ways to present the platform that would have interest and meaning. They suggested that the full platform be shortened to be more meaningful to the general public. The committee also urged that sessions of the convention be shortened and better timed. The GOP made history in Miami by starting every session close to time, a departure from the usual late start. The Democrats followed suit in Chicago.

In conclusion, this special Republican study attempted to define the nature of a convention and while conceding that some changes could make it more attractive, for the retention of the institution:

A national political convention has three major functions. The first is the nominating function, and has the public interest riding on who wins, with all the drama of the roll call of the states. However, of recent years, the excitement has been somewhat dulled by the primaries and better national reporting which frequently indicates the winner long in advance.

The second aspect of the convention is the deliberative function, including the adoption of the platform, of Party rules and similar details necessary to continue the Party. This is legalistic and dull except for the conflict between factions.

The third face of the convention is the campaign rally function. This is the only occasion on which most or all of the national leaders can be seen and heard on the same program, and along with it goes all the color, movement and excitement, not to mention the human interest of the convention. Stripped of this glitter, the convention could well be incredibly uninteresting and dull, particularly when the result is essentially a foregone conclusion.

The Committee on Convention Reforms agrees with President Eisenhower, and others who have communicated with it, that the convention system of nominating candidates for President and Vice President must be retained. With all of its faults, it has worked well for more than a century and it is expected to continue. Changes are anticipated which will improve the appearance and conduct of the convention, but it is hoped this basic system may long endure.

The special study had grappled with the problems of conventions in a television age. It decided that, as a practical matter, the coverage was so important that measures should be taken to avoid being dull but not to avoid being covered. The extremists who would curtail television access did not prevail.

Concern with TV's Conduct.

After the conventions of that year, the prestigious Committee for Economic Development issued a study, "Financing a Better Election System," which also touched on the problem. It called for drastic cuts in the number of delegates ("The huge numbers of delegates and alternates —from 2,600 to 5,600 in 1968—make these conventions wholly unmanageable as parliamentary bodies") and expressed concern over television coverage.

These are the comments of an expert in the television field and a member of the CED study group, ex-Senator William Benton:

"The glaring lights of television" do more than emphasize the "spectacular aspects of the resulting mob scenes." They also impede the view and the hearing of the delegates. The accompanying reporters interrupt the delegates on the floor of the convention. TV can be used to give immediate currency and seeming credibility to wild rumors and manufactured stories of various factions. It can even invent its own political realities by reporting such rumors, then reporting on delegate reaction to them, and so on, in the conversion of a rumor into a self-fulfilling prophecy. Television should have access to the public sessions of a party convention, but it should not be allowed to dominate the style of the convention, nor should it have unbridled privileges of access to delegates on the floor. The role of TV at our national conventions rates special study by the Congress and the two political parties.

The pervasive presence of television does irk professional politicians. F. Clifton White has expressed resentment of television's influence on convention procedure: "Television came on the scene and we started being told we can't have morning sessions because nobody will watch us... television is programming conventions ... to the television medium, it is a show, it's a production ... they want to get a rating."

He suggests that the entire convention system is in jeopardy: "I am reasonably convinced that it is not going to survive as an effective system or instrument for selecting people for the highest office in the land, if it is structured as a television production."

It might be argued that "if it is structured as a television production," it is done so by the convention itself. The rules are laid down by the national parties. They want the coverage. They express dismay about interviews on the floor of the convention that distract from podium proceedings but they don't really want to ban the interviews, especially when they grant them in hopes of influencing the public and the delegates to support the candidate of their choice.

White, concerned about the degree of emphasis on television, says that it should be restricted but not eliminated ("there are certain things that you have to discuss, in this business, that are not necessarily the sort of things you want all of the 200 million American voters to hear about").

Another observer of the American political scene, British journalist Alistair Cooke, notes that television has managed to clean up "traditional ploys and techniques in the convention system which were wearisome," notably the delaying tactics used by various supporters of candidates. "It's exposed the American people to the mechanism of the convention. I think it's been a terrible eye-opener. I think it's shown a good deal of shenanigans and corruption, but I think it's very good that people should see how it works."

Still another observer, the late Ralph McGill, publisher of the *Atlanta Constitution,* joins those who would keep newsmen off the floor of a convention:

All media should be barred from the floor during convention sessions—reporters, television cameramen and commentators, and radio reporters. It cannot be said that sessions of the Congress of the United States are lacking in meaning. But even at their more electric moment, aisles are not jammed with media reporters, cameras and mikes.

Is not a national convention entitled to as much dignity and space for its sessions?

He receives support from Herbert Brucker of Stanford, former editor of the *Hartford* (Conn.) *Courant:*

In connection with a study made of the entire electoral process, I recently interviewed some West Coast leaders in politics, newspapers, and the universities. Not one really thought the present floor free-for-all was right.

Television makes change necessary. The endless boring speeches and hoopla don't make an entertainment spectacular. Their TV crews roam the floor, picking up gossip, poking microphones into the teeth of delegates, and generally trying to find or start some action.

Newspapers check out tips and rumors before reporting them to the nation. But in the modern world, if you bar TV you will have to bar radio and newspapers as well, and maybe it's best that way. A reporter's job is to cover the news, not make it.

These comments reflect some of the newspaperman's unhappiness over the commanding role television journalism has assumed in convention and election coverage. It leaves little for newspapers to do in the way of "eye-witness" coverage. There are occasions when television falls short of adequate coverage, in part because they are on "live" and don't always have enough time for reflective reporting though Brucker to the contrary, networks are as conscientious about checking out rumors as are newspapers; their record, despite the pressures of time, is surprisingly similar to that of a good newspaper.

The emerging role for the daily newspaper seems to be that of providing a summary of what its readers have already seen ("the newspaper of record") but far more important, the interpretation that can go beyond the "instant wisdom" of television's analysts because there is more time for reflection, more time to prepare and more time (space) devoted to it.

Incidentally, in the CED study cited earlier, William Benton suggests that newspaper-television rivalry may have hurt coverage of the 1968 campaign:

A further point seems to me to be of far greater importance. In a campaign like that of 1968, journalists of the print media reported with great detail what candidates did and said before crowds of a few hundred or a few thousand partisans at Detroit or San Francisco or Manhattan, Kansas—but the candidates often made their most important statements, and best demonstrated their style and grasp and intellectual dexterity, on network television interview programs or on candidate-sponsored broadcasts and telecasts where unlike party rallies they had access to the hostile and the uncommitted. The stakes in a Presidential election are too high to allow newspapers to ignore what is going on in the rival medium of television. Prior to the recent Presidential campaign, the Republican candidate had refused all TV appearances for two years, in itself not without news interest, yet when he finally appeared on "Face the Nation," this highly newsworthy fact and exceedingly important program was largely ignored by the press. So was his appearance (and his opponents') on "Meet the Press." So were the Republican candidate's large number of wholly contrived and controlled programs. So were the Democrat's programs largely ignored. I could not even find a listing of President Johnson's speech in the *New York Times* on the Sunday before election, even though Saturday's *Times* had carried a large advertisement for it. The abdication of the press to cover candidates' TV activities is, in my judgment, a most serious indictment of the press in the '68 campaign. Perhaps a part of the explanation lies in the fact that many news editors are trained to view TV as a rival medium rather than as a major source of news.

Television has its share of shortcomings as a reporter of conventions. McGill's (and Brucker's) concerns over interviews in the aisles of the convention hall are certainly worthy of careful study. There *were* occasions in 1968 when television seemed to intrude on the workings of the convention process including moments when over-eager television reporters shoved microphones into a cluster of delegates attempting an on-the-floor huddle. In one case, the microphone, to the credit of the delegates seeking momentary privacy, was shoved right out again.

Some television reporters brashly defend their conduct on the floor. Sander Vanocer of NBC: "No doubt we are intruders, but no doubt the First Amendment to the Constitution establishes the right of intrusion, because I am sure that a lot of politicians in this country would like to have no intrusion as they exercise what they believe to be their divine right to tell the American people what's good for them."

Vanocer might have trouble establishing his interpretation of the First Amendment. It certainly does not give the right to "intrusion," just the right to a free press. Vanocer's exuberance, however, is defending the responsibility of television reporters and all others to penetrate the maneuvering of political manipulators for the education of the electorate.

Drew Pearson, the columnist, saw the television sponsor as the evil force. He concedes that, "Television has done one thing. It's made them (conventions) more interesting." He saw this, however, as a means to "keep the ratings up" to please sponsors—"a convention (is) . . . frequently very dull. This is the process of government. Government can be dull. But nevertheless, government, the parliamentary system, is a necessary function and it shouldn't be marred by what people want to have, or what the big sponsors want. It should be as it is."

There is no question that networks attempt to keep their convention broadcasts interesting ("for the liveliest, most colorful, most complete reporting, follow the convention on . . ."). Ultimately this has effect on the ability to get sponsorship of such broadcasts but the network news departments rarely concern themselves with the sponsorship question. They feel the real competition is to outdo the other networks.

There can be damaging effects from competition. There can also be immense contributions to public understanding.

There is frequent debate as to how much attention networks pay to the formal proceedings of a convention. Certain aspects of convention proceedings are sacrosanct and are always carried in full: keynote speeches, major addresses by party heroes such as ex-Presidents, nomination of major candidates, actual votes, etc. Other portions of "podium activity" are carried only sometimes.

With each network there is internal debate on how much to carry. Sometimes a network feels summary is better. CBS News, for example, devotes a significant segment of time to its own reporters outlining party platforms, what they contain, what they don't and what it means. Doing this takes less time than carrying the platform presentation in full and is easier for the audience to grasp. Carrying every word of a platform presentation does present the "historic record," it fails to present the full meaning or the shortcomings of the platform.

Some politicians feel television should not cut away at all from podium activity except when it is minor or ceremonial or a delay in convention activity such as awaiting a state caucus. A number of outside observers agree.

A convention, however, is much more than podium activity. Its main function is the nomination of a ticket. Important activity relating to the ultimate nomination takes place from the moment delegates arrive in town. Who is leading in that contest, what is happening to bolster all candidacies, what is said in relation to that, is meaty and important— often more important than officials activity at the podium.

Second, the creation of a party platform—despite one President's admonition that the platform is something to run on, not to stand on—is important as a measure of what the party stands for and, in its omissions, what it doesn't care to establish as a party position. The maneuverings to determine a platform, and the opposition to certain positions, tell much about the character of a political party at that given moment. Our history is dotted with elections won or lost over the issues debated in platform fights.

Third, a political convention is designed to create party enthusiasm, inside and outside the hall, inside and outside the party. As suggested earlier, this can be terribly important even when the choice of candidates is no surprise.

A fourth matter of convention business is electing members of the National Convention to serve until the next convention (and thus provide the continuity of the national political party). It is largely ignored by television. It is a housekeeping feature of the party.

The final concern of conventions is involved in all of the above and is perhaps as important as any, important to the party and its candidates. This is the image of the party and its candidates that the convention creates.

To cite one example of this last element, this comment Charles A. H. Thompson of the Rand Corporation in evaluating "Mass Media Performance" for the Brookings Institution study of *The National Election of 1964:*

> Probably the greatest damage to political image was suffered not by a candidate, present or potential, but by the Republican party. Television unavoidably pictured the spectacle of the pro-Goldwater mob. Far from dignity, decorum, and smooth procedure characteristic of most Republican conventions, here was the spectacle of impatience, ill-breeding, unwillingness to accord the courtesy of a fair hearing to opponents who had no chance whatsoever either of the nomination or of palpable influence on the platform. The savaging of Stassen in 1956 was muted and pale in comparison, and—more important—done behind the scenes. Almost inevitably, TV reportage of events in the hall failed to picture the efforts of the Goldwater organization to restore order in the galleries.
>
> The 1964 convention threw into sharp contrast the dignity and patience of Rockefeller speaking out for moderation, or the intellectual quality and persuasiveness of a Milton Eisenhower nominating Governor Scranton, against the unreasoning angry Goldwater delegates and galleries. Goldwater, at the moment of his nomination, failed to make the move toward party unity that might have offended some of his supporters for the moment, but that would have done much to improve Republican chances in November. This omission, which television covered with cold clarity, contrasted sharply with Goldwater's charitable and wise words to Rockefeller in his statement after the California primary. ("To Governor Rockefeller, who waged a tenacious campaign, I extend my best wishes, and I express the

hope that he will join with me in resolving to make every effort to unseat the Democrats in November.")

Television in its telling of a convention, shifts back and forth between these considerations. The official proceedings do not.

Party faithful, in convention assembled, can make or break the chances for election in November. It is television that carries their image to the electorate, more powerfully and in many respects more faithfully, than any other form of communication. Those many who see an analogy between this form of political coverage and a "town meeting of the millions" are not really wrong.

The Ultimate Clash: Chicago, 1968.

It was after the first televised conventions, in 1952, that Philip Hamburger wrote in the *New Yorker*: "Television, covering affairs of this sort, makes the viewer a member of a community vaster than his own without demanding that he sacrifice any of his individuality. It does not require him to judge, nor does it judge him—a nightmare envisioned by Orwell and mercifully not in prospect."

If it does this then any of the shortcomings of the networks, in political convention assembled, is worth the tolerance of the viewer.

That tolerance was tested in the closing week of August, 1968 when television turned its pervasive eye on the Democratic National Convention. All the criticisms of coverage, of television at political events, were brought to a boil in this most chaotic of modern political conventions.

The atmosphere in Chicago that August was volatile. There had been demands to move the convention elsewhere. First there was irreconcilable opposition to the war in Vietnam, both within and without the convention. Opponents of the war threatened to march on Chicago in the tens of thousands. Radical leaders were eager to exploit this sentiment and disrupt both the convention and the process of determining the Democratic nominee.

Within the party structure, opponents were eager to go on record attacking the war, despite the fact that it had flourished under the Administration of a Democratic President. The President himself was to come to the convention to celebrate his birthday (an immense "Happy Birthday Lyndon" cake was to be baked) but could not attend, the atmosphere having grown that tense. Divisiveness and rancor seemed the rule on the convention floor. The frustrations of anti-Vietnam Democrats and their constituencies boiled to a froth.

There was concern over Negro demonstrations. Earlier in the year, following riots in Chicago after the assassination of Martin Luther King,

Mayor Richard Daley had issued an order to police: "Shoot to kill arsonists, shoot to maim looters" which, though later amended, did nothing to
soothe the atmosphere.

Elaborate security measures added still more strain. Some felt it akin
to a "concentration camp environment."

In addition there was a crippling communications strike. For a while,
it would appear that there would be no television at all and perhaps no
telephone communication. This was amended before the convention
opened, enough to permit television from the hall and from the Chicago
studios of the networks. At one hotel, the main convention hotel, the networks could "tape" but not broadcast live. On the eve of the first convention session, those running the convention placed new restrictions on
television—cutting down on the number of floor passes and portable
cameras. David Brinkley blistered the authorities in a Sunday night broadcast; so did Walter Cronkite.

Humorist Art Buchwald, on the CBS payroll, offered a biting satire.
Dressed in a helmet and speaking from behind a wire fence at Convention
Hall, he said that Chicago was replacing New York as "Fun City" and
that Mayor Daley had shown Republicans what "law and order" really
was. This cued in Frank Sinatra's recording of "Chicago, My Home
Town" over a series of pictures of police, police dogs, fences, etc.

In that sullen, testy, nervous atmosphere, the Chicago convention
began.

It reached its climax, not in the nomination of Hubert Humphrey
but in the confrontation between anti-war demonstrators and jumpy police in front of the Hilton Hotel. Hundreds among the thousands present
used the tactic of goading police into over-reaction. The consequent loss
of control and restraint by police offered a violent scene that was carried
around the world. Newsmen as well as protesters were beaten. The conduct of Chicago's police force during the Democratic National Convention later became a subject of fierce debate in the press and elsewhere.
Though a number of columnists and some publications have taken issue
with the treatment of the convention story by newspapers and television,
few argued that the treatment of newsmen themselves was anything but
shocking.

As *Sigma Delta Chi* President Staley T. McBrayer put it in a protest
to Chicago Mayor Daley and his Superintendent of Police, "I protest
vigorously the brutal and oppressive treatment of newsmen by Chicago
police officers. Documented incidents of deliberate clubbing of accredited
journalists in the performance of their duties is a tragic disservice to the
traditions of a free press and to responsible law enforcement."

The *Chicago Daily News* said: "A Mayor Daley pathetically eager
to make things 'nice' for a convention of particular importance to him,

indulged in such security overkill that a great city was turned into a police city-state, and freedom of assembly and speech were snuffed out."

The exact number of news "casualties" was hard to determine. Many who felt the tart sting of a police billy-club did not report their injuries. Estimates vary but it would appear that some thirty-five or so television reporters and cameramen and as many newspaper reporters and photographers were clubbed during a five-day period.

The organizations represented on the casualty list read like the Who's Who of American journalism: all four Chicago newspapers, ABC, CBS, NBC, *Newsweek, Life,* the AP, UPI, the *Washington Post,* the *Milwaukee Journal,* the *Philadelphia Bulletin,* etc. The first incidents took place on Sunday with almost daily recurrences until the biggest confrontation across from the Hilton Hotel on Wednesday evening.

Claude Lewis of the *Philadelphia Bulletin* was clubbed when he refused to turn his notebook over to a policeman. Howard Berlieant, free-lance photographer for the *Milwaukee Journal,* was beaten unconscious by several policemen as he took pictures from the doorway of the building where he was staying. John Linstead of the *Chicago Daily News* was clubbed and kicked by three or four policemen, suffering scalp cuts and severe leg bruises.

Del Hall of CBS News was clubbed from behind as he filmed. He fell to the pavement and found several more police beating him. Jim Strickland of NBC News took film of Hall lying on the street and was hit in the mouth with a nightstick. An ABC News camera team reported shouts of "Get the cameras," whereupon police smashed the camera lens and clubbed ABC cameraman Charles Pharris and his soundman, Walter James.

Robert Jackson of the *Chicago American* was knocked to the ground by a policeman who hit him several times with a club. When Jackson tried to identify himself as a reporter by showing his Chicago press credentials, the officer said, "That doesn't mean a damn thing to me."

A *Chicago Tribune* photographer, David Nystrom, took pictures of a *Ramparts* magazine photographer being arrested, found himself under arrest, held in a police van for thirty minutes and then taken to central police headquarters where he was released. Numerous reporters and photographers were sprayed with mace. Jim Jones of *Newsweek* was knocked to the ground, kicked in the ribs and hit over the head while trying to identify himself as a reporter.

On Tuesday, August 27, a 17-man delegation of editors and broadcasters protested to Police Superintendent James B. Conlisk, Jr. Emmett Dedmon, editor of the *Chicago Sun-Times,* acted as spokesman and reported that police agreed to an immediate investigation of the charges and would assign officers of high rank to go to the scene of disturbances and assure protection of the rights of the press and bystanders.

Despite this there were more incidents. The general feeling among many newsmen was that police acted so because they blamed newsmen for attracting demonstrators to Chicago. In a number of cases, reporters told of police removing their badges and nameplates before swinging in on newsmen and demonstrators. This practice is against police department rules and Suprintendent Conlisk ordered it stopped.

The beatings of newsmen downtown was accompanied by severe restrictions and unusual security measures at the International Amphitheatre where the convention was held. George Murray, an executive producer of NBC's convention coverage said, "There's no question that the police are obstructing our coverage. Security regulations are five times as rigid here as in Miami, to the point of being totally unreasonable."

His statement came shortly after police ordered television mobile units off the city streets. They had parked near hotels to tape reports since a communications workers strike prevented live coverage from anywhere outside the convention hall proper. Richard S. Salant, head of CBS News, said the newest ban formed "a pattern well beyond simple labor disputes, logistics, and security problems." After strong protests from the networks, a compromise permitted the TV trucks to park in agreed areas.

At the Amphitheatre the number of floor passes was curtailed sharply. There were far fewer passes than the number granted newsmen at the Republican National Convention in Miami, a few weeks earlier. For example, the daily press was told it could have 55 floor passes and only after strong protest, received 80. In Miami, 100 floor passes went to the daily press.

Non-network broadcasters had an estimated 1,100 representatives in both Chicago and Miami. The Republicans granted them 100 rotating floor passes. The Democrats offered 25 and finally granted 45 passes. The periodical press received 25 floor passes in Miami, half that number in Chicago with half of those granted on a day-to-day basis and never the same number daily. Photographers also had 100 passes in Miami but were cut to 40 in Chicago, 15 of those for men on the podium not moving around on the floor.

The networks were also hit hard when the Democratic National Committee, in the decision revealed just one day before the convention, cut the number of floor passes to seven, insisted that only two be for reporters, and that there be only one miniature camera on the floor (in Miami there were two). Protests resulted in the granting of six additional floor passes for "messengers" which the networks quickly converted to general use. The number of floor cameras remained restricted to one, however.

Despite the severe restrictions on all news media in terms of passes, there were recurring reports of supporters of Mayor Daley having access to the floor with press credentials. On the last two nights, much of the press section in the balconies was filled with Chicago city workers and Democratic party supporters. As their signs and shouts put it, "We love Mayor Daley." Less enchanted were news people deprived of their seats.

On Tuesday night, as he sought to interview a Georgia delegate being ejected from the floor, CBS Correspondent Dan Rather was shoved around by security people, slugged in the stomach and punched in the back as he went down to the floor. All of this was seen on television by millions. Walter Cronkite, as Rather regained his feet, angrily observed, "I think we've got a bunch of thugs here."

Democratic party officials called the treatment of Rather "inexcusable" and offered apologies. The next day, several NBC and CBS newsmen were roughed up in a melee as a New York delegate was escorted off the floor for failure to have proper credentials (despite the head of his delegation protesting). CBS Correspondent Mike Wallace was incorrectly reported to have been slugged and arrested on the convention floor during this disturbance. Actually, this happened off the floor. He was hit by a police officer who misinterpreted a gesture following a heated exchange of words over Wallace's right to interview the New York delegate. Wallace was briefly under arrest and the incident ended with an exchange of apologies.

NBC Newsmen complained that men were following them across the convention floor, eavesdropping on their conversations with NBC producers and with delegates.

As the convention ended, in an unprecedented gesture, the top executives of *Time, Newsweek*, five of the nation's largest newspapers, and all three television networks, sent a protest to Mayor Daley. It read:

> We strongly protest the treatment of news reporters, photographers and cameramen by certain members of the Chicago police force during the Democratic convention. Newsmen were repeatedly singled out by policemen and deliberately beaten and harassed. Cameras were broken and film was destroyed. The obvious purpose was to discourage or prevent reporting of an important confrontation between police and demonstrators which the American public has the right to know about.
>
> An investigation by the F.B.I. is under way to ascertain whether this treatment of news personnel involved violation of Federal law. Regardless of the F.B.I. inquiry, we strongly urge that you yourself order an investigation by a responsible group of distinguished and disinterested citizens. This investigation should fix responsibility for the conduct of the members of the police force who participated in

these incidents and see to it that suitable punishment is meted out as deserved.

If America is to survive, the freedom of our news media to observe and report must remain inviolate. The police must not be permitted to suppress this freedom by clubbing and intimidation."

Critics Turn On TV.

Television was heavily criticized for reporting the problems in the streets and the dissent on the convention floor. A Chicago Congressman, Roman Pucinski, later called it "outrageous and unfair . . . the zenith of irresponsibility in American journalism." He was joined by another Democrat, Ed Edmondson of Oklahoma who said, "Network media personnel such as Cronkite, and Huntley and Brinkley have done violence to the truth by their unfair coverage at Chicago and the public deserves better at the hands of this great industry."

One criticism often heard was that television had falsely created a "boomlet" for Senator Edward Kennedy, a charge strengthened as critics noted that CBS pundits Eric Sevareid and Theodore White had speculated that the drive for Kennedy was perhaps a creation of television reporting, at least in part. Said Sevareid, "This boom for Teddy Kennedy has been, one might argue, created in part by the sheer treatment of it on TV particularly." Said White: ". . . the Kennedy boomlet has started in the past three days and I think has been enormously exaggerated, and as you say, Eric, incubating by our own medium to a large extent."

In the *New York Times*, Jack Gould ("Does TV Report News—or Make it?") said the networks had "over-responded," an interesting parallel to comments of police "over-reacting." He said, "The peril of live television is to put a story on the air at any cost without waiting even a few minutes to take a measure of its substance."

But had television over-reacted? The first story CBS News reported as it went on the air that first night of the convention was on moves by Jesse Unruh of California and former Governor Mike DeSalle of Ohio to foster a draft Kennedy movement. DeSalle was interviewed and said he had just received a call from Kennedy asking him not to place the Senator's name in nomination. Did that mean he was out of it? DeSalle's strong answer, "No, I think very definitely if a draft is a genuine draft, he's convinced of it, he would accept the nomination."

The next night, CBS News Correspondent David Schoumacher reported that Senator Eugene McCarthy had met with Stephen Smith, an aide to Kennedy about throwing his support to the Massachusetts Senator. An "insider's" story later said Schoumacher's report may have injured the Kennedy cause by giving it premature publicity. In any case, a number of Kennedy and McCarthy aides later confided that there was a move to draft the Senator. One top Kennedy advisor told me later that the most powerful figure at the convention, Chicago's Mayor Daley, had participated in the movement but had failed to rally enough support. Others claimed that Daley really wanted Kennedy to accept the Vice Presidential nomination.

Television may have played a role in exaggerating the Kennedy movement, though that is yet to be proven, but it certainly did not invent it. To ignore it (and newspapers did not either) would be as damning as to run the risk of accusation that TV was blowing it up.

The usual charge against television, that it left the podium too often, was levelled. This convention, however, had a multitude of other matters demanding attention—the street protesters, the credentials fight, the unit rule, loyalty oaths for Southerners, convention security, the Vietnam plank in the platform, and the violence to citizens and reporters.

Despite the strong protests about the police by many in journalism (a position that many other, particularly columnists, did not always agree with), there was no groundswell of public support for the media. *Broadcasting* magazine reports a study by Sindlinger and Company which judged the Wednesday night television audience at over 90 million people. Of these, only 21.3% thought police used excessive force, 56.8% thought they did not, and 21.9% had no opinion. Security measures at the convention were supported by 71.4% and only 13.4% thought them unjustified.

Further evidence of public feeling, at least in Chicago, can be judged by the appearance of Richard Nixon there on September 4 as he started his formal campaign. He was cheered as he went by. The press bus was roundly jeered.

A few days later, Mayor Richard J. Daley issued a 16,000 word report giving the city's side of the disorders. The report said, "The trusting, the innocent and the idealist were taken in and taken over. The news media, too, responded with the surprising naivete and were incredibly misused." The report blamed the news media for "any success the revolutionaries achieved in their ultimate objective of fomenting hatred and ridicule among the citizenry against the authorities."

It said newsmen sometimes encouraged protestors to prolong confrontations with the police. It called photographers particularly uncooperative in responding to reasonable police orders. The Daley report also said police found it difficult to distinguish between newsmen and demonstrators.

Ultimately, the Mayor commissioned a one-hour documentary to support his charges. His movie makers used network film extensively including portions of a 23-minute interview the Mayor granted CBS News

during the convention, one in which Walter Cronkite permitted the
Mayor to air his views extensively. Stations across the nation played the
Mayor's version of August in Chicago (the networks declined to run it).
Far fewer carried a one-hour rebuttal produced by the American Civil
Liberties Union.

The networks were stunned by the stir their coverage created. Even
before the convention ended, there was a flood of phone calls and telegrams. Many came from Chicagoans, outraged at the insult to their city.
In Chicago itself, network secretaries and young pages, male and female,
were subjected to a stream of abusive calls, the language paralleling the
worst used by provocateurs in the park, the accusations ranging from
dishonesty to observations that the networks were communist controlled.

Nationwide, the outpouring of mail was tremendous. CBS affiliates
received some 9,000 letters, the ratio critical of the coverage was 11 to 1.
NBC reported over 8,500 letters condemning their coverage, fewer than
1,100 in praise. Mayor Daley claimed he received 135,000 letters of support, only 5,000 critical.

The FCC got letters, to—about 1,500. On September 13, it asked all
three networks to defend themselves of the charges in those letters of
protest. The networks did so, reluctantly. They raised questions as to the
propriety of such an FCC request. NBC said the request "raises serious
questions under the Communications Act and the First Amendment.
Both the Act and the First Amendment bar the Commission from any
form of regulation which might constitute censorship of the broadcast
press."

NBC, to the charge that networks ignored significant activity at the
podium, documented its coverage of official proceedings and the many
other actions swirling around the convention. "Without such supplementary coverage," it said of the non-podium coverage, "a broadcasting
organization would be serving merely as a passive conduit for approved
information. This is not the function of the broadcast or any other journalistic medium."

CBS, in answer to questions about the provocation of police, documented its treatment of that matter. It even cited a telegram from two
top McCarthy aides, Blair Clark and Richard Goodwin, saying that conditions in Chicago, if anything, "were shown in a more favorable light
than they deserved."

The Walker Report and Other Studies.

Vindication of sorts came late in the year with the "Walker Report,"
a study of the Chicago convention conducted by a prominent Chicago
Attorney, Daniel Walker, for the National Commission on the Causes and

Prevention of Violence. In addition to his staff's work and statements it took from 1,410 eyewitnesses and participants, Walker had access to over 2,000 interviews conducted by the FBI.

Said the Walker Report, "To read dispassionately the hundreds of statements describing at firsthand the events of Sunday and Monday nights is to become convinced of the presence of what can only be called a police riot."

If anything, said the Report, conditions were worse than the press described them. These comments from the Report's summary:

> During the week of the Democratic National Convention, the Chicago police were the targets of mounting provocation by both word and act. It took the form of obscene epithets, and of rocks, sticks, bathroom tiles and even human feces hurled at police by demonstrators. Some of these acts had been planned; others were spontaneous or were themselves provoked by police action. Furthermore, the police had been put on edge by widely published threats of attempts to disrupt both the city and the Convention.

> That was the nature of the provocation. The nature of the response was unrestrained and indiscriminate police violence on many occasions, particularly at night.

> That violence was made all the more shocking by the fact that it was often inflicted upon persons who had broken no law, disobeyed no order, made no threat. These included peaceful demonstrators, onlookers, and large numbers of residents who were simply passing through, or happened to live in, the areas where confrontations were occurring.

> Newsmen and photographers were singled out for assault, and their equipment deliberately damaged. Fundamental police training was ignored; and officers, when on the scene, were often unable to control their men. As one police officer put it: "What happened didn't have anything to do with police work."

> The violence reached its culmination on Wednesday night.

> A report prepared by an inspector from the Los Angeles Police Department, present as an official observer, while generally praising the police restraint he had observed in the parks during the week, said this about the events that night:

> "There is no question but that many officers acted without restraint and exerted force beyond that necessary under the circumstances. The leadership at the point of conflict did little to prevent such conduct and the direct control of officers by first line supervisors were virtually non-existent."

> He is referring to the police-crowd confrontation in front of the

Conrad Hilton Hotel. Most Americans know about it, having seen the 17-minute sequence played and replayed on their television screens.

But most Americans do not know that the confrontation was followed by even more brutal incidents in the Loop side streets. Or that it had been preceded by comparable instances of indiscriminate police attacks on the North Side a few nights earlier when demonstrators were cleared from Lincoln Park and pushed into the streets and alleys of Old Town.

The Walker Report cited Mayor Daley's defense of his police department's conduct:

Chicago's Mayor Richard J. Daley held a press conference of his own late Thursday morning. He publicly criticized both the media and the protesters. Reading from a prepared statement and giving no opportunity for questions, Mayor Daley placed much of the blame for the street disorders on the news media. He said the media set the stage for the disruptions by detailing the advance plans of the demonstrators. He also claimed that the efforts of law enforcement agencies were "distorted and twisted" in news accounts. The Mayor further charged that television was a "tool" used in plans for "calculated disruption and rioting."

That night, in an appearance with Walter Cronkite on CBS, Mayor Daley challenged the television networks to cover the more positive side of the police-demonstrator story, rather than merely the violent aftermath of each incident. He contended that the cameras never showed the police reasoning with the marchers or showing them where they could move freely or safely. Nor did TV ever tell about the policemen who were hurt, he said.

"I'd like them to show the 51 policemen injured, some of them severely," he said. "I've never seen on television a picture of a wounded policeman lying on the street, seeing them badly hurt. Is this the kind of color of the news we should get?" Mayor Daley also complained that some newsmen looked so much like protesters that the police could not tell them apart. "The police have been given instructions," he said, "but one must realize that in many instances—and we have pictures of them—they (newsmen) never identify themselves. They're in the crowd and many of them are hippies themselves in television and radio and everything else. They are a part of the movement and some of them are revolutionaries and they want these things to happen."

CBS News President Richard Salant said in response to Mayor Daley: "The pictures and sound of the Chicago Police Department in action speak for themselves—louder than any words of ours or any attempts by them to find a scapegoat."

The conclusions of the Walker Report were mirrored in December of 1969 in a statement by the National Commission on the Causes and Prevention of Violence. They drew a contract between the police handling of protest in Chicago and the handling of "many of the same protesting groups . . . in roughly equal numbers" at the so-called counter-Inaugural in Washington the following January. In Washington, police used only that force clearly necessary to maintain order. In Chicago there was "excessive force not only against the provocateurs but also against the peaceful demonstrators and passive bystanders. Their conduct, while it won the support of the majority, polarized substantial and previously neutral segments of the population against the authorities and in favor of the demonstrators."

Early in 1969, the FCC issued its own report—another vindication of sorts for the networks. The FCC ruled there "is no substantial basis for concluding that the networks failed to afford 'reasonable opportunity for the presentation of contrasting viewpoints' on the issues at the Chicago convention." It did cite four alleged instances of events being "staged" for the cameras (i.e.: a "girl hippy" reportedly shouting at troops "Don't hit me!" when cued by a newsreel crew) and asked the networks for comments on those.

In September of 1969, the FCC closed the file on the convention by disposing of these four instances. It said the ABC admitted to one (a producer had placed a sign with the words "Welcome to Chicago" in a small trash fire being filmed. He was reprimanded by his network). All three networks denied any involvement in the other alleged incidents of "staging." These incidents were investigated apart from the main probe into the convention coverage, a probe the FCC said was inspired by "hundreds" of complaints about fairness. The networks, the federal agency concluded, had been fair.

The FCC stressed that it was not passing judgment on the quality of network coverage or on the "truth" of its reporting. That, it said, was beyond the proper scope of the FCC and was a matter for critics of journalism.

The networks had gone to great pains to defend themselves, before the FCC and before the Commission on Violence, before committees of the Congress and other investigators. Still, one vivid impression remained —the one that had caused the greatest outburst of protest with the general public: the networks, many viewers thought, had devoted far too much time to the violence in Chicago. This general feeling was a product, perhaps, of the frustration felt by the American majority. They were frustrated by the virulence of the anti-war protests all year long, frustrated by the brash disenchantment of the young, frustrated by the rebellion of the Blacks (who, it was said, chortled at the violence on Michigan Avenue, saying whites were finally feeling the sting of the police billy club, the smarting of police brutality).

How much coverage *had* the networks devoted to the violence? In over 38 hours devoted to coverage of the convention, CBS had used only a touch over 32 minutes dealing with the demonstrations—only 1.4% of the total. NBC in 35 hours of coverage reported about 36 minutes devoted to violence during convention sessions, 28 minutes devoted to the demonstrations outside of convention sessions. ABC, which treated much of the convention in summary rather than live, cites less than 14 minutes devoted to the disorders in over 19 and a half hours of convention coverage—1.1% of the total time.

Why did the public think it more? One suggested answer comes from Neil Hickey in the February 8, 1969 issue of *TV Guide*:

> The Chicago convention is being called the great Rorschach event of recent American history: observers of every bias are interpreting it according to their own needs and fantasies. Similarly, an impressive body of psychological literature attests to the existence of a remarkable phenomenon called perceptual selection, which means that witnesses to an event perceive it—and quite sincerely so —the way they *want* to perceive it, and reject coldly what their prejudices and presumptions find uncongenial.

Robert "Shad" Northshield, then producer of the Huntley-Brinkley newscast, said: "People have come to depend on television as their old pal, in their living room . . . in their families. It was part of the environment. And suddenly it betrayed them. It showed something that was just terrible to see, just terrible."

Friedrich Nietzche may have said it a long time ago when he observed, " 'I have done this,' says memory, 'I can't have done this,' says pride. In the end, memory yields."

Perhaps seeing it on television *did* make it more vivid than life itself. Critic Richard Goldstein, writing in *New York* magazine in March of 1969, observed that Chicago was "the death of television's most precious illusion: that vision is neutral. When I returned to my hotel on the night of Humphrey's nomination and switched on the window in my room, I realized that the scene I had just witnessed on the street seemed infinitely more terrifying on television. First, because the coverage made the horror seem legitimate. Second, because the screen was filled with concentrated violence. But most important, because the boredom of participation had been replaced by the thrill of observation."

Reuven Frank, the perceptive President of NBC News wrote this after Chicago:

A new love-hate relationship has suddenly burst forth between television and its basic audience. Not between television and the intellectuals and upper-middlebrows, the ones who talk about boob tubes and finally break down and buy one for the kids; the ones who up to 1960 bemoaned the passing of conversation in America (as though they ever listened); the ones who at cocktail parties were always importuning you to do subjects no one would watch—including them. But between television and the basic American audience, the most middle-class majority in the history of man . . .

Between 1964, the last convention year, and 1968, the average middle-class American has gone through many wrenching experiences. His tranquility has been shattered. He has been exposed to realities of war in a way no previous generation of Americans has had to face its war. He has seen ghetto riots in his living room. He has watched with horror young people of good background expressing contempt for his dearest values in the way they dress and act and what they say. Berkeley and Hough and Hue; Columbia and Newark and Tet; what he has seen on television has shaken him physically and morally, made him fear for his safety, his savings, his children, his status. The world as reported by television threatens him. It is a short and understandable step for him to conclude that television threatens him. Television has become the object of what psychoanalysts call transference.

On CBS one night, Eric Sevareid summed it up thusly:

The night of Wednesday, last August 28, was the culminating moment of the Democratic National Convention. It was also the high, agonizing point of the savage rioting in the Chicago streets.

This was the most heavily photographed and broadcast stage of the fighting. Because most of it was concentrated, by the Hilton Hotel Convention Headquarters and because most of the relatively few television cameras allowed in the streets were right there.

That night and for days following tens of thousands of angry letters, telegrams and phone calls poured into newspapers, local stations and networks. The overwhelming majority sided with the police and accused the reporters of slanted reporting in favor of the demonstrators.

It was an astounding situation. People hundreds and thousands of miles away from the scene, with no independent means of forming valid judgments of their own—knowing only what they were shown— were instantly certain that what they were shown was wrong.

The explanation seems obvious. Over the years the pressure of public resentment against screaming militants, foul mouthed demonstrators, arsonists and looters had built up in the national boiler. With Chicago it exploded. The feelings that millions of people released were formed long before Chicago. Enough was enough: the police *must* be right. Therefore, the reporting *must* be wrong.

The vehemence of public reaction and the calls for investigations on many fronts take their toll. The network news departments and the networks as a whole have defended their coverage in Chicago. Still there was a sensitiveness that comes naturally from a flow of criticism.

In replying to the FCC call for explanations about Chicago, NBC put it this way:

> If broadcasters are discouraged from covering issues or events which might require them to justify themselves to the Commission, the aims of a free press are not served. If their judgment as to what they will cover, or how they will cover it, is affected by the views of the Commission expressed in decisions, or rules, or intimations of disapproval, the broadcast press is, to that extent, no longer free.

CBS took a similar position in its reply to the FCC, stating

> When . . . as in the present instance, the passions aroused by a difficult period in our national life have brought about demands for Government censorship and control of this great medium, more than ever there is a need for the Commission to interpose itself, as we have suggested on a previous occasion, "as a shield for the defense of the integrity of broadcast journalism and as a champion of the First Amendment rather than as a willing inquisitor."

The FCC, in reply, said it was "puzzled" by the concerns of CBS and NBC, that it clearly recognized "the right of broadcasters to be as outspoken as they wish, and that allowance must be made for honest mistakes on their part."

Chicago had been a sobering experience, for television and for America. The impact of the image had shocked millions—and was sure to bear on future coverage of political events.

CHAPTER 12

PRESIDENTS AND
THE HOME SCREEN

So THEY GET nominated—and there is television. And they run for office—
and there is television. Finally, they make it, and they go to the White
House. And, still, there is television.

It's as much a part of Presidential life today as "Hail to the Chief"
when he enters a public place or applause when he leaves it. Presidents
have quarrelled with the press since the earliest days of our history when
George Washington scorned the "publick" printers. Today, they quarrel
with television as well as public printers.

Lyndon Johnson once popped in at the inauguration of a new president at the National Press Club. In his speech, Mr. Johnson noted that
Thomas Jefferson had once said that if he had to choose between a government without a free press or a free press without a government, he
would choose the latter. "That," quipped LBJ, "was before he became
President!"

Unfortunately, Lyndon Johnson did not make merry with the press
often—he was more frequently quarrelsome. One of his several press
secretaries, Bill Moyers, once wrote, "What the press and government
should seek from each other is a mutual no-poaching agreement, for the
press and the government are not allies. They are adversaries . . . How
each performs is crucial to the workings of a system that is both free and
open but fallible and fragile. For it is the nature of a democracy to thrive
upon conflict between press and government without being consumed
by it."

The nature of these adversaries is important for it tells something
about the pressures on a President and more about a President's pressures
on the press. Most modern Presidencies begin with a press-White House

honeymoon and fairly quickly degenerate into the sort of bickering not uncommon after a honeymoon.

For his part, the President rarely bickers in person (he has staff and supporters to do that); a more common Presidential posture is one of puzzled innocence, a touch hurt by press criticism. Often this is accompanied by public humility (much like W. S. Gilbert's "You've no idea what a poor opinion I have of myself—and how little I deserve it") and a brave chin, held high. In less public fashion, the President, as other centers of immense power, exerts pressures in many ways to mold news reports. "News management," that favorite cry of editors and committees on Freedom of Information, is neither new nor well-managed but it exists.

Fewer occasions of news management were more glaring than those in the early years of John F. Kennedy during that Cuban fiasco, the Bay of Pigs invasion. It is reported that a Presidential envoy to Henry Luce to complain of an account of the Bay of Pigs in *Fortune* magazine met with little success. On the other hand, Kennedy did much better with the *New York Times.*

Though the *Times* had printed much on the preparation for the Bay of Pigs invasion, it did hold back significantly at one point. White House sources had indicated that some of the suppressed *Times* material would do injury to the national security and to the forces preparing for invasions. Kennedy, it was said, later told the publisher of the *Times*, "I wish you had run everything on Cuba" and told its executive editor, "If you had printed more about the operation you would have saved us from a colossal mistake."

Such candor, after the fact, is remarkable. More typical of a President's feelings are the remarks Kennedy made prior to the invasion: "I can't believe what I'm reading! Castro doesn't need agents over here. All he has to do is read our papers. It's all laid out for him."

The Bay of Pigs story was revealed by Clifton Daniel, managing editor of the *Times*, in a remarkable speech at the World Press Institute in 1966. Daniel's own conclusion: "The Bay of Pigs operation might well have been cancelled and the country would have been saved enormous embarrassment if the *New York Times* and other newspapers had been more diligent in the performance of their duty—their duty to keep the public informed on matters vitally affecting our national honor and prestige, not to mention our national security."

Just one week after the Bay of Pigs, the President addressed a convention of newspaper publishers and said, "Every newspaper now asks itself with respect to every story, 'Is it news?' All I suggest is that you add the question: 'Is it in the interest of national security?'"

It might be argued, as the Bay of Pigs demonstrated so well, that national security is best served by not denying newsmen the privilige that Moyers talked of, the "privilege to find out all it can about what is going on." Robert Kennedy, in the spring of '67, confirmed that his brother felt wider discussion in the press might have prevented the Bay of Pigs and added, "In looking back over crises from Berlin and the Bay of Pigs to the Gulf of Tonkin, or even over the past fifteen years, I can think of few examples where disclosure of large policy considerations damaged the country, and many instances where public discussion and debate led to more thoughtful and informed decisions."

It goes back to the familiar ground-rule that so many journalists have professed (and not nearly so many have followed) that the proper relationship between a reporter and a news source is one of distance. Familiarity breeds contempt; in a newsman's life, it breeds inhibitions.

No matter how much those in power appear to be friendly for cordiality's own sake, their serious purpose is to use the media. Bill Moyers said it flatly: "Modern Presidents have realized that they can never effectively govern unless they learn to reach the people through the mass media, and the wise ones have discovered how to go through or over the press to the people."

History of Presidential News Conferences.

For Presidents, the most common means of going "through or over" is the Presidential news conference. This is especially true in an era of television where the people see and hear everything the reporter does.

It is said that Theodore Roosevelt was the first President to engage in question-and-answer sessions with the press. In press history, Teddy Roosevelt was quite an innovator: he installed the first White House press room (previously they waited outdoors in all weather for the emergence of Presidential callers) and the first press secretary (though Herbert Hoover, in 1929, was first to formalize the position, naming George Akerson as press secretary).

Roosevelt loved dealing with the press. He frequently granted scoops to his favorites. Sometimes, he wooed his critics with invitations to White House dinners. Other times, T.R. rebuked the critical ones, relegated them to the Ananias (liar's) Club, hinted to their employers that they were replaceable, or saw to it that his secretary, William Loeb, Jr., had them blacklisted at government agencies and thus deprived of access to news. In the early, happier days with the press, however, he inaugurated news conferences. They took place, it is reported, in late afternoon while his barber shaved the President. They were punctuated with Teddy pushing the razor aside and pacing back and forth, lather covering his face as he lectured the assembled few for reportorial ignorance or impudence.

In the last year of his Presidency, he was far more jaded about the press. He had his Attorney General sue the *New York World* and the *Indianapolis News* for criminal libel after published innuendo about corruption in the purchase of rights to the Panama Canal. He lost the case. He did somewhat better when he ran on the Bull Moose ticket and sued a Michigan paper for $10,000 for reporting that he was drinking heavily during the campaign. He won the case, the paper apologized, and the court awarded a verdict of six cents and court costs.

Reporters at Teddy's news conference were told that they were background-only, he was not to be quoted by name. Add to that the Roosevelt penalty system and you had polished news management.

William Howard Taft came next and was very ill at ease with reporters except for two favorites, one of them a correspondent for the paper his brother owned in Cincinnati. He met the press infrequently and was overheard to have asked his secretary before one such news conference, "Must I see those men again?"

Woodrow Wilson wanted more in his relations with the press and created the modern Presidential Press Conference, open to all accredited reporters and not just favorites or those on influential papers. The conferences were to be held twice a week and at the outset, Wilson announced that he wanted to take the press into his confidence and in turn, expected them to tell him what the country was thinking.

Unfortunately, Wilson looked upon these meetings as formal seminars. He prepared for them as he did for his lectures at Princeton and often conducted them much in that fashion. He was shocked by the questioning of reporters (200 would attend) and infuriated when questioning got personal, particularly as it related to his daughters. "Some men of brilliant ability were in the group," he said, "but I soon discovered the interest of the majority was in the personal and trivial rather than in principles and policies."

When the *Lusitania* sank in 1915, Wilson stopped news conferences, supposedly to keep foreign correspondents from leaking information to various embassies in Washington. They were never resumed as a regular thing though he held a few sessions after the war.

Warren Harding, like so many others, came in with an era of good feelings towards the press—even to dropping in at the National Press Club to play a game of hearts (a nickel a point) with reporters. He resumed the twice-daily news conference until the day he handled a question badly and had to issue a formal correction to calm an upset government, Japan. After that, Harding insisted that all questions be in writing and submitted in advance.

Calvin Coolidge continued that practice, riffling through the pile of questions and throwing away those he chose not to answer. At one such session, a dozen reporters all submitted the same question—was Coolidge planning to be a candidate in 1928? He set them aside one by one until he found a different question, answered it, and then concluded the news conference.

By the way, "Silent Cal" Coolidge was not too silent. He held over 500 news conferences during his Presidency, averaging almost two a week. Their frequency was deceiving and their results not too productive. Coolidge had little of consequence to say and like others, refused to let reporters quote him, even indirectly.

Herbert Hoover, though he was quite open with reporters and quite popular as Secretary of Commerce, retained the practice of questions submitted in advance, twenty-four hours in advance, of a news conference. With the coming of the Depression, he grew even more guarded, withheld important information, tried to punish critics, and even suggested that stories relating to the economy be submitted to the White House for clearance before publication.

Franklin Delano Roosevelt arrived and revealed himself to be the master of wooing newsmen. At his first news conference, he shook hands with every one of the 200 reporters, calling many by their first names and said this:

> I am told that what I am about to do will become impossible, but I am going to try it. We are not going to have any more written questions; and, of course while I cannot answer seventy-five or a hundred questions simply because I haven't got the time, I see no reason why I should not talk to you ladies and gentlemen off the record in just the way that I have been doing in Albany and in the way I used to do in the Navy Department down here . . . There will be a great many questions, of course, that I won't answer, either because they are "if" questions—and I never answer them . . .
>
> And the others, of course, are the questions which for various reasons I do not want to discuss, or I am not ready to discuss, or I do not know anything about. There will be a great many questions you will ask that I do not know enough about to answer.
>
> Then, in regard to news announcements, Steve (Press Secretary Stephen Early) and I though it would be best that straight news for use from this office should always be without direct quotation. In other words, I do not want to be directly quoted unless direct quotations are given out by Steve in writing.

FDR added that he didn't want to revive the Ananias Club so anything given on background was not be attributed to the White House.

This device was Roosevelt's license to float trial balloons and he sent many aloft, shooting them down later as he saw fit. He also was known to use the off-the-record technique to tie a reporter's hands if it was something he might find out anyway. With virtuoso style, Franklin Roosevent conducted 998 news conferences during his Presidency. He did not revive the Ananias Club but he created his own—the Dunce Cap Club. "Go off to the corner and put on a dunce cap."

Roosevelt reveled in being called a "newspaperman's President" or "the best newspaperman who has ever been President of the United States." He often answered questions by beginning, "If I were going to write a story . . ."

He also could get furious at the Press. When pressed to comment on running for a fourth term, he said, cupping his hands to his mouth, "You know what the answer is? None of your damned business." He also could get ugly. Angry at John O'Donnell of the *New York Daily News* whom he accused of giving comfort to the Nazis during World War II, Roosevelt awarded the reporter the German Iron Cross. In 1935, he was photographed rubbing his eyes during a birthday celebration. Somehow the picture was printed with the caption "President Ponders Farm Problem." Furious, Roosevelt banned all pictures for a period.

There was one permanent taboo involving photographs. A polio victim, FDR was never to be photographed in pain or discomfort. There was the time when he fell, full-length, on the floor. Dozens of photographers were there. Not one took a picture.

Roosevelt also created a means to go over the heads of the press. He invented the "Fireside Chat" on radio. With a magnificent speaking voice and the bedside manner of a country doctor, he spoke to the nation four times in his first year of office. Despite the great success of these, and the feeling of people that he used the device frequently, Roosevelt only gave four other "Fireside Chats," the last in 1936.

Harry Truman was not as eloquent as Roosevelt but he kept the FDR ground rules for news conferences, moved them to the Indian Treaty Room in the Executive Office Building next door to accommodate more reporters, and conducted some of the bluntest sessions ever with the press. He was not above telling reporters, "It's none of your business" or "I don't have to tell you about a Cabinet meeting."

Truman was open and candid, blunt and honest. He also could shoot from the hip and got in trouble when the Chinese Communists entered the war in Korea and Truman said the use of the atom bomb was "always under consideration." His Secretary of State, Dean Acheson, later wrote that, "We kept on hand, as a sort of first aid kit, a boxful of 'clarifications'."

Acheson said, of news conferences, "We learned from all mistakes but one—the fast answer in that nightmare of Presidents, the press conference." Truman survived over 300 such "nightmares."

Under Eisenhower, James Hagerty, an ex-*New York Times* political writer, orchestrated White House press relations with the finesse of a French cook and the efficiency of a Detroit assembly line. He said his job was to make his boss look good and he did his job brilliantly.

Ike was given to frequent vacations, particularly to golf at Augusta, Georgia. Hagerty called these "working" vacations and managed to parcel out news on demand to maintain that image. If nothing much came out of the Augusta White House and reporters became restless, Hagerty would announce appointment of a new Ambassador, or the latest Atomic Energy detection of Russian nuclear explosions, or new legislation under consideration. It was sort of a "story-a-day keeps criticism away" approach. Hagerty was the first to systematically cull potential announcements out of federal agencies and see that the President, not his Cabinet members, made the announcements.

Eisenhower, it was said, preferred their publishers to reporters. He had limited fondness for the White House press, was irritated at embarrassing questions. He never seemed able to remember very many names of White House regulars at his news conferences. Hagerty ultimately introduced a rule that reporters identify themselves by name and organization before asking the President a question.

The most brilliant performance of all by James C. Hagerty came when Ike had a heart attack in Denver. The Press Secretary would fly in Cabinet officers who allegedly were taken to Ike's bedside to "confer" with him. They then were brought to the press room for a news conference, giving the clear impression that Ike was still active in running the government when in fact he was being kept from any bad news.

Before Ike ran for a second term, he suffered still another serious health set-back, an emergency abdominal operation. It was less than a year after the heart attack and there was much speculation about the President's health and his ability to run again. Hagerty kept the President out of sight for almost two months and then produced him at a news conference on August 1, 1956. Though he was thinner and less vigorous, the President—well briefed and most candid—performed magnificently for half an hour. One magazine called it the "frankest, most searching interview since Wilson inaugurated regular conferences in 1913." Ike was obviously ready to run again.

Television Joins the News Conference.

Hagerty had felt since the beginning of Ike's first term that there should be some way to introduce television to the news conference. He did so on January 19, 1955. The ground rule was that none of the film or radio tape was releasable until it had been checked by Hagerty who had the right to edit them before broadcast. It was a restriction that Hagerty found little need to employ. And television became part of the news conference.

Ike added movie actor Robert Montgomery, an early star on television, to be his TV advisor. Montgomery introduced make-up and careful lighting for the President. He also encouraged Ike to be relaxed, to be the charming personality that had won so many friends over the years.

Eisenhower was a success on television. The Presidency had finally discovered a way to go over the heads of reporters and directly to the public.

The final step to television—live and without the right to edit content —came within a week of the inauguration of Ike's successor, John F. Kennedy. It came, not without reservations at first, but with great enthusiasm after that first one on January 25, 1961.

The suggestion for live television came from Hagerty's successor, Pierre Salinger. A few weeks after Kennedy's election, while he was resting at Palm Beach, Salinger suggested, "What do you think of opening up your press conferences to live television? I don't think there's any doubt that you can handle it. You proved that against Nixon in the debates."

The arguments against this were voiced. A slip of the lip, and there was precedent for that in the news conferences of Harding, Truman and Eisenhower among others, could create problems. In the area of foreign policy it could be a disaster. Further, shades of Woodrow Wilson, there would be reporters from Soviet bloc newspapers present. McGeorge Bundy and Theodore Sorensen thought it too dangerous. Dean Rusk, later to be Secretary of State, also opposed the idea. The President-elect, however, disagreed. He said if he were to slip, it would be impossible to suppress for very long, with or without television.

Mr. Kennedy posed different questions of Salinger. Would the networks carry them, even if they did not produce major news stories? Would newspaper reporters be antagonized by this competitive break given television? Was the President running the risk of over-exposure to the public?

Salinger argued that should the networks not be interested in carrying all news conferences or should audiences diminish, they could always review the decision. Reporters would certainly be negative if their newspapers were scooped. On the other hand, only a small number of newspapers carried a full text of any news conference—television gave Kennedy an opportunity to having "full text" revealed across the nation.

Kennedy asked Salinger to check it out with the networks. On December 27, 1960 Salinger spent five hours with the top news executives of the networks. Enthusiastically, they encouraged him. He then went to the President who agreed: "We should be able to go around the newspapers if that becomes necessary. But, beyond that, I don't know how we can justify keeping TV out if it wants in."

Salinger went to the White House regulars to announce that the first Presidential news conference, five days after the Inauguration, would be open to live television. He found his expected hostile reception. He recounts that Bill Lawrence, then White House correspondent of the *New York Times*, sarcastically beginning a statement, "Mr. Salinger, as you plunge deeper and deeper into matters about which you know absolutely nothing . . ." Salinger interrupted, shouting, and would not take the rest of the question: the decision was final, take it or leave it.

In the delicious irony of the years to come, Lawrence moved over to ABC and became one of the nation's best known White House correspondents, *because* of television.

Salinger returned from his session with the newspaper reporters and called the President-elect to report. Kennedy was laughing, "Don't tell me, I already know. I could hear it clear across town."

On January 25, 1961 President Kennedy strode across the stage of the handsome West Auditorium of the new State Department building and held the first televised news conference in the history of the Presidency.

From the start, President Kennedy prepared as carefully for news conferences as he did for the Nixon debates. In addition, this first news conference was to begin with a major news story. The Soviet Union had agreed to release the two survivors of the RB-47 reconnaissance plane that went down over Russia, Captains Freeman Olmstead and John McKone. It was interpreted as a gesture of friendship towards the new President. The day before the news conference, David Wise of the *New York Herald Tribune*, informed Salinger that he had the story. Salinger confirmed the story but asked that it be held up else the release not take place, the Russians having insisted on simultaneous announcement of the story. Wise consulted his publisher, Jock Whitney who decided to hold up on the story.

Though Salinger denies that the hold was to provide a major announcement for the President's first televised news conference, that was the effect. Mr. Kennedy was able to reveal that Olmstead and McKone had been discharged from Lubiynka Prison and were on their way home. Many reporters were convinced that Salinger had simply saved this headline grabber for the news conference. On the other hand, examination of the record showed the sensitiveness of the moment, including the toning down of a strongly anti-Soviet speech by Admiral Arleigh Burke that week to avoid irritating the Russians and ruining the release arrangement.

It soon became clear that news breaks were not essential to Presidential news conferences. Handsome John Kennedy was a perfect President for television exposure. He loved intellectual combat with the press. He had wit and grace and was always well prepared. He was an instant public success. The President was continually curious about his ratings and after the very first news conference asked Salinger to check the size of the audience. It was estimated at sixty million.

In addition to careful briefing before the news conference, the President made it a habit to view the tape of it at night (a local station carried it delayed) and would critique his performance. These self-criticisms ranged from the quality of the answers to the shortcomings of lighting and camera angles.

Kennedy held over sixty televised news conferences in the thousand days of his Presidency, the last just eleven days before his assassination. Arthur Schlesinger, Jr., called them "the central forum" of Kennedy's communication to the nation.

Salinger called the Kennedy news conferences "his most revelatory legacy. They reveal as much about the man as they do about his ideas. His grasp of the infinite detail of government; his studied refusal to look at problems in over-simple terms; his quickness of mind; his capacity for righteous anger; and his quick humor are all clearly evident."

He was so good at it that his successor had reason to avoid comparisons with Kennedy. Lyndon Johnson approached news conferences with the caution that a Texan uses in hunting rattlesnakes. He was chary of anything that might lend itself to contrast with the dead President's knack for television. For a hundred days he resisted. He'd have reporters in for coffee in the oval office of the President but did so without warning, without television. Finally, he suggested to Salinger that they go on television.

Johnson Experiments with TV.

It seems obvious that the site and the setting would have to be different or the comparisons would be inevitable. Salinger had chosen the West Auditorium at State, in part, because it could be partitioned off at the rear and there would always be the appearance of a "full house." Now, he had to choose a different site and decided on the International Conference Room at the State Department. Its 400-seat capacity was half that of the other auditorium but Salinger knew now that they would be filled. President Johnson did not stand behind a lectern; he sat behind a desk. Otherwise, the ground rules and the pattern was much as Kennedy had set it.

When the conference ended, James Reston was to comment, "President Johnson achieved his major objective in his first televised press conference: He survived."

Lyndon Johnson experimented widely in contacts with the press and television appearances. News conferences were televised first in the State Department, then in the White House East Room and back and forth including the airplane hangar at his ranch in Johnson City, Texas. Once, on May 6, 1964 he even held a news conference from an open stage on the back lawn of the White House, invited the wives and children of reporters. At the end, he called all the children up on stage with him and his beagle dogs.

Without television present, he met reporters in all sorts of situations ranging from his frequent walks around the White House grounds (at least one distinguished reporter walked into a lamp post while trying to keep up and take notes at the same time) to private meetings over sherry "upstairs" in the White House private living quarters. He tried hard to be comfortable with the press only to find them increasingly critical, especially of his "style."

Mary McGrory, the brilliant columnist of the *Washington Star* wrote that reporters "feel they have as much freedom as an attendant at the court of Louis XIV . . . They feel they are treated as an extension of his staff, which is notoriously subject to his beck and call. Some members of the hiking club bitterly refer to the unproductive afternoons on the green as 'unpaid psychiatry.' The hostilities go on, taking on occasionally the tone of a domestic quarrel, as one side complains of being misunderstood and the other of being given no consideration."

The President, himself, finally felt he had had enough of poking at his press policies. He defined them in a famous news conference on March 20, 1965 at his Texas ranch. First he revealed that it was his practice to keep records of his exposure to the press and ticked off a tabulation, a most revealing catalogue of the variety of Presidential attempts to communicate with reporters:

> Today marks the 39th on-the-record press conference that I have held; 18 off-the-record or total of 57. I have had 18 press conferences with adequate advance notice, 16 covered by radio and television. Eight of these were live television in addition to three live television joint sessions in the little over the year I have been President.
>
> There have been other occasions upon which I have seen the White House Press Corps on an informal basis in order to give them some insight into my thinking. In addition to these 56 formal meetings I have had 9 informal, lengthy walks with the White House Press Corps. Some of you who used to enjoy those walks when they were scheduled a little earlier with President Truman and from time

to time those of you who enjoy them will be invited back again. On various occasions I have had conferences with pools representing the White House Press. We have had 173 airplane flights with pools where they visited. Two pool visits while I was in the hospital with a bad cold and one pool visit in my bedroom in the Executive Mansion when I thought I was recuperating from it. I have had additional visits from 374 accredited press representatives at their request. In addition, 64 who requested meetings at Bureau chiefs, plus 200 telephone discussions that I have responded to. There have been nine other occasions where I have met with the press ranging from barbecues at the Ranch to addresses made to the American Society of Newspaper Editors, Associated Press luncheons and of course last year each one of the social affairs, White House press conference and Gridiron, etc., I believe numbered eight. I have had nine special appearances ranging from television interviews with all three networks to special statements concerning Viet Nam and the railroad strike. A considerable amount of my time has been spent with the press in this effort to discharge what I consider to be the President's responsibility to this country. I think that it is necessary to do this because the press is the media through which the American people are informed and as I said, I intend to continue to bring them all the information that is possible and to see that every Cabinet officer and every head of an independent agency does the same thing. Insofar as the President is concerned, I will continue seeing the press at different times, different places and different ways at my own choosing.

His records of televised news conferences differ somewhat from those kept by network bureau chiefs in Washington. They showed this to be his sixth on live television, not his eighth. The President, however, was promising many more:

First of all I regard my own responsibility in this field as making available to all of you all of the information that I can consistent with the national interest on as fair and as equitable basis as possible. How and where I do that is a decision that I reserve for myself, and I shall continue to reserve for myself.

Second, I consider it the responsibility of the press to report those facts to the American public as fully as possible and in the best perspective possible. The press of course also has the right and has the duty to comment on the facts in any way it sees fit but that is a right and not a responsibility.

Therefore I plan to see the press at many different times in many different ways if you are willing. I will, however, try to follow the standing practice of holding at least one press conference a month of the nature which you describe as ample advance notice, coverage by all media, full dress—even white ties if you choose.

He said he wasn't going to restrict himself to these monthly televised news conferences but this would be "a very minimum." It was not. In the remaining forty-six months of his Presidency he held not forty-six more but only seventeen televised news conferences. There were seven in the remaining nine months of 1965, four in all of 1966, four more in 1967 and two in 1968.

Johnson's first news secretary, George Reedy, once noted, "Of the few social institutions which tend to keep a President in touch with reality, the most effective—and the most resented by the chief beneficiary —is the press. It is the only force to enter the White House from the outside world with a direct impact upon the man in the Oval Room which cannot be softened by intermediary interpreters or deflected by sympathetic attendants . . . Virtually all other communications that reach him will be shaped either directly or indirectly by people who wish either to conciliate or antagonize the Chief Executive."

After he left office, Johnson was to write, "In retrospect, I believe I should have held more regular televised news conferences. I was always more comfortable meeting with reporters around my desk, as President Roosevelt did, because it often gave us the opportunity to explore questions in greater depth than in a televised spectacular. Yet broadcast news conferences are an effective means of communicating with the public and should be widely used by national leaders."

Richard Nixon entered the world of Presidential news conferences in an atmosphere of nervous network news executives, nervous for fear of a setback in the ground rules for such news conferences. He had held a number of news conferences during the campaign during which the television cameras were stopped at one point though the questioning continued.

Mr. Nixon did this twice prior to taking office as he announced appointees to the up-coming Administration. First he introduced Dr. Henry Kissinger of Harvard as his national security advisor. He made the announcement, took some questions, then the television lights were turned off as the President-elect engaged in what he called an "on-the-record backgrounder." His staff called these remarks "elaborations."

It was said this allowed the President to be more comfortable as he expanded on his earlier comments and it kept people like new appointees, innocent to such experiences, from getting too nervous. For television broadcasters, it kept them from getting equal access to Presidential remarks. They protested strongly.

The President-elect did it again in announcing Charles Yost to be

Ambassador to the United Nations. This time the network correspondents objected and CBS did more. Dan Rather appeared on the evening news with the story, running the film until the lights were turned off, continuing with darkened film as Rather explained the nature of the Nixon ground rules. He also noted that some reporters felt this was being done to permit the President-elect to duck, on television at least, any questions about Sargent Shriver who had been discussed for the U.N. post.

Washington bureau chiefs of the three networks met with Herbert Klein, Communications Director in the new Administration and later with Ron Ziegler, the new Press Secretary. There were assurances that the half-televised news conferences would be discontinued.

The sheltered, non-televised postcript to news conferences was not needed. From the moment the President began his first, on January 27, 1969, it was evident that he would have no trouble with this form of communication. As Johnson had, when in Washington, Nixon chose the East Room of the White House. He discarded lecterns and desks and simply stood before a single microphone with reporters surrounding him on three sides and smoothly fielded all questions. Nixon was thoroughly at ease. Johnson was on occasion, most particularly in November of 1967 when he, too, abandoned lectern and desk and spoke with a lavalier microphone around his neck. The result was LBJ at his most comfortable, his most persuasive.

Nixon's first news conference drew widespread praise. Late in February, he embarked on a multi-stop European trip and returning, scheduled a news conference for 9 p.m. on March 4, 1969. It was to last one hour, the longest news conference ever on television and was the first to be held in evening, prime time. Speeches had been held at night, never a news conference.

The ground rules were that the news conference would be limited to questions about the European trip and foreign policy generally; no domestic questions. This, too, was unusual.

The performance was striking. With absolute ease and remarkable candor, the President went over the full range of foreign problems, smoothly and flawlessly. Eric Sevareid called it a "virtuoso" performance. The audience was very large (40 to 50 million) and dropped off very little during the hour despite predictions that the President could not hold the attention of a television audience for a full hour.

Presidential news conferences are sometimes compared to the British custom of allowing the opposition to question the Prime Minister but it is not really that. No statutory obligation to hold news conferences exists— only a precedent that is not very old. Presidential secretaries inevitably view these confrontations as a device to reach the public, over the heads of the press if need be. Said Bill Moyers, "I don't think the press has ever justifiably felt that the press conference was any other device than one for the President to say what is on his mind."

Pierre Salinger says much the same in confessing that he often planted questions with reporters (a practice that Moyers and others also have confessed to employing): "I had two reasons for doing this. First, a Presidential pronouncement often appears more newsworthy if the press draws it out of him than if he volunteers it himself. Second, the reporters don't do as much homework for the press conference as the President. He would often come prepared to answer a question of major significance, but no one would ask it. It was important to us not only that he have the chance to express himself on such questions, but that the form of the question elicit the exact answer he had ready."

Such maneuvers are often damned as "news management" but is it really improper for a press secretary, who is there to serve his boss first and represent the press to his boss only secondarily, to try to maneuver Presidential appearances into the best possible light? If it is improper, the question is still irrelevant for it can never be any other way.

In many ways the news conference is the least satisfying way for the President to go "over the heads" of the press. He has access to other appearances on live television, many of them.

In his first two years in office alone, President Johnson was on live television about sixty times, more than Ike was in eight years and far more than Kennedy in almost three years (he made about thirty-three live television appearances in that period). He even introduced the innovation of live coverage as he signed major legislation (medicare, civil rights, immigration, etc.) with Congressional leaders around him, ready to receive souvenir pens from the signing.

He even had a live television studio installed in the White House. It was the result of a hurry-up appearance earlier that year to announce settlement of a railroad strike.

At the time, CBS News was located in the studios of its Washington affiliate, WTOP-TV. I received a call from the press office indicating that the President and representatives of labor and management were on their way over to announce settlement of the strike. I had hardly finished notifying the other networks to link to our studio when Secret Service men and police came swarming into the building. Moments behind them came the President and a very large group of White House reporters.

There was no time to isolate the reporters in viewing rooms nor any attempt to do so. They crowded into the studio with the President. All three networks were already on the air with their major evening newscasts and had to punch up live when the President began. One competing newscast did so with a bit of confusion which included an on-the-air plug for CBS ("He's ready at CBS").

When this hurried performance ended, the President and his party wanted to see the tape. Into a small conference room they went but there was some delay as the tape editor fumbled to get cued up. Labor Secretary Willard Wirtz said, "They seem to be all shook up, Mr. President." My only comment: "You should have been here thirty minutes ago!"

Inevitable post-mortems followed. There was a serious ethical question that disturbed the networks. The President had to be inserted live within the framework of newscasts with no idea of the journalistic values of what he had to say. Important, yes, but was it important enough to knock off a substantial part of a newscast before a captive audience? There is no question but that the networks would have used far less if they had had opportunity to edit the appearance.

The other question to be examined involved the rush nature of the appearance. The White House was bothered because they had to make a long drive to a studio (they did the normally twenty-minute drive in eight minutes) and the networks bothered because in all the chaos, it was quite possible that the broadcast could have been botched.

Subsequent meetings developed the idea of a studio in the White House for emergency broadcasts.

It was installed in the east wing of the White House, in a small movie theatre which FDR had installed years earlier. The room was 20 by 70 feet and one end was walled off to hold a control room while in the room proper, three cameras were set up. In February of 1965, the room was ready and the President called an 11 a.m. news conference. Unfortunately he showed up twenty minutes late, giving the networks much filling to do, but at last he arrived to face questions in a room jammed with two hundred newsmen.

The installation had cost the networks almost a quarter of a million dollars. Further, to be instantly ready, it was manned five and a half days a week, during the hours that the White House press office was open. Salary costs were expected to run over $50,000 a year.

The networks did this because of the apparent need to provide "instant television" for Lyndon Johnson. The President had gone on television as often as five times in one week, frequently with short notice. This could handle such emergencies as the Dominican crisis.

In time, however, President Johnson made less and less use of the facility. At the end of 1966, the network pool wrote Press Secretary Bill Moyers noting that the studio had been used very little over the previous nine months and then in situations that were not unscheduled "quickie" appearances. They asked for and received permission to abandon full staffing in favor of a plan to "heat up" the facility on fairly short notice and to staff it only during periods of crisis.

By the end of Johnson's term of office, the facility had fallen to complete disuse. Color television had made the equipment outdated and the "instant television" experiment had come to an end. The studio was dismantled during Nixon's first year in office.

President Johnson was fascinated by television and its power. He kept triple-sets, consoles that permitted him to watch all three networks at once with finger-tip control as to which audio he chose, both in his office and in his bedroom. He watched morning newscasts, dinnertime reports and the local news at night.

He experimented widely, and sometimes wildly, with the use of the medium. Once, in May of 1965, he delivered a speech on relations with Europe, requesting time on the Early Bird satellite and having European networks notified that the speech was available. In effect, in those countries carrying it, Johnson was talking directly to the people over the heads of the European governments.

As Walter Cronkite observed, "It seems to me that tonight there must be considerably bruised feelings among the Old World's statesmen who believe that international relations are played by that set of rules they call protocol."

In Britain, the speech was carried live. In France, it was not—and it is conceivable that Johnson's remarks about "outmoded nationalism" might well have offended DeGaulle. In Germany, there was another kind of reaction. Chancellor Ludwig Erhard requested time from the satellite people to speak to the American people.

This experiment was not repeated by the President.

Like all Presidents, Mr. Johnson found himself surrounded with staff "experts" on television. These advisors engaged in a number of experiments themselves. They leaned on network directors to shoot mostly close-ups of the President rather than medium or long shots. They even suggested that all photographers shoot the left and not the right profile of the President because someone told him that he shows up better on the left side. Aides would arrange camera positions and camera platforms to favor this "good" side.

In the end, Johnson never managed to become a successful television "personality." Late in 1969, in a Detroit speech, the television advisor to Richard Nixon, gave his own view of what went wrong. Frank Shakespeare said, "I think television destroyed Lyndon Johnson . . . (he) envisioned himself as perhaps a hopeful cross between, of, maybe Mark Twain and an Abraham Lincoln, a folksy man of the people, because that was the character that he tried to present on television. And because he wasn't those things, he came across as insincere, and that's the most devastating thing that can happen . . . he came across as a phoney. Now don't misinterpret me, it doesn't mean that he was, it just means that he came across as it."

The White House press office engaged in many moves to try to manage coverage. On more than one occasion, when the networks felt a domestic or foreign crisis warranted live capability on the White House lawn, permission to bring in live cameras and a mobile unit were denied. In fairness, after protest, this denial was generally reversed though not always. The reason for the denial? The Press Office felt that the presence of the television cameras heightened a sense of crisis or impending decision, and they wanted to dampen that image.

The White House and News Management.

Managing the news was attempted in many ways. Johnson had a personal photographer, Uoichi Okamota—an outstanding still photographer at the U.S. Information Agency. When "Okie," who took thousands of photos, came up with a particularly dramatic sequence, press officers "planted" in newspapers and magazines. Needless to say, the President always looked good in these. To the eternal discredit of some of America's most important newspapers and magazines, many of these photos were printed without identifying the source.

Okamota himself became a source of controversy at one point. Newspapers ran stories about this private photographer who had opportunities for exclusive, candid shots and speculated on how many thousands of pictures he had taken, at taxpayers expense, for the White House to use. Okie was banished back to his old job at USIA until the heat was off, then resumed snapping away at the White House.

The Press office frequently engaged in letting reporters and bureau chiefs know of their displeasure with stories (as did the President, himself, on occasion). A White House aide once called me to note that UPI had moved an item about a Vietcong mortar attack that killed twenty-seven women and children. He said he thought we ought to know about it since "everyone is doing so much reporting about other kinds of killings." I learned later that this same aide had called the other networks. The bureau chiefs speculated that the President, upset at the lack of reporting about enemy terrorism, had prompted the calls.

Once, during the Kennedy years, Pierre Salinger sent over a letter complaining about CBS news coverage. His message: "I thought you might be interested in this. We have other letters like this." Eager to make clear that this form of not-so-subtle intimidation would not influence us, I replied instantly: "Dear Pierre: Thank you for the correspondence. Does Mrs. Ehrman speak for you?"

There was no further comment from the White House.

Sometimes the anger of the White House could bite deeper. Once a CBS White House correspondent, Bob Pierpoint, reported on LBJ's reaction to some primary election results, based on the comments of an informed, but unidentified White House source. Pierpoint was called into the Press Office and refused to identify his source. Guards and others were called in and quizzed as to what people they had seen Pierpoint talking to during the day.

The source in question later called Pierpoint, asked him to continue protecting his identity. He said he thought the President was bothered because he didn't want anyone on his staff to talk to reporters without being authorized to do so. The source was protected.

Some reporters have said they believed the FBI had been used to discover the source of stories that the President did not want printed. One White House aide, after leaving the President's employe, told me that the Secret Service had once suggested that the White House pass of one CBS correspondent be lifted because he had been seen lunching with some Russian Embassy officials. It took Press Office intervention to explain that reporters did this sort of thing and were not to be considered security risks as a result. Further, they pointed out, the press protest following such a move would be extremely damaging to the White House image. The press pass remained in the reporter's pocket.

In August of 1967, CBS White House Correspondent Dan Rather uncovered a story about the so-called McNamara Wall, a barrier across South Vietnam, just south of the Demilitarized Zone. He filmed a "stand-up" piece on the White House lawn late that afternoon. This story was one that the White House hoped to sit on. Rather was called into the Press Office and after some light banter, Press Secretary George Christian inquired, "You're doing something on the barrier, aren't you?" Rather said he might be and Christian said that if he were, he would be "flat wrong."

They sparred for a while and finally Rather said, "George, I appreciate your guidance but I believe our information is solid and I'm going with it."

Christian said, "You know I speak for the President," and Rather replied that this was true but sometimes even Christian didn't know of impending moves. Christian asked that if the President said so would Rather reconsider? Christian left the room, by the door leading to the President's office area. He returned in five minutes and repeated what he had said earlier, including his comment that he speaks for the President.

Rather called CBS and suggested that the story be stopped. It was.

Less than ten days later, Secretary of Defense McNamara called a news conference. He announced the decision to build the barrier.

Christian later said he was going to check another White House staffer, not the President, and he was sorry if he left Rather with the impression that it was the President himself. The entire incident left the press with the impression that the White House was again trying to manage the timing of announcements, to prevent the press from revealing decisions before LBJ was ready for revelation.

The nature of the White House press arrangement is such that much of this sort of thing can be done. There are so many news people carrying White House passes, well over a thousand, that there must be careful regulation of where they can go and how. This power of physical limitation added to the right of controlling the moments of Presidential exposure permit White House press officers much license to manipulate.

Over at the "ladies side," the East wing, there has long been a tradition of managing coverage, of granting favors to friendly and/or important publications. There have been too frequent occasions where the press office there has had the right to "review" material before it is published.

An example of this took place in 1966. The President's younger daughter, Luci, was getting married. Under the strong hand of Mrs. Johnson's bright and witty Press Secretary, Elizabeth Carpenter, coverage was carefully controlled. The networks were told the extent to which television coverage would be permitted.

They were also invited to film certain material regarding wedding preparations, if they agreed to hold it until their "Wedding Specials" on the eve of or the day of the wedding. This material, the networks assumed, was embargoed for everyone.

A reception was held for the couple in the chambers of the U.S. Supreme Court, a reception given by Justice Tom Clark. Liz Carpenter said the networks would be permitted to film the first fifteen minutes of the receiving line.

The CBS cameraman, Tom Craven, Jr., called in and asked, "Do you know that they are saying the film is hold for release but still pictures can be printed immediately?" I told reporter Marya McLaughlin to tell Liz Carpenter that we would consider an embargo lifted if any of the media had permission to use the pictures. She reported back that Mrs. Carpenter was firm. I told her to tell Liz that if any newspaper had the right to print the photos, CBS would use the film and Mrs. Carpenter could call me if she liked. She did and my notes indicate the following exchange:

At 9 or so, Liz called said "The other networks have agreed . . ."

SMALL: "I'm in the news business. I can't be beaten by newspapers."

LIZ: "Well, if you can't be trusted . . ."

SMALL: "That's not the question. We never did and can't agree to a hold for release unless it is honored by newspapers as well. It's a good thing that this has happened over a matter so minor because there will be other stories more important."

LIZ: "Why is CBS the only one to break agreements?"

SMALL: "I couldn't face my cameraman in the morning if I allowed you to force a hold on material that will be in the morning news-papers."

LIZ: "Every media has its own problems. You should work on a magazine—their problems are mammoth."

SMALL: "Well, we can't go along with this . . ."

LIZ: "Well, we try to be cooperative . . . we try to help all media . . . we've broken our backs to help television to a good job . . . and this is what happens . . . we just won't have to work so hard to be co-operative."

SMALL: "If you're telling me that you are going to ban CBS . . . is that what you're telling me?"

LIZ: (Angry) "Listen, Bill, the President of the United States is upstairs and I'm not going to keep him waiting nor am I going to stand here in the Supreme Court arguing with you all night."

Small informed Salant . . . then called his colleagues at the other nets who agreed with the CBS position, denied ever making such a deal. Monroe of NBC said he had told his people to hold the film until he could get in the following morning and protest to Liz. He reminded Small that Liz on a prior occasion, the White House party for Princess Margaret, had banned TV coverage but permitted *Life Magazine* to shoot at will.

Such events are hardly momentous, are mostly amusing. No great injustice to the public has been done if the White House tries to orches-trate the use of wedding reception pictures or permits *Life* to have ex-clusive pictures of Princess Margaret at the White House. The incidents are revealing, however, of the day-to-day maneuvering by White House image makers, east or west wing, to create the picture of the President and his family as they would like to see it.

The Strangest TV "Conversation".

More serious and the most overtly heavy-handed example of White House intervention, as it relates to television, took place in December of 1967 when a "Conversation with the President" was taped and the editing was strongly flavored with White House suggestions. Indeed, some of this unsolicited editorial advice came from aboard Air Force One as it winged its way toward Australia, half a world away.

The first time a "Conversation with the President" was ever pre-sented was in December of 1962 when John F. Kennedy sat down with three network correspondents and talked about the problems of the Presi-dency. An exciting innovation, presented simultaneously by all three net-works, it attracted world wide attention.

This first "Conversation" was produced by CBS News for the networks, each with one correspondent participating, and with Fred Friendly producing. Friendly's bosses at that time, Richard Salant and Blair Clark, felt that the hour should be taped "to time," exactly as it would be telecast. Friendly, and ultimately the other networks, felt that more than one hour should be taped, with the best material kept, redundancy and less important material dropped. The White House was granted the right to withdraw material if it was factually in error or would adversely affect national security.

Few changes were necessary at that time and few at the first time that Lyndon Johnson permitted such a "conversation," in March of 1964 after his first 100 days in office. There was one minor deletion, suggested by National Security Advisor McGeorge Bundy that dealt with the proposed sale of wheat to India. A badly phrased sentence implied that the wheat, worthless sitting as surplus, was worthless wheat. The deletion was promptly made.

Few changes on both those occasions but not so, in December of 1967, when Lyndon Johnson's next—and last—such "Conversation" was taped.

At 10:30 a.m. on December 18, 1967 the networks gathered in the office of the President. The network bureau chiefs—Small of CBS, Bill Monroe of NBC, and John Lynch of ABC were there as a production committee along with the NBC producer, Bob Asman. In New York, an editing committee of three network news producers would tape and edit the final product. The correspondents were the White House correspondents, Frank Reynolds of ABC, Dan Rather of CBS and Ray Scherer of NBC.

Jack Valenti, no longer with the White House staff, was there that morning to give advice. Walt Rostow, the President's chief advisor on National Security was there. Other White House aides were in and out. There was some discussion of the setting inside the President's office. A rocking chair had been set for the President (in a recent appearance in a straight-backed chair, he felt he looked stern and uncomfortable). Valenti raised the possibility of Mr. Johnson walking around the room as he talked, but this was dismissed as too troublesome technically because of lighting and audio difficulties.

All but the actual participants cleared the room, the bureau chiefs and the White House advisors going next door to the Cabinet Room where television monitors had been set. They sat in the darkened room, White House servants offering coffee, and watched the monitors. As agreed to earlier, the taping stopped after ten minutes. President Johnson and the correspondents came into the Cabinet Room and the opening minutes were replayed that the President might see how he looked. There was some discussion of the length of his first reply, one dealing with the situation in Vietnam.

The participants returned to the oval office of the President and the main taping resumed. The first question was repeated and the President answered it and others for about fifty-five minutes. At this point, he left the room for about fifteen minutes to handle some business, returned to tape another twelve-minute portion, one which seemed to bring the entire "Conversation" to a normal end.

Minutes later, Presidential Aide Marvin Watson came in and said the President would be available to answer a few minutes of questioning on farm problems and taxes. This was obviously something Watson felt important to include but in the final editing none of it was used. The President invited still another brief round of questions, this dealing with Australian Prime Minister Harold Holt, who had drowned. This tribute to Holt was also excluded in the final editing, mostly because it didn't hold up. The broadcast was to be the next night, LBJ was flying to the Holt funeral the next morning and the Holt eulogy seemed to fit uncomfortably with the flow of the broadcast.

In New York, the editing committee prepared to cut the final product for air thirty-six hours later. It consisted of Wally Pfister of ABC, Ernie Leiser of CBS (a veteran at this, he had served on the editing committees of the two previous "Conversations"), and Russ Tornabene of NBC. Transcripts of the unedited tape were prepared for the New York editors. At the same time, the White House had tapes and transcripts for its own examination. Copies were also sent to the State Department by the White House.

Then came a flow of suggestions from the President's staff, most of them to Monroe of NBC to pass on to New York—some directly to the editing committee. A number of deletions in the Vietnam section were suggested for security reasons. It was also felt that some of the Vietnam materials was too long, too repetitious.

The suggestion was made, late that night, that sections dealing with the Middle East were "stale," not news. This suggestion was rejected after a reminder that there was no obligation to accept suggestions on that basis. The White House next raised a question about the sound quality in one section. New York said they would check the quality of the audio. Later still that night came a suggestion about the factual accuracy of remarks dealing with the World Bank. Since the New York committee had already deleted that material, this was no problem.

The next day the President flew off towards Australia but the suggestions did not end. From the plane came more advice on how to edit. They were passed on by Bromley Smith, executive director of the

National Security Council staff. Since the Middle East section had not been eliminated, the White House would like to see the full answer, not the section chosen. This was restored.

There were other requests. They were declined.

The final product aired at 10 p.m. EST on three networks. CBS News chose to preface their presentation with an explanation that the program had been subject to White House scrutiny for reasons of national policy and security. "National policy," of course, was not the matter agreed to before the taping. The CBS notice touched off a brief flurry of newspaper and magazine articles, most of them critical of Presidential intervention in the editing. CBS said it felt the cautionary note was needed. ABC and NBC said that since the essential journalistic integrity of the interview had not been impaired, they had chosen to avoid any explanation that might suggest White House suppression.

For broadcast journalists, it again raised the question of how to properly deal with the White House. No one would argue the value of permitting review for national security, though this is not done at news conferences, but many saw the spectre of the great big editor in Air Force One. Some argued that the only way to do these was to do them "to time" avoiding editing difficulties. Others noted that editing a longer interview permitted a fuller and better exposition of the President's thinking.

Lyndon Johnson watchers seized on this as another example of heavy-handed manipulation of the news. The members of the "Johnson Credibility Gap Club" were many in number by this time and they were crying that he was doing it again.

Adding to the suspicions and veiled implications of Presidential interference was the matter of the Tuesday morning newspaper advertisements. Appearing in the *New York Times*, the *Washington Post*, and the *Los Angeles Times* were "tune-in" ads, that looked deceptively similar to the kind networks place to build audience for special telecasts.

George Herman, on CBS that night, revealed that these ads, which gave no mention of the sponsors, were not placed by the networks at all; they were bought by influential Democratic friends of the President. There was some question as to whether they were paid for by Democratic Committee funds. There was no question that the picture in the ads were those taken by the White House photographer and were available only from the White House. If these advertisements were not White House inspired, they were at least prepared with White House help and concurrence. Newspapers in question were embarrassed at having failed to identify the sponsors.

With or without the ads, the audience was immense. It was estimated that fifty-two million persons saw the "Conversation," far more than the thirty-eight million who had viewed Johnson's earlier "Conversation" and four million more than had viewed the original "Conversation" with Kennedy.

What one critic has called the "acrimonious normalcy" of White House press relations had been demonstrated once again.

The Agnew Attack on TV News.

On November 13, 1969 the White House unleashed a blistering attack on television news with Vice President Spiro T. Agnew as spokesman. In a speech before the Mid-West Regional Republican Committee Meeting in Des Moines, Iowa, the Vice President launched into a broadside against the "small band of network commentators and self-appointed analysts," the "tiny and closed fraternity of privileged men, elected by no one" who are responsible for news on the air. The Vice President's remarks were said to be his own but the President did not disassociate himself from them when the Radio Television News Directors Association called upon him to repudiate Agnew ("Broadcast journalists are not and will not be a propaganda agency . . . The Vice President would have us ignore the problems and the dissenters of the day, and would have us swallow without criticism administration policies, all in the name of unity. Such a course would violate every tradition of Western journalism . . ."). Since the Vice President issued a second attack just one week later, it is assumed that the White House approved. In fact, White House Deputy Counsel Clark Mollenhoff told reporters, "The speech was developed in the White House. It represents White House concern about getting through to the public."

Mr. Agnew began with bitter remarks about network analysts who followed President Nixon's November 3rd speech on Vietnam. He said that the commentators engaged in "instant analysis and querulous criticism" and that "the *majority* of (them) expressed, in one way or another, their hostility to what he had to say. It was obvious that their minds were made up in advance." He was critical of the commentator (Marvin Kalb of CBS) who "twice contradicted" an exchange of correspondence between Nixon and Ho Chi Minh (the President said Ho was intransigent; Kalb said "the Ho Chi Minh letter contained some of the softest, most accommodating language found in a Communist document concerning the war in Vietnam in recent years."); critical of a commentator (Bill Lawrence of ABC) who "challenged the President's abilities as a politician" (Lawrence suggested that the Democrats vigorously tried to build up the speech as containing something new and that since it did not, the President would not influence voters in a number of areas by addressing them on election eve); and critical of a third commentator (Bill Downs of

ABC) who asserted that the President was now "following the Pentagon line."

"Others," said the Vice President, "by the expressions on their faces, the tone of their questions, and the sarcasim of their responses, made clear their sharp disapproval."

Agnew was particularly critical of one network (ABC) for including an interview with Averell Harriman in its post-Nixon analysis. He spoke of Harriman's "gratuitous advice—challenging and contradicting the policies outlined by the President of the United States." He said Harriman was the chief U.S. negotiator at "a period in which the United States swapped some of the greatest military concessions in the history of warfare for an enemy agreement on the shape of the bargaining table. Like Coleridge's Ancient Mariner, Mr. Harriman seems to be under some heavy compulsion to justify his failures to anyone who will listen. The networks have shown themselves willing to give him all the air time he desires."

ABC had felt itself fortunate to have Harriman, the last negotiator before Nixon appointed the incumbent, to comment. Some may have criticized that network for not having a pro-Administration interview as balance to Harriman (they filled the rest of their half-hour with comments from staff correspondents) but few could agree—examining his comments —that he was, as Agnew characterized it, waiting in the wings "to guarantee in advance that the President's plea for natural unity would be challenged." Though Harriman was most critical of South Vietnam's President Thieu and raised doubts about "Vietnamizing the war," the general tone of his remarks was in the spirit of his opening comment about the President: "I'm sure he wants to end this war and no one wishes him well any more than I do." Harriman criticized the approach of Republican Senator Goodell of New York who called for a full withdrawal within a year ("I'm utterly opposed to these people that are talking about cutting and running"), predicted that we would have a large force of troops in Vietnam for years to come, and said of Mr. Nixon, "I think he's got the full support of the people. He certainly has got my support, in hoping he will develop a program for peace." Harriman called for more Vietnam debate in the Senate Foreign Relations Committee, a suggestion meeting Agnew's disfavor, and ended by saying "I wish the President well, I hope he can lead us to peace." A number of prominent Democrats, including ex-Vice President Humphrey and Senator Edward Kennedy gave blistering reply to Agnew's treatment of Harriman.

Agnew, in his Des Moines speech, followed the Harriman comments with an insistence that the President had a right to go on television without "hostile critics" on his heels as he finished. He said Churchill had none as he rallied public opinion against Hitler and John F. Kennedy had none in the Cuban Missile Crisis.

The Vice President spoke of the "small group of men" who settle on "what forty to fifty million Americans will learn of the day's events in the Nation and the world." He said America knows practically nothing about those who produce and direct network news and of the commentators, little "other than that they reflect an urbane and assured presence, seemingly well informed on every important matter." He insisted that he was not asking for government censorship but asked if censorship did not already exist in this "handful of men." He pointedly noted when they were "enjoying a monopoly sanctioned and licensed by the government."

Agnew said the "views of this fraternity do *not* represent the views of America," that "a narrow and distorted picture of America often emerges from the televised news," that the networks should have a "wall of separation" between news and comment, and that the broadcasters' attacks emanate from "the privileged sanctuary of a network studio." He called on Americans (all three commercial television networks carried his speech live) to "let the networks know that they want their news straight and objective" and to "register their complaints on bias through mail to the networks and phone calls to local stations." He concluded, "The great networks have dominated America's airwaves for decades; the people are entitled to a full accounting of their stewardship."

The Response to Agnew.

The Vice President's speech sent shock waves through the mass media. Many reacted very strongly. The head of CBS called it "an unprecedented attempt . . . to intimidate a news medium." The head of NBC called it "an appeal to prejudice. Evidently he would prefer a different kind of . . . reporting—one that would be subservient to whatever political group was in authority at the time." ABC's Edward P. Morgan said, "That was one of the most significant and most sinister speeches I have ever heard made by a public figure."

Vermont Royster, Editor of the *Wall Street Journal* reacted more calmly and with a touch of amusement when he wrote:

> Well, Spiro Agnew seems to have done it again. And from all the hullabaloo you'd think he'd attacked Motherhood.
>
> What he did, of course, was to criticize the communications media, especially the electronic components thereof. What he said was interesting, provocative, traditional and as American as the Fourth of July. It was even partly true.

Royster, who also noted "the melancholy conclusion that the press

... can dish it out but quivers when it's dished back" had, with a smile, summed up the heart of Agnew's attack—it was even partly true. There was enough truth in Agnew's criticism to rouse strong public support (the mail and phone calls ran heavily in his favor though it must be noted that he solicited them and the networks did not) and some editorial support. *The Washington Evening Star* said it was not shocked or horrified, that criticism was good for the press; *The Chicago Tribune* found it "temperate and reasoned"; the *Columbia, S.C. State* said, "The networks are discovering that in trying to fool the public, they are only fooling themselves"; and the *New Orleans Times Picayune* lectured that, "Questioning responsibility does not question freedom."

On the other hand, the *Baltimore Sun* called it an attempt to suppress free criticism; the *Milwaukee Journal* saw it as "well designed to intimidate networks"; the *Miami Herald* warned, "The suppressive power of federal authority is mighty and dangerous. Mr. Agnew is toying with this dynamite as no other federal official in modern times"; and the *Louisville Courier Journal* bluntly said, "Mr. Agnew as an elected official has absolutely no business objecting to this traditional handling of comment on important speeches unless he has specific charges to make and actual inaccuracies to report."

Comment following Presidential television appearances *has* been traditional. The amount varies. Sometimes it is but a matter of minutes, sometimes it lasts much longer, up to an hour. Many factors are involved in how much time is devoted to such commentary or analysis, the prime ones being the effect on the network schedule and the importance of the speech. In the case of the President's November 3, 1969 speech on Vietnam, the importance was such that the networks decided not to limit analysis to just a few minutes and one commercial network, ABC, ran another half hour. A previous speech by the President, on his welfare proposals, had elaborate follow-up on all networks with the Administration's encouragement and with their providing Cabinet members to be interviewed.

Fred Friendly, after the Agnew speech, expressed regret about one instance when, as President of CBS News, he decided to limit analysis after President Johnson's Gulf of Tonkin speech in 1964. He permitted just two minutes of examination following the President's remarks. A dying Ed Murrow called to deplore the decision, demanding, "What do you mean by going off the air?" Murrow's biographer, Alexander Kendrick, called it the "sole major occasion of their entire association that Murrow had so angrily passed sentence on him." Friendly, in 1969, said "I shall always believe that if journalism had done its job properly that night and in the days following, America might have been spared some of the agony that followed the Tonkin Gulf resolution."

With this practice as with others in broadcast journalism, there has been a great deal of self-examination. Some on network news staffs feel uncomfortable with this form of "instant wisdom" but most would agree with former Presidential News Secretary Bill Moyers who said, "To give a President, who remains a politician at all times, thirty minutes of uninterrupted and unanswered access to sixty million Americans, is too great a power to give one man no matter how honest his motives, no matter how valid his concerns. And I came to the conclusion while I was in the White House, that these commentators provided a very good balance in making us responsible in those speeches."

Agnew dramatically noted that Churchill had no such criticism as he rallied public support against Hitler but many have since noted that this was not true; Churchill had much criticism. As for Kennedy during the Cuban Missile Crisis, it had elaborate network follow-up. Ex-CBS News Correspondent David Schoenbrun who, post-Agnew, said he opposed such analysis and suggested a three-day moratorium before analysis, was one of those who appeared after Kennedy that day as several others.

Time magazine which suggested that the power of television to decide which event to cover is awesome "and must be kept under scrutiny" noted that on November 3, a few hours before Nixon's speech, both NBC and CBS carried film of atrocities committed by South Vietnamese troops. *Time* implies something wrong in this but surely it would be more "wrong" to suppress news stories simply because a Presidential address, not yet made public, is to be given later that night.

The Vice President called the analysis "instant" (though elsewhere he talks of correspondents ready to pounce on the President) and suggests that this is a problem. It has been noted that the subject, Vietnam, was hardly new—the network men had been dealing with it daily for half a dozen years. There had been speculation about this speech for weeks. In addition, though the Vice President did not note it publicly, the text was released two hours before the President had concluded and, for about forty-five minutes, a Presidential advisor had conducted a "backgrounder" in the East Room of the White House explaining the Presidential point of view. This effort to influence the thinking of the press was ignored in the Agnew speech. Incongruously, Agnew talked of analysis being instant in one place but, in another, says the newsmen were ready with minds made up in advance ("Those who recall the fumbling and groping that followed President Johnson's dramatic disclosure of his intention not to seek re-election have seen these men in a genuine state of non-preparedness. This was not it.").

He spoke of the great power of television—"no medium has a more profound influence over public opinion"—but if this power is so great, why did Nixon's popularity after the speech rise to new levels according to pollsters? Should this power have resulted in the opposite if we concur with the Agnew thesis? Similarly, as several observers noted, if TV reporting of the Chicago Democratic Convention was—as Agnew also suggested—damaging to the authorities, particularly the Chicago police, why did post-Chicago polls show the majority of Americans nevertheless supporting Mayor Daley and his police?

The Vice President, handpicked by the Presidential nominee as were almost all running mates in recent decades, talked about the newsmen who are elected by no one, who are self-appointed to the tiny and closed fraternity. Anyone who has observed the process of journalists, on the air and behind the scenes, getting jobs at the network level, rising through the ranks, and then facing the competition from their counterparts at the other networks knows that the process is neither simple nor the goal easily achieved. Columnist Max Lerner, hardly a friend of Mr. Agnew, made this observation:

> When Agnew raises the question of TV power, he exposes himself to a counterquestion of government power. He says the power of news selection and total power over the destinies of the nation is in the hands of an even smaller group, and the power over the Vietnamese war and peace today is in the hands of one man. In the hangman's house, be wary of talking about death . . .
>
> In our own day, the media are part of the system of countervailing powers. The administration still has all the power over foreign policy and a good deal of the power over domestic policy. But it is subject to the independent opinion of editors and commentators in the media among which TV has the biggest impact. Would Agnew prefer a system of fused powers rather than one of countervailing powers? If he would, he is a more foolish and dangerous man than I think he is.

The *Washington Post*, after correcting the Vice President's historic references to Churchill and John F. Kennedy, said, "Much of the rest of what Mr. Agnew had to say was either trivial or churlish or both. Mr. Reynolds' raised eyebrow or the tone of Mr. Sevareid's voice will not sway 200 million Americans. Mr. Kalb's contention that Ho Chin Minh's letter was moderate in tone is shared by a good many people in government and out, and is legitimate comment. What Mr. Agnew does not appear to grasp is the difference between respect for the President's views and unquestioning acceptance of the rightness of those views. A thing isn't necessarily true because the President says it is true; and ditto, in spades, for the network commentators."

The official response of one network, CBS, came from its President,

Dr. Frank Stanton, in a speech on November 25, 1969 before the International Radio and Television Society. After rebutting Agnew's criticisms in detail, Stanton said:

> In my judgment, the whole tone, the whole content and the whole pattern of this government intrusion into the substance and methods of the broadcast press, and indeed of all journalism, have the gravest implications. Because a Federally-licensed medium is involved, no more serious episode has occurred in government-press relationships since the dark days in the fumbling infancy of this republic when the ill-fated Alien and Sedition Acts forbade criticism of the government and its policies on pain of exile or imprisonment.
>
> In the context of this intimidation, the self-serving disavowal interpolations of no censorship, no matter how often repeated, are meaningless. Reprisals no less damaging to the media and no less dangerous to our fundamental freedoms than censorship are readily available to the government—economic, legal and psychological. Nor is their actual employment necessary to achieve their ends; to have them dangling like swords over the media can do harm even more irreparable than overt action. If these threats implicit in the developments of the past week are not openly recognized, unequivocally denounced and firmly resisted, freedom of communications in this country will suffer a setback that will not be limited to checking the freedom of television or to barring critical comment on government policy.

What was Agnew after?

It is difficult to ascribe motives to the Agnew speech. It may be, as Richard Wilson—a columnist friendly to the Administration—said, "This has been a bold and calculated move which can be seen in its true perspective as a part of President Nixon's attempt to hold public opinion to his measured course of liquidating the Vietnam war at his own pace and then proceeding with broad governmental domestic reforms and his own re-election in 1972. The move is bold and calculated beyond anything previously dared by a President."

This may be so. The White House did nothing to disown the Agnew attack. The President's Director of Communications, Herbert Klein, told a CBS audience (*Face the Nation*, November 16, 1969), "I think that any time any industry—and I include newspapers very thoroughly in this, as well as the networks—if you look at the problems you have today and you fail to continue to examine them, you do invite the government to come in. I would like not to see that happen."

It may be that Agnew, whose views on the media are familiar to those found in conservative writings (the *Baltimore Sun* in one report said large segments were lifted word for word from a right-wing publication), was simply expressing the frustration of those who disagree with the news coverage. One network commentator says he receives thousands of letters a year, many complaining about his remarks. The complaints are always from those who disagree; no one ever writes that "I agree with you but you are unfair to the other side." Yet every network news operation has continual soul searching over this very question: Are we fair to the other side? Is there another view of this matter which should be included?

An interesting theory was offered by Meg Greenfield, brilliant editorial writer for the *Washington Post*, who suggested that there is a bizarre kinship between Agnew and Herbert Marcuse, the apostle of the left who is in such favor with young revolutionaries. She notes that the language and tone of Agnew's attacks are similar to the attacks on the mass media from the left. Indeed, networks find themselves attacked continually from the left for being "captives of the Establishment," attacks in language which mirrors the views of conservative Spiro Agnew. He would undoubtedly be astonished and appalled to find himself in their company.

Miss Greenfield noted that in Joe McGinniss's book, *The Selling of the President 1968*, Nixon's TV advisor, Frank Shakespeare, muses about going to NBC and complaining of bias in coverage of Nixon's campaign. Shakespeare, a CBS executive who later became Nixon's Director of the USIA, is quoted as wishing he could say, "We are going to monitor every minute of your broadcast news, and if this kind of bias continues, and if we are elected, then you just might find yourself in Washington next year answering a few questions. And you might find yourself having a little trouble getting some of your licenses renewed." McGinniss says Shakespeare paused and smiled, "I'm not going to do it because I'm afraid of the reaction. The press would band together and clobber us. But goddamit, I'd love to."

The Nixon Administration did engage in a touch of influencing broadcast opinion. After the November 3rd speech, they called at least twenty important television stations to ask if they planned on local editorials dealing with the President's speech and if so, what they planned to say and would they mind sending a copy to the White House. No such calls were made after the Agnew speech.

There was considerable agitation over the action of Dean Burch, newly appointed to the FCC as chairman. He telephoned each network for complete transcripts of their post-Nixon analysis. Burch insists that he just wanted to see the texts without waiting for the more traditional and slower method of requesting them through normal FCC channels. Norman

Isaacs, President of the American Society of Newspaper Editors, who saw the entire Agnew affair as an attempt to intimidate and muzzle the American press, demanded that Burch be fired.

Burch, after Agnew, said he approved of the Vice President's remarks which he termed "thoughtful and provocative." This is in direct contrast to the FCC Chairman's very first speech in office, a speech given two days before Agnew gave his, in which Burch said, "I think all of us will agree that the finest hour of television is in its news and public affairs reporting . . . For all the criticism of journalism, possibly there's not enough in the way of thanks to the individuals who do contribute so much to our way of life."

The entire FCC, however, refused to get involved in the controversy. A few weeks after the Nixon speech, Burch signed a unanimous letter on behalf of the FCC to Mrs. J. R. Paul of Houston who had written that the men of the three networks "*must* be watched carefully." The FCC letter spelled out policy on matters of "truth" and fairness, repeating positions stating that "no Government agency can authenticate the news, or should try to do so." Of the issue at hand, the letter said "The issue which was here involved—Vietnam—is one to which the networks have devoted, and continue to devote, substantial amounts of time for contrasting viewpoints. Indeed, that was the case as to the broadcast in question. The fairness doctrine requires no more."

The Agnew thesis and the resulting controversy at the end of 1969 brought to public attention more information about how network news operates than anything else had in the decade. It also brought to prominance the growth of network news. Mr. Agnew contended that the First Amendment did not apply to networks in the same manner as it did to newspapers because they are different. He noted that the *New York Times* reaches 800,000 people and NBC twenty times that number. This is just short of being accurate. At the time of Agnew's address, Walter Cronkite's audience numbered about 18,400,000, NBC's about 16,500,000 and ABC's major newscast about 7,250,000. In contrast, the *Times* had a circulation just under 900,000. *Time* magazine had 4,164,021 readers and *Newsweek* had a circulation just under 2,500,000. No conduit of news reaches more people than a network newscast.

Taking on this mammoth of the media, the Vice President was safe considering the concern of broadcasters over government control. Also, he somehow had chosen the right moment in terms of public support. A public tired of the disruptions in the decade of the 60's—the racial unrest, the festering war, the rebellion of the young—this public was ready to welcome the man who placed the blame with the messenger who delivered the news. If he chose the moment because this resentment was recognized by the Administration, if he chose it because they felt the need to keep public opinion in line, if he chose it because of the resentment of a conservative with a conservative's paranoia about the men who run the media, or if he chose this moment simply by accident, he was not telling.

There is one other possibility. In his thoughtful book, *The Twilight of the Presidency*, former Presidential aid George E. Reedy offers this thought:

> There are very few politicians who do not cherish privately the notion that there should be some regulation of the news. To most of them, "freedom of the press" is a gigantic put-on, a clever ploy which has enabled publishers as an economic group in our society to conduct themselves with a degree of arrogance and disregard of the public interest that is denied to other groups. The "ploy" has succeeded to an extent where it cannot be challenged publicly and therefore must be accorded formal deference. But the deference is purely formal and rarely expressed with heartfelt enthusiasm.
>
> If censorship ever comes to the United States, it will explode out of the frustrations of a political leader convinced that the public good is being thwarted by self-serving reporters distorting the news.

Spiro Agnew protested too much that he was opposed to censorship but the outcry by the media indicated that he is not convincing them. There is irony in television being the target. In the last twenty years, television has been the means for political and ideological leaders to get their views across to the people and it has served to minimize and correct the biases of politically motivated newspapers.

Once an astute politician, it was the year 1962, said, "I think it's time that our great newspapers have at least the same objectivity, the same fullness of coverage, that television has. And I can only say, thank God for television and radio for keeping the newspapers a little more honest."

The author of those words: Richard M. Nixon.

CHAPTER 13

OTHER POLITICAL FORCES AND THE HOME SCREEN

RELATIONS WITH THE White House with the coming of television created a whole new body of problems for Presidential image-makers. In the Congress, always a bit slow to catch up with the times, there were also new problems with the press—because broadcasting was now an important element in that press. The more traditional press, the printed press, was uneasy.

It was Joseph Pulitzer who said that accuracy is to a newspaper what virtue is to a lady. It was Adlai Stevenson who added, "but a newspaper can always print a retraction."

Newspaper men in Washington have been slowly retracting some of the precious myths of past years, myths about the competition, television. Not without traces of bitterness do they now concede that a few television reporters are "good enough" to work on a paper. Even more damaging to tradition and galling to ego, they now grumble about the growing influence of electronic journalism in the nation's capitol, about television "taking over." Once newspapers complained of television as a nuisance with those eye-squinting lights, those never-ending cables, and those untrained, naive, golden-voiced correspondents. Now the newspapers complain of television as a different kind of nuisance with those specially-timed appearances by news sources, those accommodating favors, and those pampered, much-courted (still golden-voiced) correspondents.

There was a day, less than thirty years ago, when a network reporter covering Capitol Hill had no more privileges than a tourist. He could walk the Congressional halls but could not enter the Press Gallery. He could sit in the balcony (in the unreserved section) but was bound by the rule banning the taking of notes except in the press section.

Today, the network reporter in Washington finds things different.

There are studios just off both House and Senate chambers with direct audio lines, occasional live television cameras and daily film activity. A gallery staff serves him and special seats are reserved for him in that balcony where he now can take notes without leaving the chamber. In fact, if that reporter is peripatetic enough, he'll find that his network has similar facilities available at the White House, the State Department, the Pentagon and, on occasion, in almost every federal agency, airport facility, historical site, and—when needed—every hotel in Washington. In the more frequently used locations, lines are permanent. In the others, installation is quickly arranged.

How actively is the capitol covered by television? Network television averages more than one "remote" day every two weeks. The network "pool" also assigns "mults" to facilitate audio pickups and minimize the number of microphones placed before Presidents or U.S. Senators in committee. In a typical year, over 550 such "mult" assignments were made. These are minor manifestations of a growing truth: in terms of news coverage by television, there is more activity in Washington than anywhere else in the world. The exceptions are during those temporary periods of feverish activity in cities temporarily with political convention or race riot or other natural and man-made disasters.

The heart of broadcasting remains in New York and most news *production* is there but the busiest place for news *coverage* is Washington. With the exception of the AP, UPI, local Washington newspapers (including that local favorite, the *New York Times*), the networks have the largest staffs, the greatest output and the most prestige in this capital.

In addition to directing their own coverage, network bureau chiefs are members of a formal pool with a rotating chairmanship. It is this pool which coordinates and assigns constant coverage of major events including Presidential appearances (a conference telephone line connects pool members and the White House). These men also represent the networks in arranging coverage of events at the "Hill."

Broadcast Access to Congress.

It was 101 years after the printed media did so before electronic newsmen won entrance to the Congressional galleries. The first Press Gallery goes back to 1838 and the 25th Congress when local newspapers were given floor privileges. A year later, six out-of-town reporters were similarly accommodated. Exactly 100 years later, radio reporters gained access.

A small committee of four organized the effort. Led by the late Fulton Lewis, Jr. (who became first President of the Radio Correspondents Gallery), it included Fred Morrison of the new defunct Transradio

Press Service, Albert Warner of CBS (later to go to *U.S. News and World Report*) and Carleton Smith of NBC (later an NBC Vice President). After the gallery committee was formed, Smith was replaced by the late William McAndrew (erroneously listed in one of the early membership lists as "Tom" McAndrew). He became President of NBC News.

This small group prevailed upon Congressman John J. ("Jack") Dempsey of New Mexico to put through an enabling resolution in April of 1939. Five days later, Iowa Senator Guy Gillette offered a similar Senate measure and the Radio Gallery was in business.

Radio was not new to the Congress. The opening of Congress in 1923 was broadcast as was President Coolidge's State of the Union message to that Congress two days later, on December 6. Actually, one month earlier, radio had carried ex-President Woodrow Wilson's Armistice Day message. In February of 1924, Wilson's funeral services were broadcast and in March of the following year, Coolidge's Inauguration. In 1939, however, the broadcaster became a Congressionally recognized force. On June 26, 1939, H. R. Baukage of NBC gave the maiden broadcast from a gallery "studio."

The original gallery had twenty-six members (some records say thirty). Today there are almost 450 active members of the Radio and Television Gallery, and broadcast reports are filed daily by all networks and independents. When the gallery had its formal opening in July of 1939, FDR sent a message hailing its members as "pioneers in a great adventure." With a suspicion shared by political figures ever since, the President added that he urged them to be "fair" in their coverage.

Television came later, Harry Truman delivering the first State of the Union telecast in January of 1947. That same year saw the first televised hearing—that of a House (note: *House*) Labor Committee. The main witness was colorful Jimmy Petrillo, grand master of all union musicians.

The real impact of televised hearings, including the great political impact, became evident in 1951 when the late Estes Kefauver held his crime investigation hearings. Early the following year, Speaker Sam Rayburn forbade television from covering Un-American Activities Committee hearings in Detroit. Republicans were upset by the Rayburn ruling, in part because a member of the committee, Rep. Charles E. Potter, was a potential candidate for a Michigan seat. Potter's supporters called it an underhanded means of keeping their man off television in his home state.

In Washington, Minority Leader Joe Martin, Jr. asked for a formal ruling. Speaker Rayburn said the rules of the House are the rules of its committees "and as far as the Chair knows, there is no rule granting the privilege of television."

Since Senate committees establish their own parliamentary procedures, the Senate continued to permit television but the now famous
Rayburn Rule became the law of the House. There was exception to come
a year later when the GOP won control of the 83rd Congress. Joe Martin
became Speaker and without formal ruling, allowed House committees
to permit television but in 1954 the Democrats regained control. They
reverted to the earlier ban under Rayburn himself and since his death,
under Speaker John McCormack.

On the House side, it is still "stake-out" in the hall outside and no
television inside. One can make a case for this contributing to diminishing House influence on the national scene. Not many House members are
true national figures. Ironically, Adam Clayton Powell is almost the only
exception though some Representatives are known for their specialties
(i.e.: Wilbur Mills in tax legislation, John Moss for freedom of information
activity, Gerald Ford for party activity, etc.). In contrast, many Senate
figures are household names (Dirksen, Fulbright, Edward Kennedy,
Mansfield, Morse, etc.) and even freshmen can achieve quick national
prominence (Percy, Brooke, etc.).

Without comparable exposure to television, the House is destined to
growing obscurity. This is unfortunate. Its work is of equal importance
and coverage of the committee, since the floor of the House has limited
debate, is all the more vital. One can see the same witnesses say the same
things before two committees. On the House side, it is worth a mention;
on the Senate side, it can create a national stir.

Press agentry at the Hill being what it is, it seems inevitable that
someday the House will open its hearings to television. Back in 1913
Congress passed a bill to ban the use of press agents, the main target
being Woodrow Wilson (who once said our form of government is "government by the chairmen of the Standing Committees of Congress") but
today, every Congressman has at least one press assistant.

A Mississippi Senator once reminded his staff, "Every day we don't
get in the papers is a day lost." That flavor exists in many Congressional
offices today though many old timers look upon newsmen with suspicion
and prefer anonymity. Just how far the publicity seekers will go is demonstrated in a bit of advice circulated among members of one House investigating committee which somehow got into the hands of reporters:

    1. Decide what you want the newspapers to hit hardest and
then shape each hearing so that the main point becomes the vortex
of the testimony. Once that vortex is reached, *adjourn.*

    2. In handling press releases, first put a release date on them,
reading something like this: "For release at 10:00 AM EST July 6,"

etc. If you do this, you can give releases out as much as 24 hours in advance, thus enabling reporters to study them and write better stories.

3. Limit the number of people authorized to speak for the committee, to give out press releases or to provide the press with information to the *smallest number possible.* It plugs leaks and helps preserve the concentration of purpose.

4. Do not permit distractions to occur, such as extraneous fusses with would-be witnesses, which might provide news that would bury the testimony you want featured.

5. Do not space hearings more than 24 hours or 48 hours apart when on a controversial subject. This gives the opposition too much opportunity to make all kinds of counter-charges and replies by issuing statements to the press.

6. Don't ever be afraid to recess a hearing for even five minutes, so that you can keep the proceedings completely in control so far as creating news is concerned.

7. *And this is most important:* don't let the hearings or the evidence ever descend to the plane of a personal fight between the Committee Chairman and the head of the agency being investigated. The high plane of a duly authorized Committee of the House of Representatives *examining* the operations of an Agency of the Executive Branch for constructive purposes should be maintained at all costs.

The brunt of this guidance is directed at newspapers. Savvy press aides offer comparable advice today as to handling television. The broadcast galleries of House and Senate are busy places.

Television Covers a Filibuster.

One of the most interesting examples of television influence on the Congress occurred in 1964 when CBS News arranged to put correspondent Roger Mudd on the steps of the Senate. The idea was to have Mudd report on every single newscast on CBS radio and television, report on the progress of the filibuster over civil rights legislation.

Fred Friendly, then President of CBS News, announced the extraordinary coverage thusly: "The pending civil rights debate and the anticipated filibuster in the Senate give every indication of becoming one of the most important running news stories of the decade. It warrants continuing coverage in the same manner we have dealt with the space shots and with primary elections. The fact that cameras and microphones will not be permitted access to the Senate floor does not affect our responsibility of reporting the debate and filibuster as completely as possible."

The first Mudd report almost aborted. Though CBS News received the necessary permissions, someone forgot to inform the Capitol police and they would not permit the remote truck to park. In a growing snow storm, the mobile unit circled the Capitol parking lot as CBS desperately tried to find someone in authority to get word to the police. Those in authority were fighting the snow on their way to work. Finally, approval came and the technicians raced to set up the cameras.

They would be ready with minutes to spare. Meanwhile, Mudd emerged from the entrance beneath the steps to the Senate with his first interview guest, Senator Hubert Humphrey—Democratic Whip and Floor Leader for the Civil Rights bill.

Humphrey stepped back immediately—he didn't know about the growing snowfall, he had no coat. "I'll have to get my coat," he said. There was no time. I stepped into the hallway, took off my raincoat and we slipped it on Humphrey. It was several sizes too big, especially as it hung toward his fingertips. We promised to keep a tight shot on him— and did. The Mudd odyssey on the Capitol steps had started.

Actually, before it was over, he had to leave the steps. Growing unhappy with his constant reports, some influential Southerners had prevailed upon the Senate authorities to move Mudd. They said he might attract crowds and obstruct the entrance to the building. We ran a cable underground to the sidewalk across the plaza. Mudd did his reports from there, the steps as a background across the street.

Why were the Southerners unhappy? Some observations by John Horn, then writing for the *New York Herald Tribune*:

> It was only several weeks after Mudd took up his vigil that the full significance of his careful TV watch was appreciated. Caught at all hours, on a minimum of four TV programs daily, giving the latest debate report and time count or interviewing Senators on both sides of the argument, Mudd has been as faithful as a postman. Neither snow, nor rain, nor heat, nor gloom of night has stayed this TV courier from the swift completion of his appointed rounds.
>
> His continued presence at the scene of Washington inaction has personalized and dramatized the halting processes of our government to the average viewer in a way no amount of words or secondary reports could have. A viewer could identify with Mudd, stand on the steps with him, and have brought home in a compelling way the Senate stall and sitdown against effective government led by Southern Democrats.

Roger Mudd had been meticulous in seeing that both sides *were* heard. He saw to it that Southerners expressed fully their views as well as Northern Senators who favored the bill and that key to passage, Republican Everett Dirksen, who would ultimately come up with the accepted compromise.

The effect of the coverage was telling, however, with a clock mercilessly superimposed under Mudd as he reported, ticking off the hours, minutes and seconds of the "extended debate" (as Southerners loved to characterize a filibuster). A nation felt that this was not a normal process of government—this was the minority delaying a bill badly needed in a period of growing Negro protest.

A leading and powerful Southern Senator paged me to his office one day and asked me to give reason why the Senate should not stop Mudd's reports. They were, after all, being televised on Senate property.

I answered that the series had gone on too long for that. If banned from Capitol grounds, we would place Mudd on the Mall at the Smithsonian with the Capitol behind him. The publicity would certainly not help the Senate establishment. Furthermore, thanks to Mudd's care, there had been fully as many Southerners interviewed as proponents of the bill.

Luckily, I had checked the list of Mudd's interviews. The one Senator interviewed more than any other was the distinguished gentleman from Georgia, Richard Brevard Russell. Russell was at once the head of the Southern bloc and also the most powerful man in the U.S. Senate.

My Southern friend ended our discussion with a mild plea that "you all continue to be fair to us, you heah?" We were.

Sixty-seven days after it and he started, the filibuster and Mudd came to an end. The Civil Rights Bill was passed.

A good reporter had done a fair and thorough job. He did it under conditions that reached people across the country. The Senate respected him for it. The Senate also sensed that television had been strongly felt.

That influence is now felt daily. When live hearings are telecast, Senators are as conscious of the audience at home as they are of their duty in the room. Often these days, you will hear a Senator tell a witness, "I want that answered while the cameras are on." The business of the U.S. Senate hasn't changed much over the past fifty years but the eyes watching the business have new lenses—and Senators know it.

In a Congressional hearing room, late in 1968, Richard Salant of CBS News told a Presidential commission, "If this hearing had been held ten years ago these television cameras couldn't have been in the room and I think that as we learn how to use this medium and by using it, I mean living with it and adjusting to it, I think that the public will be much better served. Television is the first thing, I believe, that has happened in the governmental process that has taken government back to the people because it has been moving further and further away."

TV and Local Government.

As it is in Washington, so it is becoming in state capitols and cities, large and small, across the country. Television is becoming more and more a presence—and in its way is bringing government closer to the people.

In many states, television cameras film the actions of state legislatures. In some states, unlike the Congress which limits live television to special joint meetings and to Senate hearings, local television cameras cover open hearings of both houses. In a number of states, actions in the chamber itself are filmed. Increasingly, local stations devote time to live coverage of a Governor's "State of the State" message or similar major appearances in the legislature.

The pattern across the country is erratic, the prohibitions and permissions vary widely. Whereas there is more not less television coverage, there is more not less citizen interest. Coverage of legislative action is often supplemented by special interview shows with major participants in the legislature or the state administration.

The vast growth in population in this country had accentuated a drift towards government being distant from its constituency. Even experiments in "taking government to the people" by moving state government to different cities or local government to different neighborhoods, touches only a few members of the electorate. But they all have television sets to watch. This is not to suggest a form of "participatory democracy" for the citizen plays a passive role here. Television is simply an aide to understanding—it is not a device to permit the kind of dialogue held in a town hall atmosphere. Even telecasts that encourage viewer questions can only embrace a tiny number of participants.

As suggested earlier, the emergence of broadcast news has served to provide divergent views to communities at a period when the number of daily newspapers has remained static and the number of broadcast stations has grown rapidly. If the community is served by a diversity of reports, the future will rely more on broadcasting than on print for this diversity.

The Broadcast Editorial Emerges.

One remarkable trend has been the growth of editorials on the air. Back in 1940, the FCC placed a ban on broadcast editorials saying "the broadcaster cannot be an advocate." The question was re-opened in 1948 when the FCC held hearings and heard a series of arguments in favor of editorials on the air: (1) freedom of expression on the air was as important as freedom of print, (2) at that time the number of stations was already twice the number of daily newspapers, (3) in many communities, the stations had facilities and resources equal to a newspaper's, (4) this would encourage fuller discussion of vital and of controversial issues, (5) advocates of strong views in the community would have far more freedom to be heard than newspapers alone could provide.

In 1949, the FCC reversed its ban on editorials and introduced the Fairness Doctrine which called for broadcasters to play a positive role in bringing forth opposing views when it engaged in editorial advocacy. It was a major step forward for broadcasting.

Today, well over half the radio and television stations in the nation engage in editorial presentations. Many have been doing it for fifteen years, some for twenty. Only about one in eight editorials, according to a 1966 study, dealt with national or international matters—the vast majority deal with local (almost 70%) or state (15%) issues. It is the practice of these stations to invite proponents of opposing views to respond to their editorials.

On the network level, editorials are almost never used. Individual stations owned by the networks, however, are encouraged to take editorial positions. Only CBS has engaged in network editorials and has done so only four times: in August, 1954 when Dr. Frank Stanton urged television access to the Senate committee considering censure of Senator Joseph McCarthy (with a rebuttal broadcast over CBS facilities on September 2 by Judge Harold R. Medina of the U.S. Court of Appeals); on January 5, 1958 when Howard K. Smith on television and—three days later—when George Herman on radio, urged greater U.S. space efforts in the wake of Russia's success with the Sputnik satellite; in July of 1959 when Dr. Stanton urged amendment of Section 315, the "equal time" provision of the Communications Act (with a rebuttal one week later by three opponents: Dr. Daniel M. Berman, a Political Science professor; Dr. Timothy Costello of the Liberal Party of New York; and Eric Hass of the Socialist Labor Party); and on June 6, 1962 when Dr. Stanton again took the air, this time to oppose a bill increasing magazine postal rates—this editorial broadcast only over CBS owned and operated stations and, over the same stations one day later, answered in rebuttal by Postmaster General Edward J. Day.

Why are networks reluctant to editorialize? They serve hundreds of stations in hundreds of communities. Few issues would be common to all, few positions would be compatible to all.

A study of public acceptance of editorials shows that two out of three persons favor editorials on the air. At the same time, an equal percentage—two out of three—oppose endorsement of political candidates in these editorials.

When eight CBS owned stations announced endorsement of political candidates in 1966, there were powerful voices in the Congress calling for a federal ban on such endorsements. They feared undue influence in political races despite the assurances that stations, following Fairness Doctrine, played an active role in providing time for advocates of opponents of those endorsed. The ban never came to be. It was noted that the provision of time to reply was quite different than newspaper advocacy where endorsing a candidate rarely gave his opponent a chance to be heard.

It is an interesting footnote to the controversy that in two states, Illinois and California, the CBS radio and television stations disagreed and endorsed opposing candidates. CBS, at the time, said in a memorandum to all officers of the company, "We are convinced . . . that the practice of endorsing candidates increases the interest and involvement of listeners and viewers and in so doing results in a more widespread exercise of the voting franchise. We believe these gains outweigh the arguments of those who want television and radio to be mere passive observers of the election scene."

Studies show that broadcasters are far less likely to use "canned" editorials handed out by vested interests than are newspapers. Broadcasters, however, are as guilty as newspapers in presenting soft editorials, attacking safe issues such as safe driving, crime prevention, brotherhood, etc.—or, in the words of Newton Minow: "in favor of greener grass, mother love, canoe safety and milk for children."

Minow, when Chairman of the FCC, encouraged broadcasters to editorialize and not to fear FCC handling of complaints. He said to broadcasters, "If you get a letter from the Commission asking about a complaint, don't panic. Integrity will protect you better from the federal troops than a regiment of lawyers." He noted, "Complaints prove you are communicating, not toe dancing with issues."

The FCC Chairman, in that encouragement to stations, cited several good examples of editorial influence. He told of WTVJ in Miami, which under Ralph Renick's leadership, pioneered in editorializing and, in 1961, aroused community reaction against the city commission firing a city manager who—said Renick—"was too good for his own good." The station ran a series of editorials and moved live cameras into the next city commission meeting. On live television, the dismissal of the city manager was reversed. In Minow's words, "There is a moral in this story. You can fight city hall—and most effectively, too—with television cameras."

He also told of WDSU and WDSU-TV in New Orleans which presented over fifty editorials dealing with school segregation during the civil rights crisis in that city. The Louisiana State Advisory Commission to the U.S. Commission on Civil Rights bemoaning the lack of newspaper leadership wrote, "The editorial leadership that did exist in New Orleans during the school crisis was provided by television station WDSU-TV and its companion radio station, WDSU . . . their editorial position has seemed to be a full acceptance of the concept of editorial responsibility to interpret the facts and to advocate constructive lines of action."

Added Minow, "This is broadcasting making its voice ring!"

Perhaps the most famous editorial battle by a broadcast entity was that of New York radio station WMCA (which in 1960 became the first station to endorse a candidate for President). It engaged in a series of editorials dealing with legislative reapportionment, then supplemented its position with a suit, as a taxpayer, to force the issue in court. This ultimately led to the famous June, 1964 Supreme Court decision on reapportionment, the landmark ruling on "one man, one vote."

Few editorials will lead stations dramatically to the highest court in the land and to decisions affecting the very fabric of the democratic system. They do, however, have remarkable impact on the local scene and make the broadcaster additionally important in the lives of all.

CHAPTER 14

WHO RUNS TELEVISION?

TELEVISION. It troubles the real world for it is powerful. It sends out charges. It makes waves. It matters.

Sophisticates decry television ("the boob tube") and say they don't watch it. Intellectuals try to ignore it. These are minorities. Too many people watch it too many hours to leave it ignored. Men of power sense its power and they seek to examine it, measure it, and control it.

Who does control television? Who makes the big decisions? How are they made?

Lyndon Johnson had answers to those questions during the 1966 Congressional campaign. He spoke at a rally in Wilmington, Delaware and declared that two or three men determine everything America sees on television. A few hours later, at a news conference, he brought up the matter again and spoke critically of "what three networks put on the air and what three men decide you can observe from Vietnam and all of the international incidents."

Asked about this Presidential jibe, Richard Salant, President of CBS News, said, "I wish I had that much power. In electronic journalism there is probably the greatest dispersion of authority in the news business."

Presidents and lesser politicians are not the only ones to raise questions about the power in broadcasting. A kindly critic, poet Archibald MacLeish, told a group of broadcast newsmen in 1959: "You people in television and radio are fair game in all seasons and to any hunter—including hunters as inexperienced as myself. The reason is one you can take pride in. Your fellow citizens care about you. They may not always love you but they care. What you do matters."

Control of television is found in many places, LBJ notwithstanding. Government sets some of the control by law. A government agency exercises a considerable degree of restraint in its regulatory function. Congress often threatens, sometimes acts to restrict television. Within the industry, executives play roles, producers and editors exert decision-making power. The cameramen and reporters who gather the raw material have the greatest influence. The audience, the critic, the news source all contribute to the patterns of non-fiction television.

Since broadcasting is licensed, ultimate control rests in the hands of government. Networks, the prime source for programming, are not regulated as such but are accountable since their member stations are licensed. In addition, each network owns the full number of stations, seven in radio and five in television, permitted a single owner. Since they are the source of great profit to the network, control over their licenses is a most effective lever on any given network.

The affiliates are held responsible for the network broadcasts they carry so, as CBS's Salant has noted, "Whatever we do at the network has 200 or more bosses—every one of our affiliated stations." The FCC, which holds these and other stations responsible, holds one absolute weapon— the threat to remove a license.

The Role of Government Regulation.

The seven members of the Federal Communications Commission have one of the toughest policing jobs in the entire federal constabulary. Big as broadcasting is, it is only a minor part of the FCC's domain. The seven commissioners, and their staff of 1,500 employees, have much more than just commercial broadcasting to worry about. While there are some 7,000 or so station licenses, they must also worry about 1,700,000 or more fixed, portable and mobile transmitters.

The annual number of applications for such radio authorizations alone exceeds 800,000 a year. The number of complaints received by the FCC dealing with only one question, interference with radio signals, alone approaches 50,000 a year.

The scope of FCC activity was once summed up by Chairman Newton Minow when he noted,

> The FCC is constantly appearing before Congress. In 1961 and 1962, for example, we participated in fifty-two congressional hearings. These dealt with: political broadcasting and the requirement of equal time for political candidates under Section 315 of the Communications Act; educational television; patent practices; international telecommunications conventions and radio regulations' television boosters; FCC reorganization; juvenile delinquency; horse-

racing and gambling; all-channel receiver legislation; the merger of common carriers; space communications and communication satellites, wiretapping and eavesdropping; appropriations; crime and racketeering; efforts to influence FCC decisions by improper means and off-the-record contacts; consent decree and antitrust matters; problems involving daytime broadcasting; the licensing of radio station operators (subversive activities); clear channel broadcasting; various FCC legislative proposals dealing with forfeitures, oaths, permissive early renewals; and foreign embassy radio stations.

Seven men must oversee all this and more. Each is appointed for a seven-year term and not more than four of the seven may belong to one political party. They operate in what Minow called "a quixotic world of undefined terms, private pressures and tools unsuited to the work." Their basic directive, in the Communications Act of 1934, is to look after the "public interest, convenience and necessity."

The language is purposely vague and comes from similar regulatory standards in the Interstate Commerce Act. The latter, however, deals with public utilities and broadcasting is not that. The author of the Communications Act, Senator Clarence Dill of Washington state, sought legislation to encourage investment in broadcasting without fear of the kind of regulation that public utilities faced. At the same time, he felt a firm measure of public control was needed.

Minow feels that the FCC works "in a jungle of procedural red tape that flowers wildly out of the quicksands of constantly changing public policy."

When Minow was named to the Chairmanship, he told a veteran of Washington's ways, Thomas G. Corcoran, that, "Everybody tells me this job is like trying to hold a barrel of snakes." Tommy the Cork, as FDR called his Congressional liaison man, laughed and answered, "Son, you've got a barrel of snakes all right. Only, there's no bottom to the barrel."

Of the 1,500 FCC employees, only one in six—just 250 people—are in the Broadcast Bureau which oversees the broadcast industry. Though their problems proliferate, their numbers and their budgets expand slowly and sometimes not at all. The strength of the FCC is more in the threat it can pose than in actual actions. License revocation rarely takes place. The threat to revoke or the suspension of the license has been the power of the FCC. It is frequently accused of "legislation by raised eyebrow." One observer, R. H. Coase of the University of Chicago, compared its actions to "a professional wrestling match: the grunts and groans resound through the land, but no permanent injury seems to result."

A more brutal comment came from James M. Landis, former Dean of the Harvard Law School, in a report on regulatory agencies made for John F. Kennedy. He said the FCC "has drifted, vacillated and stalled in almost every major area."

The stalling is a result of FCC rule-making proceedings which can stretch over long periods of time. The Commission invites industry comment on proposed rules, replies to the comments, oral arguments, etc. Once rules are made, industry representatives can file petitions for reconsideration and the process is repeated. If the issue is complicated enough, the process is repeated several times. One case, a rule involving the use of clear channels by a second station during nighttime operation, took seventeen years to settle. Another, involving the grant of a license in Texas, took nine years and included three sessions before the U.S. Court of Appeals along with the numerous FCC considerations. After what they thought was a final decision in their favor, applicants had gone on the air and faced six more years of litigation before their approval was final.

A license must be renewed every third year. That means that the FCC must handle almost 2,000 renewals annually. It is no easy task.

FCC Commissioner Nicholas Johnson, an outspoken critic of broadcasting ("I'm one of seven men and what you need to do to function in the FCC is walk around the corridors until you can count up to four which I had difficulty doing") sums up FCC's watchdog role thusly:

> It is a pretty big event, you know if a license ever gets turned down. It is generally for an offense, say an antenna tower painting. We feel strongly about that at the Commission. We imposed high fines for failure to paint antenna towers. But programming is not viewed with quite that much interest by and large. We not only don't do investigations on our own but it is not even the case that we will necessarily go ahead and prosecute like your district attorney if someone brings us the evidence. We get fifty or sixty thousand complaints a year of one kind or another. We have three investigators. They travel in pairs. Their responsibility is the U.S. The number of these that can be investigated is somewhat less than it might be with what one would call more rigorous investigation in pursuit of complaints.

The history of broadcast regulation shows a number of incidents where Congress, not the FCC, uncovered broadcast scandals. The payola and quiz-show rigging exposés in the '50's were such. Indeed, some of the most squalid episodes of FCC history came in that period. They include the indictment of an FCC Commissioner, the late Richard A. Mack, on charges of criminal conspiracy in connection with the award of a television allocation. Channel 10 in Miami. Mack had accepted an $82,000 "loan" from Thurman Whiteside, a longtime friend but also the attorney in the Channel 10 case. Their joint trial ended in a hung jury. Whiteside, who was acquitted in the second trial, committed suicide. Charges against Mack was dropped.

The stakes, in allocating broadcast licenses, are high. A television license is worth millions.

Sometimes the pressures on the Congressional side are high. In 1943 a Congressional investigation of the FCC resulted from an exchange between Representative Eugene Cox of Georgia and FCC Chairman James Lawrence Fly. Cox called the FCC "incompetent, arbitrary, inefficient—a danger and a menace to national security." Chairman Fly accused the Congressman of accepting a $2,500 legal fee from a Georgia radio station.

The hearings were wild. The general counsel of the FCC, 27-year-old Charles R. Denny (later to become an FCC Chairman), kept jumping up, demanding to be heard. Cox threatened to throw him out of the room. Representative Will Rogers took to the floor of the House to demand Cox's resignation. Cox replied by pulling Rogers' hair and Rogers threw a punch at Cox. In that undignified atmosphere, the hearings dragged on for six months inconclusively. Cox finally resigned with a bitter denunciation of the Commission and said "poisoned shafts of slander have been driven into my heart."

Someone else continued the investigation. It evaporated some months later. The FCC had survived.

It survived other moments under fire. When the *New York Herald Tribune* revealed that FCC Chairman John C. Doerfer had taken a six-day cruise on the yacht of a prominent broadcaster, Doerfer insisted he was not compromised and would continue in office. Editorial comment blistered him. He resigned.

Most of the time, the FCC is not engaged in such colorful adventures. It tends to get broadcasters excited but when the loud groans and grunts subside, it takes little strong action. Perhaps it acts in the spirit of Benjamin Disraeli's observation that, "Decision destroys suspense, and suspense is the charm of existence."

The Fairness Doctrine.

The FCC's greatest influence in the field of non-fiction broadcasting deals with the concept of fairness. It is not in any law. It is not in any FCC rule (except for the debatable "personal attack" clarification) but it is FCC policy. It is called the "Fairness Doctrine."

Many attribute its beginning to 1949 when the FCC reversed the Mayflower decision of eight years earlier to permit and encourage editorials on the air. It said then that editorials, in fairness, ought to be accompanied by a right of reply. Thus was born the doctrine of fairness in broadcasting. Actually, historians of the broadcast word can find earlier precedents regarding fairness. In 1928 for example, in renewing the license of WEVD in New York City, the Commission said a station must be operated "with due regard for the opinions of others."

The Mayflower decision involved a move by the Mayflower Broadcasting Company to gain the frequency used by WAAB which had been editorializing since 1937. The FCC ruled in that case that "a broadcaster cannot be an advocate" though it denied Mayflower and renewed the WAAB license. The condition of renewal was discontinuance of editorials.

The second Mayflower decision came in 1949 when the FCC issued a report on editorializing. This permitted advocacy, editorials, but laid the basis for modern day "fairness." Stations were to "seek out, aid and encourage" the broadcasting of opposing views on matters of public controversy.

The Fairness Doctrine is different from "equal time," the Section 315 provision which deals with political candidates. Indeed, when Section 315 was amended in 1959 to exempt newscasts and documentaries, the amendment clearly stated that the exemptions "did not relieve broadcasters of the obligation to afford reasonable opportunity for conflicting views."

Aside from matters of personal attack, fairness is determined by the broadcaster and not limited to exact equality in the placement or timing of the "other" side of an issue. In general it calls for the broadcaster to present various sides of an issue over a period of time—unlike "equal time" which says it must be done on the same program time for the same number of minutes involved in the original presentation.

The FCC sought to define its terms in one area, personal attack, with a ruling in 1967. It attempted to equate the right of reply to personal attack with a politician's equal time guarantees under Section 315. The Radio Television News Directors Association and two networks, CBS and NBC, took it to court. The Seventh Circuit of the U.S. Court of Appeals ruled against the FCC guidelines.

The Court did not declare the so-called Fairness Doctrine unconstitutional but it did declare FCC rules on personal attack a violation of the First Amendment. In July of 1967, when the FCC issued the guidelines, it spelled out the method and terms of offering rebuttal time to persons attacked on the air. Exempting newscasts, live coverage of bona fide news events, and news interviews, the guidelines had concentrated on editorials and documentaries.

The Court called the rules vague and warned that, "Strict compliance with the rules might result in a blandness and neutrality pervading all broadcasting arguably within the scope of the rules. Apparently the Commission views programming which takes sides on a given issue to be somehow improper or contrary to the public interest." Noting that the Commission invited stations to seek its advice to clarify the rules, the Court called this a serious "threat of Commission censorship . . . it follows that the Commission, through interpretation of its own vague rules, has the power to effectively preclude the expression of views."

The matter went to the U.S. Supreme Court which, in June of 1969, overturned the actions of the Seventh Circuit and strongly endorsed the Fairness Doctrine. In a 7 to 0 ruling, the Supreme Court said the FCC regulations "enhance rather than abridge freedom of speech."

The ruling, written by Justice Byron R. White, dismissed the argument that the First Amendment was violated, stating that nothing in that Amendment keeps government from requiring a licensee to share his frequency with others. "It is," the Court ruled, "the purpose of the First Amendment to preserve an uninhibited market-place of ideas in which truth will ultimately prevail, rather than to countenance monopolization of that market, whether it be by the Government itself or a private licensee."

On the matter of personal attack, the Court upheld the distinction from the Fairness Doctrine generally and said it was not good enough for the broadcaster to present the views of those attacked, they must have the opportunity to do it themselves or have their representatives give reply. A footnote quotes John Stuart Mill (*On Liberty*) who noted that it is not enough to "hear the arguments of his adversaries from his own teachers, presented as they state them, and accompanied by what they offer as refutations . . . He must be able to hear them from persons who actually believe them; who defend them in earnest, and do their very utmost for them."

The Court rejected the contention that the FCC regulations would result in self-censorship and ineffective treatment of controversial issues. It cites the FCC conclusion that such a possibility was "speculative" and quotes Dr. Frank Stanton who said in a keynote address to *Sigma Delta Chi* in November of 1968, "We are determined to continue covering controversial issues as a public service, and exercising our own independent news judgment and enterprise. I, for one, refuse to allow that judgment and enterprise to be affected by official intimidation."

The Supreme Court said, "This is not to say the First Amendment is irrelevant to public broadcasting. On the contrary, it has a major role to play . . . (but) it is the right of the viewers and listeners, not the right of the broadcasters which is paramount."

It reversed the U.S. Seventh Court's contention that it is a fallacy to think of broadcasting as a "privilege" limited to a few and therefore subject to government control since the "airways belong to the public." The lower court had discarded but the Supreme Court reaffirmed that the scarcity of licenses was a meaningful factor in freedom of the airways. The lower court reasoning is worth examining, however.

The Seventh Circuit Court had noted that the concept of public ownership of the airwaves to distinguish the broadcast press from the printed press is logically meaningless, that a number of allocated broadcasting frequencies are inoperative for the same kind of economic reasons that limit the number of newspapers. It cited data showing that there are more commercial broadcasting stations (6,253 AM, FM, and TV stations) in this country than daily newspapers (1,754). It said that radio and television may be major vehicles for discussion of controversial public issues but are not the only vehicles, that exposure of all sides of a given issue is achieved by the combined effort of several media of communications.

The lower court ruling also touched on a matter often overlooked by some in printed media—that of FCC reliance on the "public ownership" concept as a means to "sanction inhibitory regulation." This could be extended logically to other media, namely in the use of second-class postal rates. This decision cited Supreme Court precedent (*Hannegan v. Esquire, Inc.* 1946) saying "under that view the second-class rate could be granted on condition that certain economic or political ideas not be disseminated."

The Right of Reply.

There are those who feel the "right of reply" *should* be extended to newspapers. This view was spelled out by Professor Jerome S. Barron of George Washington University's Law School in the June, 1967 issue of the *Harvard Law Review*. His article, entitled "Access to the Press: A New First Amendment Right," advocates a legally enforced right of reply for persons attacked in newspapers.

Two states, Nevada and Florida, have right-of-reply laws on their books, have had them since 1911 and 1912 respectively. Little known and rarely invoked, the Nevada law was used only twice in its history. Once an Ely, Nevada councilman was permitted to reply to the *Ely Record's* charges that the town was trashy. Another time, in Las Vegas, a lawyer demanded the right to reply to a story involving prohibition in the 1920's. He dropped his demand when the editor of the newspaper threatened to test the law in court.

In Florida, the law permits political candidates to reply to newspaper attacks. It, too, was rarely invoked. On the other hand, efforts to repeal the law or declare it unconstitutional have failed.

Attempts to pass similar legislation in Wisconsin, Illinois and Louisiana have not succeeded. The general argument of advocates was that such laws don't hamper freedom of the press, they supplement it and compel the press to be accurate. The fairness issue, thus proposed, is not just a broadcast issue but affects all elements of mass media.

The right of reply, say its proponents, is much better than libel protection for it gives a private citizen a cheap, expeditious and convenient way to combat misstatements about himself in the press. Unfortunately, say its critics, it places serious and novel burdens on the press. If invoked frequently, it would mean newspapers full of replies. Further, a newspaper could add additional insult by offering editorial footnotes to the reply, a practice sometimes seen on editorial pages in regard to letters to the editor. Most serious is the possibility of demoralizing existing practices, inhibiting news media from reporting controversy.

In addition, unfettered right of reply could mean publication of libel or slander. At the very least, in a complication that broadcasters share under existing regulation, it could start a chain reaction: the reply to attack could itself contain further attacks.

Professor Barron, however, contends that present protection of the right of expression in the press is really repression of unpopular and unorthodox ideas. He derides the "free marketplace of ideas" as a "romantic conception" that really means press control of ideas.

In broadcasting, the Fairness Doctrine demands the presentation of contrasting viewpoints. Many broadcasters feel this a violation of the First Amendment and NBC presented this position when the Supreme Court accepted arguments appealing the "personal attack" decision of the Seventh Circuit Court in Chicago. NBC called the Fairness Doctrine "directly contrary to our tradition of a free press."

CBS, on the other hand, in a separate presentation to the Supreme Court, said the basic principal of general fairness in the doctrine matched CBS's own standards of journalistic responsibility and have not significantly inhibited its journalistic freedom. This is not to say that CBS agreed with the personal attack guidelines. It did not; it called them "mechanical," "inhibitory," and in violation of the First Amendment.

As for the "inhibitory" nature of such doctrines, Reuven Frank, head of NBC News, told a House subcommittee:

> I truly believe that as the Fairness Doctrine or as the personal attack subhead of the Fairness Doctrine get more and more specific in their application, there will not be more diversity but there will be less.
>
> We can always do programs about rivers and creeks, and I guess somebody could object to that, though not too many. I am worried about self-censorship, by professionals and journalists. I am

worried that each one of them must so concern himself, improperly or unjustifiably, with the threat of somebody catching him short, that he will hold back his training, his instincts, his talents, and the result will be less and less challenging, and less stimulating, television journalism . . .

Enough of this regulation would reduce journalism—television news presentations in various forms—to the dull and frivolous.

How do you administer fairness? A distinguished communications lawyer and former FCC Chairman, Paul Porter, told the same Congressional group:

> I remembered the comment some years ago of a really great Kentuckian by the name of Alben Barkley, when on one occasion I asked him in a very hot primary in the State, "Senator, where do you stand?" He said, "Well, I am for everybody some." I suspect that that is the dilemma that we all find ourselves in in considering this very vexatious problem of where protected speech begins and where it ends . . .
>
> I have had some limited experience in attempting to administer a statute that had a similar standard, and I refer to the late and unlamented OPA. I was the last Price Administrator of OPA. The standard in the Emergency Price Control Act was that there should be no price schedule that was not "generally fair and equitable."
>
> You could measure that. You could take raw material costs, manufacturing costs, historic profit margins, and by a process of arithmetic you could come out to where you thought you were reasonably being generally fair and equitable. My recollection is it took a staff of 70,000 people in the agency to assure that we were being generally fair and equitable as Congress had demanded.

As noted earlier, the FCC Broadcast Bureau has a staff of 250, not 70,000.

Fairness, however, is a matter that serious journalists have held to be vital from the earliest days of news reporting. Even without statutory or doctrinal exposition of fairness, it is deserving of serious concern. The remarks of CBS's Salant in a 1969 speech:

> In the last analysis, if the First Amendment rights are granted only on condition that the journalist meet some Government condition of responsibility and impartiality, then we have read the First Amendment right out of the Constitution. Maybe some may think the First Amendment *ought* to say that it is a privilege to be granted

by the Government to those who meet certain standards of eligibility. But that isn't what it says. If the First Amendment's umbrella covered only the impartial and the responsible, there are a number of newsmen, rabble-rousers, pamphleteers, movie producers, publishers of lurid magazines, muckrakers, and yellow journalists whom the Courts have erroneously protected under the First Amendment . . .

. . . the unconditional freedom which I am convinced the Constitution gives us imposes on us an immense and awesome responsibility which we *must* fulfill. We must be accountable. We must be responsible. We must do our level best to be fair, accurate, impartial. And we must never forget that while we *do* have the Constitutional right to be wrong, to be unfair, to be inaccurate, to be biased, we have no such right, no such ethical or moral or journalistic right, no such right as citizens and as decent human beings.

Whether or not fairness, in FCC doctrine or personal broadcaster inclination, remains prominent there are other forces to inhibit or restrict the broadcaster. Congress itself has frequently moved into this area. In past years the Congressional intrusion, as in the payola or quiz scandals, dealt with television generally. In the turbulent days of Vietnam protest, college campus uprisings, and other tumultuous public occurrences, Washington turned its attention to the non-fiction aspects of television.

As the decade of the 1960's drew to a close, there were many who questioned the role and the style of the press. A genuine credibility gap had been created. There was much call for reform, for government intervention. When investigators could seize on events they felt the press had created—be it the anti-war protests or the disturbances in Chicago during the '68 Democratic convention of the growth of the hippie movement— the investigators demanded controls be imposed over the media.

The Case of the "Pot Party".

A fine study of Washington investigators panting to impose greater control on the media was exhibited in Washington's interest in the so-called Pot Party story in Chicago. WBBM-TV had done a two-part story on marijuana in a campus atmosphere and government investigators insisted that it was staged. They demanded that safeguards against such deception be instituted.

The two broadcasts, entitled "Pot Party at a University," were aired on several newscasts over a three-day period, November 1st through 3rd, 1967. Each of the two parts were about five minutes in length. The reporter was John Missett, a young reporter fresh out of Northwestern. There was strong insistence by both Missett and his station that the Pot

Party was not staged. A special investigating subcommittee of the House Commerce Committee disagreed. An FCC investigation, reported by its chief hearing examiner James D. Cunningham, also charged that it was "pre-arranged for the benefit of the television station."

Missett admitted discussing the proposed party with some of the participants but insisted that the invitation to film came from them. As *Sigma Delta Chi*, in objection to the FCC findings put it, "Faced with conflicting testimony, the examiner had rejected the testimony of the reporter, and has resolved all conflicts in favor of the students who admittedly arranged the party."

Who started it all is always tough to determine after the fact. In a most unusual move, the president of *Sigma Delta Chi*, William B. Arthur, editor of *Look* magazine, wrote the FCC and on this point noted:

> As in most instances where inside informants are used, it may be difficult to determine whether a pattern of questioning and direct or indirect suggestions may have stimulated the arrangement for the party, or whether the party host had conceived a plan for a party and volunteered an invitation for the reporter to attend. Even at the time of such events the differences may be so subtle that the two parties may have a misunderstanding about what triggered the party invitation or the party. In the period after the event, it is virtually impossible to reconstruct the case, particularly where circumstances have changed and each person tends to view the past events to his own advantage.

The motives expressed by the participants were to illustrate how widespread marijuana usage had become and to question the existing laws prohibiting it. The motives of Missett and WBBM-TV were to illustrate widespread usage and the extent of a social problem.

One of the things that offended the federal investigators was the failure of the broadcasters to call the police. They quoted the chief of Evanston police, Bert Giddens, as saying, "I know for a fact that this is a rarity, and by showing this film the impression is given to the community that this is a common thing. This is a malicious reflection of our community that does not exist."

Despite the assurances of local police, the long history of investigatory reporting is dotted with the need to refrain from first reporting to the police. Chairman Rosel Hyde of the FCC testified that a reporter could expose widespread criminal activity but notifying the police could prevent, at best, a single violation. This brought strong response from Commerce Committee Chairman Harley Staggers (Dem., W. Va.) who interjected, "Yes, sir, but that is just exactly what is happening in this nation today. So many are breaking the law and saying they are trying to change it and there is a wave of it across the land and a lot of it has to do with TV, Chairman Hyde, and you know that yourself."

Hyde insisted that he was not defending the right of a reporter to encourage a crime but insisted that coverage of illegal activity, activity that would have taken place anyway, could be defended as an "exercise in judgment." He insisted that broadcasters needed the same latitude in investigative reporting as did newspapers.

An interesting point this, since reporter Missett had contacted one of the participants because the man had been involved in a series of articles on drug usage on college campuses, a series published in the *Chicago Daily News.* Indeed, the kinds of questions being raised with the television exposé of marijuana usage were not raised when similar investigative reporting was conducted by Chicago papers, by two newspapers in Washington, D.C., that same year or by the *Albany Times-Union.* In fact, a student newspaper at Kent State University won a *Scholastic* Magazine award for journalism that year because of a similar series of articles. In all cases, reporters attended pot parties, maintained the anonymity of their interviewees, and engaged in attendance at these marijuana get-togethers without informing police before or after.

In the *Sigma Delta Chi* protest on this matter, President Arthur makes these observations about the relationship of the reporter and the police:

> In some instances, of course, the newsman has an unmistakable duty to give the police any information he may have regarding criminal acts, or crimes about to be committed. If, for example, a reporter were to learn in advance of an assassination plot, or a clear threat to national security, or a robbery attempt, the public interest would require that he notify the police. Even where the prospective illegal acts are minor, and involve no clear and present danger, newsmen often have cooperated voluntarily with law enforcement authorities; individual reporters and the organizations they represent have frequently received official praise for significant assistance in combatting crime and corruption. But circumstances vary and, within reasonable judgment, they often can serve the public interest more effectively by reporting their information directly to the public.
>
> The need for news media to act independently of the police is obvious in some cases. An investigation, for example, may be directed at law enforcement officers themselves, or at illegal activities that could only exist with their knowledge, and perhaps active conniv-

ance. At other times, investigations have concerned activities which are too widespread to be controlled effectively, such as the use of "pot" by young people.

The Commerce subcommittee was disturbed by the failure of WBBM-TV to make available the out-takes of the film. It said that it was virtually impossible to ascertain bias or prejudicial editing without looking at all the footage, not just that on the air. This brought sharp comment from CBS President Frank Stanton who testified, "We stand by what we had on the air and that is the thing I think we should be judged on and not what is on the cutting room floor."

"Pot Party" was of special interest to broadcast journalism, and to all media reporting, because it marked a confrontation of government action with an event that was not spontaneous news. Investigative reporting never is. Hard news coverage deals with the spontaneous. Investigation is an attempt by journalists to get behind the facade that protects a social ill.

This was stated by four dissenting members of the Commerce subcommittee when they wrote, "The press does not lose its right to publish because what it may publish may be untrue. In other words, the press has the right to be wrong. And that right is in the 'public interest.' To suggest that WBBM's 'pot party' may have been prearranged or 'staged' does not, *per se*, indicate that it was not a reasonably accurate representation of an occurrence worthy of public attention and concern."

The full subcommittee, however, was far less lenient towards "Pot Party." They recommended, in March of 1969, five things:

1. Amending the Communications act prohibiting on falsifying quiz programs to include prohibiting deceptive news broadcasts.

2. Amending the Act to permit loss of license if a station violates *any* law, not simply the Communications Act itself.

3. Adding to the Act a provision calling on stations to retain all film and tape—both that included in news and documentaries and the out-takes which never saw air—over a period of six months "for inspection by duly constituted public authorities."

4. All preview of news material is prohibited unless all interested parties, on request, are accorded equal opportunity to preview such programs.

5. A call for a study of what limitations, if any, should be imposed on commercial sponsorship in newscasts, documentaries and live coverage of news events.

Of the first two recommendations, Congressman Robert C. Eckhardt of Houston suggested that we might as well change the First Amendment to read, "Congress shall make no law . . . abridging freedom of speech . . . which is not deemed a falsification by the Court of the Federal Communications Commission."

Other dissenters on the subcommittee noted, "All news is to some extent a 'falsification,' if for no other reason than time forces someone to decide what 'news' to disseminate and what 'news' not to disseminate. By its very name, news implies that someone determine what is immediate and important. This process inherently means that someone else will think that the news presented is in some sense a 'falsification.' "

As for the recommendation that broadcasters hold on to out-takes for six months to permit government investigation of what they did *not* put on the air, Congressman Lionel Van Deerlin of California noted, "numerous judgments go into the preparation of a televised news program, as they do in the editing of a newspaper. A TV editor orders his film or tape cut and sequenced for clarity, for effect, and always for staying within the limitations of air time. Much of his cameraman's product remains unused. But do we really wish to tell a newsman that some government sleuth, in effect, is looking over his shoulder as he edits his film or script—that he may be judged by some future court of inquiry not alone on the basis of what he puts on the air, *but by what he decided to omit* as well?"

Van Deerlin concluded, "I should feel far safer with a few demonstrated liars on the air than I could possibly feel with a government agency going over their scripts."

Four dissenting Congressmen—Ottinger of New York, Harvey of Michigan, Brown of Ohio, and Hastings of New York—hit the idea of investigating the question of advertising on newscasts, noting that the courts long ago settled against the idea that one forfeits his First Amendment rights if his publication is for profit. The continued existence of motion pictures, newspapers, magazines and broadcasting all relate to "pecuniary profit."

These four concluded, "Our dissent from the recommendations of the report is reached without regard to any issue of culpability, irresponsibility, or bad judgment on the part of any party in collecting, editing or airing 'Pot Party.' It is the recommendations of the report which we find intolerable."

The majority of Commerce Committee members disagreed. The vote was over two to one supporting the report.

Television had become so powerful, in the eyes of some Congressmen, that there had to be means of checking it. At various times in 1968 and 1969, other Congressmen called for various measures to control broadcasting: laws to license networks as well as stations, laws to guarantee the right of reply, laws to limit networks to only 50% of the prime air time of their affiliated stations, laws to enforce balanced programming and objectivity.

Senator John Pastore, Chairman of the Senate Subcommittee on Communications, leaned heavily on the networks to submit all their entertainment broadcasts to the Code Authority of the National Association on Broadcasting. The Authority would become a censoring agency like the old Hays office that cleared movies.

The Question of Network Courage.

On another occasion, the Senator ruminated on the question of network bosses—and the oft heard accusation that they are really frightened men when Congress asserts itself. Said Pastore, "Well, my experience, and I have talked to all of the presidents of the networks—they're not easily scared—and I don't think they're intimidated at all . . . I don't know who's frightened them if they've been frightened. They are strong powered-minded, men. As far as I know, I don't think they are intimidated at all."

Network bosses have not always been courageous. Their submission to the pressures of blacklisting during the McCarthy era was a shameful chapter in the history of the broadcast art. On the question of defending their news departments, however, they generally show admirable courage. Perhaps this is because news is an achievement that they could always point to when anything else was being criticized.

Whatever the reason, the courage of networks in the field of nonfiction, despite occasional lapses, is in the spirit of that famous Kansas editor, William Allen White, who admonished that "nothing fails so miserably as a cowardly newspaper."

Walter Cronkite, in receiving the 1969 William Allen White Award (first broadcaster to earn it), said, "I can testify that the executives of my network are far less meddlesome in the news process than the publishers for whom I've worked. When the history of our branch of communications is written, the names of William Paley and Frank Stanton of CBS and David Sarnoff of NBC should loom large. They came to the ownership and management of the most powerful communications medium ever without journalistic background—just as have some publishers. But by their wisdom they have created one of the freest news systems yet. From the very early days of radio they kept the advertisers and the political power wielders off our backs until today we have established our independence."

The independence that Cronkite speaks of is real. There is an old leftist shibboleth that sponsor control is at the heart of broadcasting.

That has not been the experience at the network level and is rarely seen in local news presentation.

Sociologist Herbert J. Gans, who has made careful study of broadcast news, says, "Despite the old stereotype that media employees report the news as their owners and advertisers see fit, this is not true of national television and magazines, however true it may be of the local press. People who work in the media I have studied so far are surprisingly free from outside interference on the part of non-professionals and business executives, and can decide on their own what to cover and how to cover it."

While the left worries about conservative, monied interests affecting news, the conservatives are convinced that it is a liberal bias which distorts the news. Frank Shakespeare, Nixon's key television advisor in the '68 campaign, one year later spoke to the Radio Television News Directors Association as they met in Detroit. He said bluntly, "It's my view that television news, as it exists in the country today, is rather clearly liberally oriented." He said that no matter how hard those in his audience tried, "You sweat blood trying to be decent and objective and fair—the problem is, in my view, that you cannot be." He said TV news attracts liberals and no matter how hard liberals try to be fair to the conservative position, it could not be done. "I suppose," he continued, "that you could say that it would be shocking to take into account the man's ideology when you hire him. You want to hire him because he's the best . . . and not because he's a Republican or a Democrat or for Wallace or a member of the John Birch Society or the ADA or whatever he is—those are his private views and he's entitled to them. But, if out of fifty or one hundred men you hire, purely on the basis of ability you're going to end up in the box." He suggested that television, as newspapers, include known conservatives, "specifically because it represents the other point of view."

Since the earliest days of broadcasting there have been suggestions that commentators come from all shades of personal philosophy to compel balance. Most networks have chosen to follow another route, hiring men of integrity who do not automatically take or represent a specific point of view. They are chosen for ability, intelligence and most have shared broadcasting's desire to be fair to all points of view. Shakespeare feels this can be accomplished only with the addition of more conservatives. When Vice President Agnew attacked the presentation of analysis following Presidential addresses, Shakespeare offered another suggestion: that local stations drop network interpretation and cut away to permit local newsmen to analyze the President's remarks.

The Vice President in his Des moines speech of November, 1969 raised another question which conservatives have long defined as one of the evils of network news coverage. He said, "We do know that, to a man, these commentators and producers live and work in the geographical and intellectual confines of Washington, D.C. or New York City—the latter of which James Reston terms the 'most unrepresentative community in the entire United States.' Both communities bask in their own provincialism, their own parochialism. We can deduce that these men thus read the same newspapers, and draw their political and social views from the same sources. Worse, they talk constantly to one another, thereby providing artificial reinforcement to their shared viewpoints."

It is inadequate for defenders of the broadcasters to point out that very few correspondents are from New York—i.e.: Walter Cronkite of St. Joseph, Mo., David Brinkley of Wilmington, N.C., Chet Huntley of Cardwell, Mont., Howard K. Smith of Ferriday, La., and Eric Sevareid of Velva, N.D. This argument is specious. They do live and work in Washington and New York. They do because the center of network television is in New York, the center of American news is in Washington. They all travel widely, on assignment and to give speeches, and they do receive extensive mail from across the country. These are the same means of keeping contact with the people as those employed by Vice Presidents and other national political figures, who all live in Washington, "read the same newspapers, and draw their political and social views from the same sources (and) worse, they talk constantly to one another." There is one difference: while they share the same sources for understanding the currents that run through the nation, newsmen—unlike politicians—do not have to serve special interests that are the base of their support nor do newsmen have to worry about the kind of popular response necessary for re-election.

How the Decisions are Made.

The control of the news product, of television examination of the real world is spread across many people, directly in the hands of journalists but influenced by many others. The multiplicity of this responsibility is the greatest protection for the public.

At the highest level in the network structure, executives frequently know of news coverage at the same time as 20,000,000 viewers do: when it is on the air. They are concerned with broad principles of fairness, some are active in defending the First Amendment rights. They are not involved in day to day decisions.

At the bottom level, that most important point, a reporter and his camera crew are first to make the measure of a story. This is the rubbing point, the actual confrontation with what is happening. It is also the point of greatest influence. The reporter's observations and the camera crew's documentation are the most powerful influence in how a story is played. Editors and producers work with the reporter. The executive producer of a news broadcast measures the pressures of time and competing stories to determine how much "space" it gets in a newscast. Though each of these influences on the final treatment can be frustrating, they also can serve to help balance the influence of that given report.

News administrators get involved in questions of policy and in reviews of the final record, the broadcast. These, too, are influences on how television views the world. They are part of the checks and balances of broadcast news.

Within the hierarchy of a network (or local) news department, there are numerous checks and balances. The men involved are professional journalists. The involvement varies and on occasion (always during live situations) there is only the single involvement of the single man on the air, the reporter on camera. That involvement reflects confidence in the reporter, his ability, his honesty and his professionalism.

The quality of such checks and balances vary, of course. Others—outside the news departments—come into play. The audience is more powerful than it knows. One hundred letters, if spontaneous, can change the course of reporting. Indeed, a single, thoughtful letter can have such impact.

Professional critics can be important molders of broadcast opinion. Unfortunately, there are not too many critics. In newspapers the critics concentrate on entertainment programs, deal largely with news documentaries and rarely with day-to-day coverage. That is, of course, sadly true of newspapers as well. Except for some CBS experiments in a few major cities, no one has criticized daily press performance other than in occasional articles in the *Columbia Journalism Review*.

Broadcasting networks have still another check: their affiliates—those 200 "bosses" that Salant referred to. On the whole, these particular bosses are far more interested in the business and entertainment ends of networking than in news. Still, many station owners and managers have made thoughtful criticisms of the news product of their network.

All of this is not to suggest a perfect system of journalistic integrity. As in any bureaucracy, the networks have men who hear different drums and often find the news departments troublesome and frustrating. Many network sales executives tend to feel this way. They can't quite go along with G. K. Chesterton when he says, "I believe in getting into hot water. I think it keeps you clean."

Nor is it true that all newsmen are pure. Despite the exuberance of one network newsman that "I think our medium—television—is the freest and most nearly independent news medium on earth," there are those within news departments who can be less than virtuous about their product. Considering the size of network staffs, it comes as little surprise that there are little men included: men who fear controversy, men who would stifle dissent or at least muffle it, men who try—inadvertently or not—to breed fear into other men.

Overall, however, broadcast journalists are terribly careful to enhance the integrity of their trade, to taste what Cronkite calls "the heady fruit of respect that can be won by the fearless conveyor of truth."

The Young and Advocacy.

Mencken said journalism's job is to comfort the afflicted and afflict the comfortable. That is not true though it reads as well as any other epigram. Journalism's job is to try to determine what is real and what is not.

A growing number of young journalists or would-be journalist prefer the Mencken dictum. They feel that the media must carry forth social "good."

Young activists are impatient. They see the sham that sometimes suffocates what little fact is ascertainable. They are impatient. They "know" truth and they feel journalism should support truths, with or without ascertainable fact.

The one constant in life is change. Despite the fact that each development leads us to feel we have been there before, change is always there. It may be in the sense of the old saying that "Everything changes and everything is the same" but is changing nevertheless.

The angry young, of course, are swept up in change—real and anticipated. Their influence is being felt in journalism.

They are not always attractive to the eye or the mind. They don't care much for their elders. Example: the view of the angry young might be summed up in the observation of one such, "We were convinced that everyone over 25, with perhaps one or two remarkable exceptions, was 'hopeless,' having lost the *elan* of youth, the capacity to feel, and the ability to distinguish truth from falsehood."

That's the way they feel, lots of the angry young. Of course, that particular quotation was from the autobiographical works of British author Leonard Woolf, and he was talking about the year 1903. Everything changes, everything is the same.

He also noted "No doubt to those whom we did not like or who did not like us we must have been insufferable."

Today's young journalists or would-be journalists may seem insufferable, just as young protesters in the political and social field do at times. They engage in a so-called "Journalism of Involvement." They call it the "New Journalism."

It's not terribly new but it certainly gets them involved. Their basic principle is simple. Objectivity has failed. The old virtues of journalism haven't worked. It's time to be involved. Don't fret about fairness or full reporting—use the media to get the message across. Correct social ills, as you see them, by reporting only the news that fits the reform.

It's very popular on college campuses. There's a good deal of talk about it in Journalism schools. There's a good deal of evidence of it in college newspapers.

These publications are often exciting, the makeup and style innovative. They are also exasperating—the substance being slanted, distorted and guilty of bad taste, bad writing, and bad reporting.

I spoke before some journalism students at Columbia in 1969 and they expressed excitement about the *Village Voice*, a Greenwich Village publication which believes in the New Journalism. The editor of the *Voice* had described his participation in anti-Vietnam demonstrations and how he wrote them up as one involved in the action, not just as observer. One student offered the thought that upon graduation he would rather write for the *Village Voice* than the *New York Times*. That, in journalism, had to be classed as blasphemy.

Campus publications rage over their right to use obscene words— as if the heart of Freedom of the Press lies in the divine right of the four-letter idiom. The essence of New Journalism, they feel, relates to being daring and fearless.

Involved journalism is the personification of a vision.

That idea, the rage among the young, is unfortunately neither new nor journalism.

Examining substance in the daily press or on the air reveals that much or almost all of what we call news is not really that, not in the sense of news as a spontaneous happening. Most of "news" is contrived, planted, managed, massaged, manipulated but it is still "news" in that the men reporting it are not managed, manipulated or themselves contriving. Their vision is one of fairness and honesty.

The New Journalism has different visions. Basically, it is old-fashioned "do-goodism" with the good they do being the private visions of their own. Though it would make them uncomfortable to think it, they have plenty of company among conservatives and "old" liberals. In these camps, too, are those who would have journalism "do good."

Reuven Frank, President of NBC News, addressed himself to this when he wrote:

> Today, in the United States, facing a fighting jigsaw of crises for which we are unprepared, many people seem to think that American journalism, and above all, American television journalism, should be governed by enobling purposes. We are castigated for not

promoting unity, for not opening channels of interracial communication, for not building an edifice of support for our fighting men, for not ignoring dissent, for not showing good news.

Our system does not now provide for working toward social good. Let us even postulate that there is a unanimously accepted social good which television journalism should set itself to achieve or promote. And the decision would be made by five Albert Schweitzers sitting around a table. Whoever put them there could, in time—perhaps far, far off in the future—replace them with five Joseph Goebbelses, or five Joseph Stalins, or five George Lincoln Rockwells. You see, it's not the five Albert Schweitzers who are important, but the table.

I say the table itself is evil. To those who worry about television, or television news, being too powerful, I say there is no doubt that there is great potential power here, but only if used. The only safeguard is free journalism, journalism without directed purpose, because whether that purpose represents good or evil depends on who you are.

The impatience of the young with ancient virtues of journalism, like their impatience with so many old fashioned virtues, reflects a lack of understanding of what journalism really is.

Journalism is not truth. It is a seeking after truth. It is a searching for truth that journalism can never fully achieve. Almost half a century ago, Walter Lippmann called it a search for "reportable" truth. He noted that governing forces are imperfectly reported and "the theory that the press can itself record those forces is false."

Wrote Lippmann, "The press is no substitute for institutions. It is like the beam of a searchlight that moves restlessly about, bringing one episode and then another out of darkness into vision. Men cannot do the work of the world by this light alone. They cannot govern society by episodes, incidents, and eruptions."

The Nature of "News."

The matter is further confused by the role of the press itself as an institution. It has become woven into the being of current democracy. It often provides episodes and incidents itself, further complicating any hopes of journalism singling out truth.

The news media make news.

That is an uncomfortable truth but a truth to reckon with in the 20th Century. As the conduit of what is happening, the news media is not only imperfect but frequently shapes or re-shapes happenings.

Examine that most common journalistic device, the interview. Simply seeking the interview is an intrusion into fact. This doesn't mean that the reporter is wrong in doing so nor that his motivation is base. It simply mean that his action in conducting an interview does, in a primitive way, constitute "making" news.

Those who have explored the beginnings of journalism, credit Horace Greeley with the first modern interview with a major public figure when, in 1859, he interview Brigham Young in Salt Lake City. Even a century ago there was concern that interviews were a contrived matter. In 1869, the *Nation* summed up the journalistic interview as "the joint product of some humbug of a hack politician and another humbug of a reporter."

The interview led to the press conference and the initiative shifted from the press to the politician. Is this a "real" event or contrived? Admittedly it is contrived, but is it thus unreal? Is there not reality in the non-event that then makes it an event?

A step from news conference—which permits the press to raise questions which do not always please the interviewee—is the news release, a means to eliminate the questions. If the release contains news, the content is controlled by the source to a considerable degree. Certainly the embargo, the time of release, is his. Rarely is the timing violated. The content is his but the press is, of course, free to question it, to seek associated comment, to offer opponents a chance to comment, and most important, to reject it completely.

The release itself, however, is not a real event. It may be pertinent, it may be important, it may bear upon real events but in itself, it is manufactured. Even this form of counterfeit, however, achieves a role, a life of its own—and may rival reality in its pertinence. Sometimes, when the release is the text of a speech, the "real" event ends up differently. A President might not stick to his text. He may abandon it completely. The release, however, has that life of its own. The press makes much of the departure from text, sometimes concentrates its entire attention on the fact that it was changed, that the prepared text was dropped. Analysis of the differences sometimes replaces reporting of the remarks themselves.

In a similar way, failure to comment on something, takes on a meaning of its own. "No comment" in the parlance of current journalism can mean much, never means what it says.

The "overnighter," that story filed by the wire services to accommodate newspapers that publish the next day is similarly "unreal." Its content and its quotations are being held, not by the news source this time, but by the press agency to serve its special needs.

The "background" interview, which flourishes in Washington and has spread across the country and the world, is another unreal event. A prominent public figure gives his views to the reporter with the understanding that they are not to be reported as his views. Out come the stories quoting "a top Administration source" or "high government sources."

One group of prominent journalists in Washington lunches periodically with top government officials on such a basis. The interlocutor of the group explains at the start that, "This luncheon did not take place. You are not here. Nothing is to be quoted. Anything you use is to be on your own authority."

More than once, when such sessions produced highly controversial material, the real source has emerged from his anonymity to deny his own statements. At one "backgrounder" dinner "a very high public official" refused to rule out the use of atomic weapons in Vietnam. This was widely and sensationally reported. Subsequently this same "high authority" issued a public statement denying that atomic weapons were *ever* considered for Vietnam.

One prominent reporter, who had not been at the dinner, chastised his colleagues for printing and broadcasting such a patently false story. He quoted Mr. High Authority's public statement as evidence of how silly it was, never realizing that Mr. High Authority was the original source of the speculation.

Every day's news budget is heavy with non-events. Every newspaper, every broadcast is full of "news" created by news sources or news reporters. Even the play of such news, in print or on the air, changes the nature and the importance of the non-events. Reality must sometimes pursue this simulated news and doesn't always catch up. The new reality of the nonevent then becomes actual, factual, the permanent record.

It is not just content but form that affects this news coverage. Example: the photograph. James Russell Wiggins, distinguished ex-editor of the *Washington Post* and former chief delegate to the United Nations, spoke to journalism students at the University of North Dakota early in 1969 and observed, "It has been said that the camera does not lie, but the camera does lie. It is a notorious, compulsive, unashamed and mischievous liar."

Wiggins cited several examples to carry his point. One: he said that cameras were conveying portraits of police forces throughout the country which were distortions. Police were shown acting with brutal aggression but little was shown to indicate what the object of that aggression had done prior to resisting police. "In this and other matters, the camera does not tell the truth," said Wiggins, "and because what it tells is not the whole truth, skepticism about the media rises in the minds of readers who know that policemen, whatever their undoubted faults, are not always wrong."

Secondly, Wiggins cited photo coverage of the war in Vietnam and the restrictions on what photography could show. "The camera has told many lies about the war in South Vietnam," he said, "and readers, who are increasingly biased about the war, have difficulty in understanding that the camera is a congenital liar, condemned to prevarication by the mechanical limitations of a contrivance that could only tell the whole truth if it were equipped with lenses as all encompassing as the very eye of God."

The Wiggins speech sparked off violent reply by newspaper photographers. Sam C. Pierson of the *Houston Chronicle,* President of the National Press Photographers Association, said, "We must shoot what is there. The bad cannot be covered up or sweetened up with words . . . It would be ideal if there was such a thing as a camera that would shoot people's feelings, their character, and all the many other intangibles but this will never be the case."

Other photographers noted that it wasn't their role to picture interpretive matter nor could they. No photography could explore the role of Vietnam beyond what is available to see—no photographer can weave into his pictures speculation about the war, about its rights or wrongs, about its possible role in preventing wider war.

Of police, said Charles Scott of the *Chicago Daily News,* "Wiggins condemns news photography for showing police in the wrong light. Careless use of the camera and its pictures can do honorable police officers an injustice. However, suppression of all pictures of police charging into demonstrations and making aggressive arrests would do the public an injustice. When police brutality isn't exposed by a conscientious and vigilant press, who is going to call attention to it and help keep the practice from spreading? The police aren't apt to correct their faults voluntarily. Their victims aren't in a position to do much about it."

Wiggins, of course, was not questioning the right to expose police brutality or the truth about a war. He really was raising questions about the honesty of photo reporting. The former editor cited an incident during the Korean War when he declined to print a picture of President Harry Truman walking across a train platform against a backdrop of caskets of Korean War dead.

"What the camera said," insisted Wiggins, "was that the Korean War was 'Truman's War,' just what thousands of the President's critics were saying. But this was not the truth. It wasn't Truman's war. He didn't start it. He didn't will it. He tried to stop it. And the camera that pictured the caskets of Korean War dead did not have a lens capable of photographing those who might have died elsewhere if there had been no Korean War."

A *Chicago Daily News* photographer, Paul Sequeira, later observed, "Of course, Wiggins realizes that a man can lie with words; obviously we all do. But it is somehow less colorful and more ludicrous to coin the phrase, 'The typewriter lies.'"

What the battle of Russ Wiggins versus the press photographers involved was both the actual creation of the false or non-event and the very process of the press being involved in that creation in the manner of reporting. The war coverage, he seemed to imply, involved a subtle staging of events to make a point—a point with which he disagreed. One assumes that if he agreed he would have printed the Truman-casket photo.

Abe Lincoln once warned of war reporting that when it appeared in the press, "all the little Colt's revolvers will have grown into horse-pistols."

Journalists all know that photos, in the print media, and film in television or tape in radio, can be cut to fit an editorial bias. The ancient virtues of journalism say that bias must be tempered with an honest seeking of truth. The "new" journalism of the '60's advocates encouragement of the bias.

The so-called "new" journalists would encourage an editor to cut his raw material to fit the mold of his prejudice. This is not really new, of course. The penny press of the earliest days of this country were full of this. Anybody with a printing press and a prejudice could put out a paper. These publishers would admit to printing the little news they had and filling the rest with their opinions. It compelled Thomas Jefferson to note that "the most truthful part of a newspaper is the advertisements."

So the new journalism is really the old journalism. Perhaps it is a mix of those revolutionary era, opinionated polemics and the spirit of "yellow journalism" of the early part of this century. It is the latter in the sense that current us of profanity and or lurid themes, in sex *or* politics, is the equivalent of the sensationalism of early Hearst and Pulitzer. It is "shock and titillate" journalism. In keeping with Pavlov's dogs, however, the reader shocks less with each exposure. The titillation level declines with too much exposure.

An observation of early American newspapers might fit some of the product of the "new" journalism. Henry David Thoreau said, "If words were invented to conceal thought, newspapers are a great improvement on a bad invention."

Loose use of personal opinion, escalation of permissiveness, the increase in subjective writing have created exciting journalism but often careless reporting. Add to that the subject matter of the late '60's—a portrayal of unseemly events to audiences who really wish a more seemly world—and you make the audience uncomfortable.

A distinguished sociologist, Professor Daniel Boorstin of the University of Chicago has examined the nature of today's news product. He finds much of it is what he calls the "pseudo-event." Boorstin sees the daily press full of pseudo-events. He says, "Pseudo-events from their very nature tend to be more interesting and more attractive than spontaneous events.

Here are the Professor's characteristics of the pseudo-event: (1) It is more dramatic—a television debate can be more suspenseful than a casual encounter between candidates, (2) Participants are selected because they are more newsworthy and dramatic, thus pseudo-events are more vivid, (3) Pseudo-events can be repeated and thus their impression re-enforced, (4) They can be advertised in advance, (5) Being planned, they can be more intelligible and hence more reassuring than spontaneous events, (6) They are more convenient to witness, (7) They can spawn other pseudo-events in geometric progression—they are discussed and analyzed, they are a measure of being informed, they are like walls of mirrors— each reflection repeating the original event.

Concludes Boorstin, "By this new Gresham's law of American public life, counterfeit happenings tend to drive spontaneous happenings out of circulation." He adds, "This is the age of contrivance. The artificial has become so commonplace that the natural begins to seem contrived . . . Fact itself has become 'non-fiction.' " Dr. Boorstin feels that the pseudo-event is so much the substance of daily reporting that the world of crime, and to a lesser extent sports, are the "last refuge of the authentic, uncorrupted spontaneous event." Newsmen who invite comment or incite inflammatory statements are themselves generating the event. It is hard to distinguish between who does the deed and who reports it, who is the history and who is the historian.

Boorstin is especially aware of the role this played in the career of Senator Joseph McCarthy. He wrote, "Newspapermen were his most potent allies, for they were his co-manufacturers of pseudo-events. They were caught in their own web. Honest newsmen and the unscrupulous Senator McCarthy were in separate branches of the same business."

Now the key word in that paragraph is "honest." The newsmen may have unwillingly been creating the McCarthy influence but they did so in innocence. They were in pursuit, honestly, of their profession. They reported, honestly, material they may have found distasteful. This virtue, honesty, even when a result of culpability, is strengthened when Boorstin distinguishes between pseudo-events and propaganda. Propaganda is information intentionally biased, a pseudo-event is ambiguous truth. Pseudo-events thrive on an honest desire to be informed, propaganda feeds on a willingness to be inflamed, on "appealing falsehood." Propaganda oversimplifies experience, pseudo-events overcomplicate it.

It may be that the grist to journalism's mill is the pseudo-event, that the need to fill pages of newspapers and hours of newscasts has spawned these counterfeit items. But the motivation is more information not falsehood.

Difficult as it may be to distinguish, the heart of what constitutes staging a news event is intent. An interview is staged if the intent is to support a pre-determined view. The news release is staged if it succeeds at distorting. The photographic display is staged if it intentionally falsifies. The television film is staged if it is meant to deceive. And if contrivance, at the source or in the reporting, is part of the nature of non-fiction, then it is important to know. Ideas, however, do bubble forth —serious ones and others. They are heard. As someone once noted, a single sparrow fluttering about the church is an antagonist that the most profound theologian is unable to overcome.

Broadcasting and Seeking for Truth.

In May of 1969, *Fortune* magazine published a study of television news. It concluded, "The networks' unique commitment to news has always carried with it some unique risks. Because they are licensed and because they are demonstrably so powerful, TV newsmen have been held to high standards by an understandably concerned public, the FCC, and Congress. The imposition of standards is appropriate, to be sure . . . But few newspapers or magazines can stand comparably close scrutiny and display a better record over the years."

Despite the handicaps of its licensed birthright, broadcasting has done much to foster ideas for it is returning diversity to an age of dwindling news sources. Newspapers are less in number and fewer and fewer of them invest in the kind of overseas, Washington and even local coverage that is needed.

The wire services are down from several to just two, the Associated Press and United Press International. The emergence of the national and worldwide broadcast news staffs (and those of the news magazines) have added to the diversity of national and foreign reporting. Even more significant is the multiplicity of local broadcast news departments, adding new eyes and ears to local reporting.

This is the heart of broadcast journalism's contribution to our times.

It is foolish to call it all good. Oscar Wilde warned us that, "It is only an auctioneer who can equally and impartially admire all schools of art." It is equally foolish to call it all bland or bad. The new reporting of broadcasting contributes to the general store of knowledge that each of us has about our society, our intimate community, ourselves.

Those who fear the power of the media do so needlessly. The nature of the reporting and diversity of the sources contradicts this. It sells soap, says former FCC Commissioner Lee Loevinger, but that doesn't mean the media exposure sells ideas in the same manner. In a speech at the University of Wisconsin in early 1969, he said:

> The American citizen today has access to more information about the world, has available a greater range of choice and decision, and has a wider area of personal freedom than any other group of citizens in the world in all history. This is a fact which does require to be proclaimed and emphasized. For responsibility is a product of freedom. You cannot tell a man that he is unfree and urge him to be responsible. Those who insist that we are pawns in the hands of the media deny not only our freedom but our responsibility. If we have no power, we are not responsible for what happens.
>
> This is exactly the wrong doctrine for our time. We are—all of us—responsible for what is happening in our society and what we need now is greater emphasis on our sense of personal responsibility and less talk about our hopeless helplessness. That, at least, is my faith; and if this faith is misplaced then democracy is an illusion and the American dream is a false hope.

This is an imperfect world. Television has no lock on what the world is all about and it is sometimes guilty of distorting the vision of what is real. Television's failings, its shortcomings, are often obvious for the product is highly visible. If one follows the route of some critics, you can take enough examples of failure and shortcomings to paint an ugly picture of television. Many do just that.

There is the other picture, of course, of television contribution. It can and it does contribute to the dialogue of what we are all about. It does so a hundred ways in each of our days.

This volume has attempted to round out the picture, the good and the bad. The medium is wanting in many ways but constructive in many others. It is woven into the fabric of our being so, for good or bad, television is a social force worthy of everyone's understanding, of everyone's caring. It cannot be wished away, it will not waste away.

The poet Archibald MacLeish said, "A free society lives and must live in and by the imagination. Freedom itself is an imagined thing—a dream never realized—a vision always about to be made true. To quicken the imagination should be the great end of a society which moves towards freedom.

"And," he added, "no instrument ever devised holds such promise for that quickening as radio and television."

INDEX